Ralph Ellison's *Invisible Man*

Recent Titles in
Greenwood Guides to Multicultural Literature

RALPH ELLISON'S
INVISIBLE MAN

A Reference Guide

Michael D. Hill and Lena M. Hill

Greenwood Guides to Multicultural Literature

GREENWOOD PRESS
Westport, Connecticut London

Library of Congress Cataloging-in-Publication Data

Hill, Michael D., 1971–
  Ralph Ellison's Invisible man: a reference guide / Michael D. Hill and Lena M. Hill.
       p. cm. — (Greenwood guides to multicultural literature)
  "First published in 2007"—T.p. verso.
  Includes bibliographical references and index.
  ISBN 978–0–313–33465–8 (alk. paper)
  1. Ellison, Ralph. Invisible man.   2. Ellison, Ralph—Study and
teaching.   3. African American men in literature.   4. African Americans in
literature.   I. Hill, Lena M.   II. Title.
  PS3555.L625I53525   2008
  813'.54—dc22   2007037492

British Library Cataloguing in Publication Data is available.

Library of Congress Catalog Card Number: 2007037492
ISBN: 978–0–313–33465–8

First published in 2008

Greenwood Press, 88 Post Road West, Westport, CT 06881
An imprint of Greenwood Publishing Group, Inc.
www.greenwood.com

Printed in the United States of America

The paper used in this book complies with the
Permanent Paper Standard issued by the National
Information Standards Organization (Z39.48–1984).

10 9 8 7 6 5 4 3 2 1

CONTENTS

PREFACE

Scanning the blurbs on Colson Whitehead's novel *The Intuitionist* (2000), one quickly notices its conspicuous comparison to Ralph Ellison's *Invisible Man* (1952).[1] A similar experience awaits the person who looks at the jacket of John Edgar Wideman's *Philadelphia Fire* (1990).[2] These kinds of allusions are hardly new. At least since Toni Morrison's *Song of Solomon* (1977), introducing serious African American fiction entails connecting it somehow to *Invisible Man*.[3] Observe for instance the paperback cover of David Bradley's *The Chaneysville Incident* (1981).[4] Whether by content affinity or shared acclaim, a link to Ellison's masterwork seems a mandate of savvy marketing and a synonym for lofty artistic ambition. In part, these practices reflect editors' and reviewers' penchants for associative thinking; nevertheless, *Invisible Man*'s status as a gold standard in black narrative depends on more than habit. It stems from a durable, sternly disciplined talent.

2007 marks the fifty-fifth anniversary of *Invisible Man*. Despite the passing years, this omnibus novel retains its prominence, existing like James Joyce's *Ulysses* (1922) as a much admired, yet incompletely under stood work. From the moment of its publication, the book has inspired spirited dialogue. Reviewers alternately hail and disparage it, and as biographer Lawrence Jackson has noted, Ellison almost came to blows when a friend impugned its artistic method (17). The testiness that *Invisible Man* causes partially reflects its author's cantankerous ways; still, its orneriness chiefly stems from the combustible theme that powers its picaresque, namely racial identity. Commentators buzz at the intimate portrayal of what Adrienne Kennedy has since termed the "funnyhouse" of African American experience (1). Readers manifest ceaseless wonder and epic confusion because here is a genuine mystery story, the life of a third generation emancipated black. Starting with John M. Reilly's *Twentieth Century Interpretations of "Invisible Man"* (1971) and continuing to Patrice D. Rankin's *Ulysses in Black* (2006), a prodigious string of scholars wrestles the angels that animate this classic. The volume and skill of prior efforts beg the question, why is one more book on Ralph Ellison's *Invisible Man* needed? Facing this query, the authors of the present study offer a simple defense: accessibility.

Invisible Man confers an aura of intellectual brio. Like the coffee shop patron who pulls Friedrich Nietzsche's *Thus Spake Zarathustra* (1883–1885) from a bruised attaché, the reader spotted with Ellison's book is instantly deemed deep. The writer no doubt would be tickled by this. Likewise, he would be gratified that critics still mine his first novel for fresh insights. Despite his satisfaction, Ellison, the son of literate, working-class parents, might also covet a non-specialist audience. His imagination pierces myriad vibrant cultural spaces; therefore, witnesses of his treasures should constitute an equally diverse group. By promoting fuller appreciation for high school students, college undergraduates, and general readers, the present study invites new voices to join the conversation about Ralph Ellison's *Invisible Man*. In doing so it aims not only to perpetuate affection for this great literary work, but also to democratize the contours of its reception.

In 1989, Susan Resneck Parr and Pancho Savery edited *Approaches to Teaching Ellison's "Invisible Man."* Conceived as a pedagogical resource for college professors, this book includes a précis of relevant background materials, several articles about instructional strategies, and a series of insightful literary critical essays. Its editors expressed a desire "to represent as many approaches to the novel as [they] could," and by providing a comprehensive point of entry for *Invisible Man*'s readers, they succeeded admirably [x]. While this volume's merits are redoubtable, substantial changes have occurred in the nearly 20 years since its publication. Methodological and thematic innovations have transformed literary criticism about *Invisible Man;* two full-length biographies of its author have appeared; *Juneteenth* (1999), an incarnation of Ellison's long-awaited second novel, has been published; and no fewer than 40 volumes that in some way, form, or fashion, address the writer and his work have been penned and printed.

Ralph Ellison's "Invisible Man": A Reference Guide builds on the foundation poured by all prior Ellison researchers, but in key ways, its purpose most closely resembles that of Parr and Savery's collection. Maintaining the earlier study's implicit interest in empowering undergraduates, the present guide eschews any explicitly pedagogical commentaries and in tone and perspective emphasizes the needs of lay readers. Its organization allows quick retrieval of relevant information, a thorough index speeds the pinpointing of details, and its summaries not only examine individual works but also place those works within the context of ongoing debates and other historically significant events. All of this is undertaken with the hope of delivering to every reader who wants it an intimate encounter with a supremely rewarding text.

Ralph Ellison's "Invisible Man": A Reference Guide consists of eight narrowly focused chapters. These provide thorough, yet concise overviews, and at the start of each, its contents and organization are clearly announced. Although analytical trends complete with conflicts and controversies are explored, the guide preeminently tries to ease one's journey through the thicket that is *Invisible Man*. Thus, its presentations incline toward selectivity rather than exhaustiveness. Such selectivity does not stint any major development regarding the novel; however, it does mean that the final riches of a particular suggestion are often reserved for further research by the reader. Works cited pages conclude each section of this text, and in particular, those for the "Contexts" and "Reception" chapters indicate exactly how fruitful such supplemental reading might be. These features give adventuresome personalities varied avenues down which to wander. For the bulk of the book, the practical concerns of the anxious interloper hold sway.

The guide's initial chapter is an introduction. It presents a sketch of Ellison's biography that concentrates on Oklahoma, Tuskegee, Harlem, and his status as a public intellectual. By intimating the impact of these areas on his relationship with *Invisible Man,* it establishes the centrality of this novel not only to the writer's career, but also to the development of post–World War II African American and American literature. Stressing the paradoxical continuities and divergences that fill Ellison's pre- and post–*Invisible Man* life, the introduction finds that such complexities may be the haphazard engine of his most stellar achievements.

Chapter two, "Content," summarizes the events of the novel. Using Kenneth Burke's notion of purpose, passion, and perception, a triumvirate that Ellison says spurred his efforts, it shows the patterns in the chaotic experiences recounted in *Invisible Man*. Moving carefully through the entire novel, "Content" clearly explains what is happening, and by presenting Ellison as a meticulous arranger who orchestrates single scenes and entire sections, it clarifies just how disciplined an execution *Invisible Man*'s narrative is.

The third chapter, "Texts," offers a history of *Invisible Man*'s publication starting with the 1947 appearance of an excerpt in *Horizon* and ending with Ellison's fine-tuning of his prefaces for later editions. It also devotes considerable space to analyzing the differences between his drafts of sections of *Invisible Man* and the novel's final published form. Benefiting from extended archival research, "Texts" suggests that *Invisible Man* in its various packagings is not merely the result of chronic tinkering; rather, it reflects its author's systematic investment both in managing how the novel is interpreted and in deciding what kind of book to present to the public.

"Contexts," chapter four, provides information on the cultural and historical backdrop that informs and surrounds *Invisible Man*. Considering events from chattel slavery up to the nascent civil rights movements, it explains how Ellison's novel alludes to these situations and, in doing so, emphasizes the inextricable link between the past, the present, and the future. This chapter testifies to the book's encyclopedic evocation of American culture and demonstrates how its references demand the sort of integrative imagination that Ellison sees as a symbol of the nation's spirit.

The fifth chapter, "Ideas," explores three master themes that structure Ellison's portrayal of an identity quest in *Invisible Man*. Focusing on inner blindness, cultural complexity, and artistic responsibility, it relates these concepts to crucial characters and scenes showing again how the maelstrom that appears to rule the novel's landscape yields considerably when the author's design is discovered and analyzed.

Honoring the sort of close scrutiny that Ralph Ellison proclaimed would edify his readers, chapter six "Art" notes the dominant rhetorical devices that fuel *Invisible Man*'s narrative effects. It ranges over mainstays of figurative language, among them metaphor, irony, symbol, and satire, describing how the novelist's engagement with these fundamentals reflects his intent to simultaneously tell the story of his protagonist and inscribe the tale of his own artistic tutelage and maturity.

"Reception," chapter seven, chronicles over 50 years worth of critical responses to *Invisible Man*. Initially examining the novel's reviews, it then summarizes major voices and trends in the book's analysis in African American and American literary history and criticism. Articles, chapters in longer works, and single author books all receive attention as do anthologies and other collections. By placing discrete interpretive pieces against the background of broader discussions and controversies, "Reception" conveys the still-growing intellectual ripples that *Invisible Man* inspired upon it descent.

The final chapter "Bibliographical Essay" presents the best resources for further research on *Invisible Man*. Favoring anthologies and collections, the bibliographic essay glosses those books that provide a wealth of information on the novel. Turning to more recent developments, it explains the differences in scope and archival access between the two biographies of Ralph Ellison.

Ralph Ellison's "Invisible Man": A Reference Guide joins an illustrious lineage both at this press and in Ellison studies more generally. If it enables new assemblies to tarry within a worthy work's trance, then its kinship claims will be gratified.

NOTES

1. The excerpt on the cover of *The Intuitionist* is taken from Walter Kirn's review of the novel. It suggests that Whitehead's book is "the freshest racial allegory since Ralph Ellison's *Invisible Man*" (Book Jacket).

2. On the front of its paperback version, a quote from *Time* suggests that *Philadelphia Fire* is "reminiscent of Ralph Ellison's *Invisible Man*" (Book Jacket).

3. On the first page of *Song of Solomon*'s blurbs, an excerpt from the *Book-of-the-Month Club News* proclaims that "it is the best novel of the black experience in America since *Invisible Man*" (Book Blurb).

4. Since it went to paperback, *The Chaneysville Incident*'s front cover has featured a quotation from the *Christian Science Monitor* suggesting that Bradley's book "rivals Toni Morrison's *Song of Solomon* as the best novel about the black experience since Ellison's *Invisible Man*" (Book Jacket).

WORKS CITED

Book-of-the-Month Club News. Book Blurb. *Song of Solomon.* 1977. By Toni Morrison. New York: Plume-Penguin, 1987.

Christian Science Monitor. Book Jacket. *The Chaneysville Incident.* 1981. By David Bradley. New York: Perennial-Harper, 1990.

Jackson, Lawrence. "Ralph Ellison's Invented Life: A Meeting with the Ancestors." *The Cambridge Companion to Ralph Ellison.* Ed. Ross Posnock. Cambridge: Cambridge UP, 2005. 11–34.

Kennedy, Adrienne. *Funnyhouse of a Negro.* 1964. *Adrienne Kennedy in One Act.* Minneapolis: U of Minnesota P, 1988. 1–23.

Kirn, Walter. Book Jacket. *The Intuitionist.* By Colson Whitehead. New York: Anchor-Random, 2000.

Parr, Susan Resneck, and Pancho Savery, eds. *Approaches to Teaching Ellison's "Invisible Man."* New York: MLA, 1989

Time. Book Jacket. *Philadelphia Fire.* 1990. By John Edgar Wideman. New York: Vintage-Random, 1991.

INTRODUCTION

Suggesting a central accomplishment of *Invisible Man,* Eric Sundquist writes: "No book...sums up the psychological and cultural effects of segregation in the United States more thoroughly than Ellison's" (2). His statement edifies on two accounts. First, it notes the novel's ingenuous meditation on the absurd ironies of America's separate-but-equal society. Second, it appreciates *Invisible Man*'s quirky, yet undeniable exemplarity in fictions about twentieth-century black life. Seeing Ellison's freewheeling burlesque of tragically miscarried democracy requires much discernment, yet sensing his precise spot in the contemporary literary pantheon is even trickier. When a spectator ponders the Ellison of post–*Invisible Man* celebrity, who lectured widely, served on the boards of cultural institutions, and received prestigious awards, he perceives a writer firmly ensconced in mainstream American culture. The post-1950s Ellison looks securely, if always tempestuously integrated. Still, behind the deft intellect and sartorial refinement that permeated Ralph Ellison's later persona, vague remnants of the desperate, fighting writer always remained. This fighter is a wordsmith who anticipates Ishmael Reed's pugilistic prose, and he is a Midwesterner with a temper, a man ready to knuckle up over the seriousness of his craft. To truly comprehend Ralph Ellison and his prodigious triumph in *Invisible Man,* one must acknowledge the perilous straddling that typifies his life and his literary career.

Encapsulating Ellison has proven so daunting that only recently have extended biographical treatments of him begun to appear. Given this reality, trying to paint a full picture of this complex man in the brief space of an introduction seems misguided. This section abandons any pretense toward exhaustiveness; instead, it selectively recounts the broad contours of Ellison's existence. Devoting considerable attention to Oklahoma, Tuskegee, Harlem, and his post–*Invisible Man* public intellectualism, this account strives to give the reader glimpses of the crucible in which Ellison's literary sensibility evolved and the backdrop against which his professional identity coalesced. Suggesting the heterogeneous encounters and the sober, measured reactions that filled his life, these remarks hint at the underpinnings of a pluralist, yet fiercely independent character. Such peremptory work should thin the thicket that ensnares Ralph Ellison's masterpiece, a needful preliminary if one is ever to leave this forest happy.

Ralph Waldo Ellison entered the world on March 1, 1913, inheriting not only the name of one of America's first towering intellects but also the robust expectations of his parents.[1] Reared in South Carolina and Georgia respectively, Lewis Ellison and his wife, the former Ida Millsap, each carried candid impressions of their Southern origins. Lewis had seen the ebb and flow that Reconstruction occasioned in the life of Alfred, his father. He knew that the South could propel a black man to a seat of power and then in an instant dash that seat to indistinguishable pieces of kindling. Although her experiences involved a different gauntlet, Ida also appreciated the limits of early twentieth-century Dixie opportunity. She was raised in Walton County, a rural farming community that in the wake of World War II would be the site of the Moore's Ford lynching. While this high profile eruption of racial violence would not occur until 1946, seeds portending such calamity were already germinating in the years before World War I. Aware of these realities, the young couple, even before they had children, decided to live in Oklahoma City thereby demonstrating a daring and a practical creativity that aptly foreshadowed the literary exploits of their second-born son.[2] Many critics have noted the profound lessons that Oklahoma frontier life taught Ralph Ellison; nevertheless, the fullest story of the novelist's roving imagination must consider the duo that conceived him amid the wide open spaces. The mixed results of Lewis and Ida's Ellison's Western odyssey reveal much about the winding and not always glorious trek that their son took to success.

As Maryemma Graham and Jeffrey Mack have noted, Lewis Ellison possessed "an enterprising spirit" (21). Predisposed towards independent entrepreneurial ventures, his efforts took the form of selling ice and delivering coal. Lewis's family prospered when his businesses did well, but his unanticipated death in 1916 became a material and a metaphorical gap that the Ellison household and Ralph, in particular, would struggle mightily to fill. Because of Lewis's passing, Ida Ellison not only entered widowhood but also poverty. Her resourcefulness allowed her to secure a domestic position that included residence in the parsonage of Avery Chapel African Methodist Episcopal Church. Notwithstanding an employment history dotted with such housekeeping jobs, Ida Ellison took pains to ensure that her sons grew into well-exposed young men. John Callahan expressed this woman's character aptly, writing that "Ida Ellison worked as a domestic, but she was never domesticated" (5). Callahan mentions her political activism, noting that she campaigned for Eugene V. Debs's Socialist Party and opposed Oklahoma City's restrictive housing covenants, and stressing that her actions were not confined to the public sphere, he states that she "regularly brought books and magazines home from the white houses she cleaned" because "she was determined that her son become acquainted with the widest possible world of culture, music, and politics" (8). No doubt, this fact informed Ralph Ellison's fierce insistence that depravation should not excuse mediocrity. Despite believing this with all of his being, he could not shake the irrefutable facts of his upbringing. Ralph Ellison was a child who became fatherless at three, and he was a precocious boy whose mother only narrowly kept her family fed and sheltered. These circumstances blessed him with a richly textured vision of resilience, and they bred within him a proud sensitivity that marked his entire life. The same reservoir of chutzpah that allowed his withering reaction to Irving Howe's black test essays about *Invisible Man* also pushed him for years to fudge his age and the details of his high school matriculation so that he could conceal the fact that he graduated a year late. Personality indisputably infuses these decisions, but the specifics of his situation often made maneuvers necessary. Just as much as the elastic sensibilities of the frontier, these needs also fueled Ellison's intimate appreciation of irony.

Commentators from Hollie West to John S. Wright have eloquently extolled the heterogeneous treasure that frontier life constituted for Ellison (West 11–14; Wright 6–7). Aside from providing him with variegated male role models who could to some degree dim the effect of his father's death, the Deep Deuce, as Ellison's black Oklahoma City neighborhood was called, also initiated him into the disciplines of artistry. His earliest experiences focused on music, and his bifurcated tutelage reveals much about the dichotomous aesthetic that pervades his celebrated fiction. While Mrs. Zelia N. Breaux formally introduced Ellison to music theory as part of the Oklahoma City school curriculum, her efforts were complemented by the young Ellison's wide circulation among the acts that filled the town's musical landscape. In particular, he frequented Slaughter's (a cabaret) and the Aldridge Theater, listening to the sounds of Charlie Christian, Lester Young, and blues icons like Gertrude "Ma" Rainey (Graham and Mack 23). Just as Ellison later blanched at attempts to segregate modernist experimentation from vernacular structures, he resisted any temptation to fault the musicianship of the black purveyors of gospel, blues, and jazz. If Ellison's aspiration was to write a "symphony encompassing his varied experiences," then his determination to capture the "rocking power" of his life in "classical form" stemmed more from the epic potentialities of symphonic composition than from an inherent suspicion of the nobility of jazz and the blues (Graham and Mack 23). As his experiences at Tuskegee suggest, Ellison's ambitions often partook of his subtle appreciation of excellence's spoils.

Ellison's trumpet-playing earned him all sorts of gigs in Oklahoma City, and in 1933 it also resulted in a state scholarship for him to attend Tuskegee University. If the symmetry between this detail and the similar, albeit modified odyssey of his nameless protagonist in *Invisible Man* seems pregnant, then other facets of Ellison's time at Tuskegee refine the contours of the institution's impression on him. Ellison ultimately matures to a lampooning of Booker T. Washington's cultural architecture, yet one notes, perhaps best in his reaction to the New York performance of the Tuskegee Choir, a genuine appreciation of acclaim. He is no spectacle-hound in the P. T. Barnum mold, but Ellison's delight in opulent achievement, fueled no doubt by his exposure to the music-drenched world of cutting contests and trash-talking virtuosity, finds something seductive in specific Tuskegee examples. For instance, William Dawson, the organizer of the Tuskegee School of Music, possessed skills as a director and a composer that fired Ellison's ambitions. Listening to the performances of Dawson's choir, Ellison fantasized about limitless creative possibilities and the satisfaction of earned repute. Ironically, the budding Oklahoma City composer never became Dawson's star pupil.[3] Like so many aspects of his Tuskegee tenure, Ellison's initial intentions miscarried. Despite such drifting, the equivocal treasures of the institution never escaped his notice. This is true for a variety of reasons, but a basic one is too seldom mentioned. Tuskegee was Ellison's direct, extended confrontation with the torturous, yet resplendent dimensions of black existence in the American South. Although the university vexed him, as the site of another full fledged African American community, it also challenged and refined his curiosity. The vigor of an encounter in 1942 where he, his friend Mike Rabb, and soon to be close acquaintance Albert Murray gabbed about the old stomping ground suggests how intensely Ellison marveled at not just isolated relationships but also the entire Tuskegee phenomenon (Ellison and Murray xxi). The variety of his experiences tells a compelling story of why.

If Ellison at first believed that William Dawson was going to be the master teacher who delivered him to virtuoso status, then he soon discovered that Hazel Harrison and Morteza Drexel Sprague were more pivotal players in the abbreviated, yet integral drama of his matriculation.[4] Harrison, the inspiration for a recurrent wizened voice in several of Ellison's essays, arrived at Tuskegee after studying in Berlin and circulating among some of Europe's leading pianists. Catholic in musical taste and unrelenting in matters of artistic discipline, Harrison not only encouraged her students to incorporate all sorts of influences into their performances, but also she literally introduced them to the brokers who were in the 1930s helping to thrash out the priorities of black cultural production. Robert O'Meally describes such an encounter: "One afternoon [Harrison] gathered students in her studio to meet her personal friend, Alain Locke...Locke, an intellectual stimulus to Ellison for several years, had just returned from Paris, and at Tuskegee he talked informally about artistic and intellectual trends in Europe." This kind of first-hand access made a mighty impression on Ellison because it showed him "the world of [creative] pursuits of the highest order" (20). Although he ultimately traded his horn for a pen, Ellison's appreciation for Harrison's tutelage never waned. The same could be said of his exposure to another member of the Tuskegee faculty.

In his sophomore year, Ralph Ellison took a literature class with the head of the English department, Morteza Drexel Sprague. Young and energetic, Sprague became something akin to a guide through and an emblem of literary possibility. Ellison would discover T. S. Eliot's "The Waste Land" on his own, and he would always be a voracious and a self-motivated reader. Despite these tendencies, he benefited immeasurably from Sprague's instruction and from his administrative presence. Robert O'Meally identifies Sprague as a part of Tuskegee's "intellectual avant-garde" (19). Waxing poetic, Albert Murray, in *South to a Very Old Place* (1971), avers that the school's "post-Booker T. Washington Liberal Arts Emphasis...was the very self and voice of Morteza Drexel Sprague" (126). In many ways, personalities like Harrison and Sprague simultaneously extended and foiled seminal Tuskegee traditions. Their approaches ruptured the institution's enduring pragmatism and at the same time exemplified why it could always lay some claim to intellectual vitality. Even as Ellison filled his fiction with unstinting critiques of Tuskegee's malicious myopia, he always included lyrical details that symbolized a lingering wistful romanticism.

It was forever paradoxically the site of startling disillusionment and glimpsed artistic liberty. If Tuskegee marked a second point of Ellison's tripartite initiation into public blackness, then Harlem, both in artistic and in cultural terms, indicated the final corner of this triangle.

Aside from catapulting Ellison into the company of elder statesmen like Langston Hughes, Alain Locke, and Richard Wright, Harlem also exposed him to the leftist circles that would allow his earliest forays into publishing. Although he would eventually minimize their importance to his artistic development, when Ellison reached New York in the summer of 1936, his posture towards these contingents acknowledged their generosity and betrayed an enthusiasm that bordered on giddiness. His cheeriness was not difficult to understand. Due to some confusion regarding his scholarship, he had been forced to leave Tuskegee. Sensing that New York might be a place to earn money and further his studies in sculpture and music, he packed up, in the throes of the Great Depression, and headed to the spot dubbed the capital of black America. He was not without contacts in the metropolis, yet anticipating the fate of his famous protagonist, Ellison's brace of introductory letters fell on barren ground (Jackson 168). To a young man with so few concrete prospects, consistent and substantive contact with literary luminaries and cultural agitators must have seemed like manna indeed. Ellison still viewed himself as anything other than a writer when he arrived in Harlem. Arranging composition lessons with Wallingford Reigger and sculpture instruction with Richmond Barthé, he clung to earlier incarnations of his artistic destiny (Busby 11). After his mother's death in 1937, writing's prominence as a career option increased dramatically.

The emotional toll of losing a parent as a toddler differs decidedly from the anguish that such an event unleashes in the life of a promising, yet unproven man in his twenties. Probing the shape of these differences provides clues about Ellison's art and his disposition that are beyond the scope of this introduction; nonetheless, what can be stated unequivocally is that Ellison's emblematic orphaning immediately preceded his decisive turn to the life of the pen. Perhaps, the infinite field afforded by composition suited the ironic possibility within his plight. More likely, he felt motivated to honor the enduring faith of his progenitors, one of whom he knew and another whose presence an intense reverence made almost palpable. Whatever explains the cause and the quality of Ellison's embrace of writing, the fact that it had begun is evident in his activities in 1937. After attending his mother's funeral in Dayton and spending over half a year there, he returned to New York and, at the request of Richard Wright, wrote a review of Waters Turpin's novel, *These Low Grounds*.

This review marked the beginning of a period where Ellison would discover both the thrill of getting published and the parameters of his artistic praxis. Between 1937 and 1945 when he began work on *Invisible Man,* Ellison, according to Mark Busby's selected bibliography, published over 20 non-fiction prose pieces and some 10 or so short stories (155–157). Often placing these works in radical publications like *New Challenge, New Masses,* and *Negro Quarterly,* he acquired during this interim a sophisticated perspective on the American socio-cultural landscape. In part, this sophistication arose from the broad exposure offered by his employment. For example, Richard Wright pulled strings to get Ellison a position with the Federal Writers' Project (FWP). Aside from foraging through the archives of the Schomburg Library, Ellison, whose chief assignment was a book intended to be entitled *Negroes in New York,* also interviewed elder denizens urging them to yield up the stories of their lives. This exercise shaped Ellison's aesthetic proclivities and introduced him to vivid scenes, portions of which are recycled in his fiction (Busby 12; Foley par. 7).

Ellison's FWP job extended from 1938 to 1942, and through it he not only surmised an artistic calling but also a season of economic security and social vitality. Ellison later describes the leftist ideology and lifestyle as one by which he was seduced. The cosmopolitan spaces and the urbane philosophies that defined pre–World War II radical New York may have held for him somewhat the status of a potential lover whose mysterious, alluring contours are at first only glimpsed; still another reason for his evocation of seduction could have been the memories of the intensity and the rapidity with which his relationship with his first wife, Rose Araminta Poindexter, blossomed. Rose Poindexter was born in 1911, and by 1935 she had fashioned an acting and dancing career that had taken her to Europe. Though he described her as "politically alive," yet "not an intellectual," Rose combined an activist mindset and a domestic sensitivity that contented Ralph Ellison (Rampersad 110). After meeting her in the spring of 1938, the two moved in together. By the fall of that same year, they were married. Practically, this marriage, spanning from 1938 to 1945, was symptomatic of "a young man involved in his first significant sexual and emotional commitment," but symbolically, its coincidence with Ellison's professional and political evolutions ignited wonderment (Jackson 212). Why did Ellison the novitiate gravitate towards one type of woman while a more seasoned Ellison desired another? Certainly, these types of questions extend beyond the realm of political creeds and socio-cultural convictions; nonetheless, their proliferation amid the variegated experiences of his unfolding life is noteworthy.

In 1943 seeking to control the circumstances of his participation in World War II, Ellison joined the U.S. Merchant Marine, which he considered the least prejudicial branch of the military. His tour of duty exposed him to Wales and London, producing dramatic situations and perspectives on citizenship that would color his writings. More than that, his armed forces interval allowed the buzz around his artistic stock to grow. After placing several pieces, both critical and creative, in non-mainstream venues, Ellison in 1944 began to crack the circle of middle-brow journals and anthologies. *Tomorrow* had accepted his short story "King of the Bingo Game" in 1943, and based on the efforts of Ellison's literary agent Henry Volkening, the publication in 1944 purchased a second piece "In a Strange Country." Aside from these developments, Edwin Seaver, who was compiling a fiction collection, decided to include Ellison's "Flying Home," a work that he had completed "in Stanley Hyman's living room...literally hours before shipping out" to the war (Jackson 296). This publication flurry combined with his growing public acclaim as a shrewd cultural critic made Ellison a hot commodity, and in the summer of the year, he received the flattery of being courted with book contracts by Atlantic Monthly Press; Harcourt Brace; Little, Brown; and Reynal & Hitchcock (Rampersad 178; Jackson 299). Such pursuit even with the damper of a steadily crumbling marriage stroked the confidence of the trumpeter turned writer. Other personal and professional events buoyed him even further.

On the advice of Horace Cayton, Ellison applied for and in 1945 received a Rosenwald Fellowship. The generosity of this grant combined with the boon of his burgeoning romance with Fannie McConnell Buford proved a convenient portal through which he could step into the imaginative universe of his novel. As Virginia Woolf has seriously, yet wittily observed, writing requires "five hundred a year" and "a room of one's own" (106, 108). While Woolf's quip ostensibly addressed the plight of women writers, its relevance for Ellison cannot be gainsaid. Where the Rosenwald and a book advance dented the economic strain in his life, it was Fanny who diligently and consistently carved out for Ellison the monetary and spatial liberty necessary for creation. Not only was she steadily employed, a ready typist, and a fastidious filer, but also her zeal in insulating him from distractions was indispensable. Introduced to one another in 1944 when both were slogging through failed marriages, the couple bonded instantly, and within a short time they were living together. By 1945 their devotion was so complete that each expedited a divorce. Fanny and Ralph Ellison were married in 1946 (Rampersad 209).

The story of how *Invisible Man* arrived to the public in the form that it did perhaps begins with Ellison's decision in 1944 to sign a contract for his first novel with Reynal & Hitchcock. At that time the subject of the book was a black pilot who after being shot down spent time in a Nazi prisoner of war camp. Arnold Rampersad has determined that between this incarnation and its definitive draft as the tale of an invisible man, there exists another tentative effort about Bard, "a black man," and his experiences at "a Southern college" (194). While it is difficult to know exactly when these three options were reduced to one, Ellison's feelings about his time in Vermont during the summer of 1945 are quite lucid. From the moment that he and Fanny first moved in together, they, as would be the case for the bulk of their life together, resided in Harlem. This arrangement given its duration suited the couple, yet the constraining effects of the environment occasionally led first Ralph and then the duo to seek relief outside the city. The generosity of their friends John and Amelie Bates at times afforded them a country vacation. It was on Ralph Ellison's second such Vermont getaway in August 1945 that the coalescing germ of *Invisible Man* appeared. From these origins, the route to the novel's publication in 1952 meanders prodigiously.

The initial agreement with Reynal & Hitchcock identified a September 1945 delivery date (Rampersad 179). Although the summer had been productive, it also pushed Ellison into the peculiar situation of working on a text that was dramatically different than the one he had proposed. He requested and received a six-month extension, but by mid-1946, it became clear that he would need more time to tame both his intentions and his vast output. Deliverance arrived for him in the form of a balky transition and some key defections. Frank Taylor, the editor who had secured Ellison's Reynal & Hitchcock contract, left the company after a succession generated some ripples. Persuading his new employer Random House that Ellison's first novel was worth its attention, he negotiated a new contract and along with it a new deadline, November 1947 (Rampersad 211). *Horizon,* a British magazine, published the first chapter of *Invisible Man* in October 1947, and many spectators, among them his editors who by now at least tacitly included Albert Erskine, assumed that the balance of the text was in the works. Such was not the case, and no other sections of the novel in progress would be published for five years. Like his protagonist, Ellison's journey to an authoritative word would deploy him all over New York.

From haunting Harlem bookshops to toiling away in Fifth Avenue apartments, Ellison during his work on *Invisible Man* existed in an array of concentric orbits (Jackson 331; Ellison viii). His and Fanny's apartment provided a stable base, but appearances on television shows, installing high fidelity stereo equipment, and taking pictures demanded that he venture out into the city's maelstrom away from his notebooks. Occasional loops to the New England countryside, usually to visit Stanley Edgar Hyman and his wife Shirley Jackson, peppered this routine, and over a long, yet steady interval Ellison amassed the manuscript of his first novel. The core chapters of the book along with the Prologue were produced roughly sequentially. By 1950 he submitted these to Erskine who was now the point man on the project. Erskine's reactions were overwhelmingly enthusiastic, yet the editor and the writer sensed within the manuscript a pivotal lack. With Ellison's contrivance of an epilogue, a complement to the prologue's frame, an ingenuous solution materialized. Thus, 1951 marked an end to a season of artistic toil, and unbeknownst to the laborer, it simultaneously portended scarcely imaginable rewards.

Published in 1952 to several remarkably appreciative reviews, *Invisible Man*'s most propulsive honor was its choice as the recipient of the 1953 National Book Award.[5] Gwendolyn Brooks's poetry collection *Annie Allen* (1949) broke new ground for African Americans by capturing the 1950 Pulitzer Prize, and Ellison a few years later joined her with his unprecedented achievement in fiction. Founded in 1950 by the American Book Publishers Council, American Booksellers Association, and Book Manufacturers Institute, the National Book Award immediately became one of the most coveted literary distinctions in America. Ellison's feat in garnering this prize is made more impressive when one considers that in order to do so he had to best novels by Ernest Hemingway and John Steinbeck, two bona fide artistic titans. Although Richard Wright's *Native Son* and *Black Boy* broke barriers when they were adopted by the Book-of-the-Month Club, Ellison's distinction singularly placed him in the mainstream of both popular and critical opinion. His life changed incalculably on the crest of such success. In many ways Ellison's receipt of the National Book Award inaugurated his slow, yet inexorable transition from a creative writer into that potentially allied, yet more anomalous figure, a public intellectual. A large part of that intellectualism stemmed from his almost obsessive need to manage the reception of his masterwork. Notwithstanding that seemingly interminable and eventually distracting assignment, Ellison pursued other rich opportunities.

Just as the news of the *Brown v. Board of Education* decision (1954) was fitfully making its way into the national consciousness, Ellison and Fanny exhausted by the welcome, yet strident rigors of literary celebrity, also weighed the prospect of a protracted stay abroad. Chosen for a Prix de Rome Fellowship, Ellison thought that the award would give him space to work on his next novel. The interval in Italy from 1955 to 1957 emerged as one of the most tempestuous of both his personal and professional life.

Serious marital problems developed as Ellison became intimately involved in an affair (Rampersad 341–346). On top of this, his habits of
composition and his peculiarly sensitive intellect did not completely synch
with his environment. Europe for Ellison, contrary to the experiences of
a host of black expatriate artists, would remain a space of cerebral rather
than direct physical engagement. While his appreciation for its palpable
historicity survived, after he left in 1957, he would only return once.

Ellison's battle to complete his second novel extends from the mid-
1950s all the way to the end of his life. As early as 1958, he sent a lengthy
excerpt to Saul Bellow who accepted and eventually published it in a new
journal *The Nobel Savage.* Despite this fortuitous start, the book would
not give; thus, for more than four decades, the writer would calculate his
travel plans, accept and deny employment, begin and end friendships, and
ultimately craft narratives of apology all for the sake of a never-completed
work. Speculation as to why this novel was not finished will continue un-
settled for as long as Ralph Ellison is discussed, yet the array of activities
that surrounded and at times competed with his efforts to craft a follow-
up to *Invisible Man* offer their own intriguing conjectures. After initially
spurning offers of visiting positions at colleges and universities for fear
that they would hamper his progress, Ellison in 1958 gave teaching a try
through an appointment at Bard College. From then on, he would be af-
filiated in succession with Rutgers (1962–1964), Yale (1964–1965), and,
after a five-year hiatus dotted with sporadic appearances elsewhere, New
York University (1970–1979). These appointments immeasurably buoyed
Ellison's financial stability, and they gave him a firsthand perspective on
the alternately pedestrian and profound circuits of academic exchange.
Still, in sum they, as he had initially feared, did not solve the riddle of his
work in progress. That is not to say that he did not draft pages during his
stints; rather, the necessary compass of inspiration could not be summoned
to preside. If the novel stubbornly lagged, then other efforts were more
fruitful.

Ralph Ellison's first essay collection, *Shadow and Act,* hit bookstores
in 1964, and as an instrument to burnish his mainstream man of letters
credentials, the collection functioned deftly. Composed between 1942 and
the beginning of the 1960s, the book, while varied, persistently reveals its
writer's belief in America's pluralist ideals. Such faith looked for many
audaciously courageous, and the book's admirers proclaimed it insightful and inspirational. In the context of increasingly militant civil rights
demands and rumors of war, others saw its premises and conciliatory energy as puzzling. The flurry of prominent public service appointments and

social honors that fell to its author and his zealous investment in them did little to quell the perplexity about his true allegiances. From 1960 to 1969, Ralph Ellison not only joined elite arts organizations like the National Institute of Arts and Letters and the Century Association but also received appointments from President Lyndon Johnson to the Carnegie Commission on Educational Television, the National Council on the Arts, and the Board of Directors for the inchoate John F. Kennedy Center for the Performing Arts. These associations were not inherently debilitating, but they fed Ellison an image of himself as something other than a fiction writer. For a man who often harnessed desperation to shape himself professionally, the effects must have been pronounced. To an intermittently vexed creator of a chronically unruly book, the commitments provided distractions that were by turns flattering, frustrating, and seductive.

In 1969 Ellison earned the Presidential Medal of Freedom, for distinguished civilian service, and in 1970 he garnered the Chevalier de l'Ordre des Artes et Lettres, a French honor created to recognize contributions to the arts. These accolades cemented his status as an intellectual luminary, a status that only grew when he was elected to the elite American Academy of Arts and Sciences in 1975. While these honors gratified the proud Ellison, their palliative effect could not blunt the growing suspense about the fate of his second novel. A 1967 fire at his and Fanny's summer home in Plainfield, Massachusetts, consumed some of his revisions and notebooks; nevertheless, hiccups in his work could not solely be explained by the trauma of this event. In fact the astounding reality of the second book as a dream deferred might be the sheer number of pages that Ellison was able to draft for it. By 1977, eight sections of the novel constituting "approximately 150 pages" had been published in different venues (Graham and Mack 44). Notwithstanding this output, the will to fuse these disparate elements forever remained thwarted. Even in the throes of this kind of paralysis, Ellison's professional legacy while hotly debated attained a vintage where retrospectives were appropriate. Looking over the landscape of his career, most spectators could not deny his role in liberating certain vistas.

If the 1960s occasioned attacks on Ellison's heraldic advocacy for technical mastery and animosity about his critiques of Black Power, then by 1970 a special issue of the magazine *Black World* at least hinted that attitudes towards the demanding elder were more complicated. *Black World* was not alone in its backward glance. That same year the *College Language Association Journal* the print organ of the black literature and language professional organization devoted its entire March edition to articles about Ellison. These gestures not only marked the first stages of what would be a protracted taking stock but also signaled a highly equivocal, almost initiatory rapprochement between him and some of the fledgling writers born into the post–World War II America in which he composed *Invisible Man*. These artists regardless of their ideological stripes for the most part deemed Ellison the supreme yardstick of black potential. At the beginning of the 1970s, they were tentatively exploring the parameters of his example. By the decade's end, they were ready to weigh in eloquently and affirmatively.

The Ralph Ellison Festival at Brown University took place in November of 1979, and its proceedings captured in the 1980 issue of the journal *Carleton Miscellany* bespoke a moment of coronation (Wright 3–6). Not a half decade before three brash youngsters from Hollis Queens would proclaim themselves kings, a significant crop of intellectuals and writers were giving Ellison the royal treatment. Within a few years, their sentiments would become a consensus, as a slew of literary critical books accorded the writer a foundational position in the development of late twentieth-century novel-writing. The seeds of this centrality could be glimpsed in a 1978 *Wilson Quarterly* poll of American literature professors. Asked which novel published since World War II was the most important, the majority chose *Invisible Man* (Posnock xiv). The literati were not the only ones boasting a feting mood. In 1985 President Ronald Reagan awarded Ralph Ellison America's highest artistic tribute, the National Medal of Arts. Ellison's inclusion in the first group of citizens ever to be so honored speaks volumes about his stature. At 73 years old, his climb to the heights of creative eminence was not only complete, but it was as he had steadfastly hoped working itself into the fabric of the nation's memory. No firmer testimony could be secured that history would not forget him. As a valedictory gesture, the publication of his second essay collection *Going to the Territory* (1986) complemented this season of encomia. It reinforced the guiding principles that distinguished his unique slant on life.

Succumbing to pancreatic cancer, Ralph Waldo Ellison passed away on April 16, 1994. Within a year, three compilations *The Collected Essays of Ralph Ellison* (1995), *Conversations with Ralph Ellison* (1995), and *Flying Home and Other Stories* (1995) appeared. By 1999 *Juneteenth: A Novel* supplemented this bevy, and in 2000 *Trading Twelves: The Selected Letters of Ralph Ellison and Albert Murray* came out. *Living with Music: Ralph Ellison's Jazz Writings* (2002) is to date the most recent posthumous publication of Ellison's writings. Surveying this harvest one must acknowledge the heterogeneous intellect required to produce so much, so well. Despite this admission, *Invisible Man*, when pitted against its author's other works displays a higher order of excellence than any them. It is the realization not only of a sophisticated aesthetic ideal but also of an epoch's prevailing spirit.

To fully grasp what Ralph Ellison accomplishes with his first novel, one must ponder the anonymity that enshrouds most African American novels written between 1945 and 1960. The prominence of James Baldwin's *Go Tell It on the Mountain* (1953) and the keen anticipation that preceded Richard Wright's *The Outsider* (1953) give an impression that black fiction in the civil rights era was all about nascent literary fame. A quick glimpse at Nathaniel Hooks' *Town on Trial* (1959) belies any such notion. Hooks, a Navy veteran, saw his first novel manuscript destroyed aboard a ship. Later, when he found employment as a welder, he would cap a long shift at the plant by turning to his new project, a slowly unfurling courtroom drama. Hooks believed deeply in the significance of publication. Even though the journey required hard sacrifices, he derived exquisite joy from Exposition Press's printing of *Town on Trial.* Ultimately his enjoyment would be the novel's most illustrious legacy since it brought him nothing by way of wider acclaim. This neophyte and his odyssey exemplify the complex interplay of aspiration and achievement that pervades African American fiction in the middle of the twentieth century. The more than 200 novels by blacks that surface from 1945 to 1960 show that a legion of sable scribes earnestly bent their pens toward enduring approbation.[6] Ironically, few if any of them joined Ralph Ellison in crossing the finish line. Ellison forever conquered obscurity through the singular act of composing *Invisible Man,* and in doing so he simultaneously embodied and transcended the strivings of his frequently indiscernible peers.

NOTES

1. Controversy surrounds Ralph Ellison's birthday, but following the arguments outlined in Lawrence Jackson's *Ralph Ellison: Emergence of Genius* (2002) and Arnold Rampersad's *Ralph Ellison: A Biography* (2006), this guide will retain the 1913 date (1; 5–6). See John Callahan's introduction to *Ralph Ellison's Invisible Man: A Casebook* (2004) for arguments in favor of March 1, 1914 as Ellison's birth date (7, 19).

2. Ralph Ellison is the first of Lewis and Ida's children to reach adulthood, but the couple lost their firstborn child, Alfred. See Jackson (1) and Rampersad (5).

3. Robert O'Meally's *The Craft of Ralph Ellison* (1980) mentions that in 1934, William Dawson was the musical director for a production of Willis Richardson's play *Compromise* (19). Ralph Ellison was cast in this production. Although this association seems promising, it is clear that Ellison never became one of Dawson's favorites (Jackson 148, 149).

4. Beyond the well-known duo of Harrison and Sprague, Arnold Rampersad discusses the importance of Walter B. Williams a college librarian to Ellison's Tuskegee days (61–74).

5. While the National Book Award understandably dominates public perception of Ralph Ellison's plaudits, Arnold Rampersad makes clear that the novelist deeply treasured accolades from African American organizations like the Robert S. Abbot Memorial Award from the *Chicago Defender* and the Russwurm Award from the black National Newspaper Publishers Association (280).

6. At Kansas University, Maryemma Graham heads "The Project on the History of Black Writing." She has compiled the best extant database of African American novels. Throughout this book, her list informs all of the numbers related to publication.

WORKS CITED

Busby, Mark. *Ralph Ellison*. Boston: Twayne, 1991.

Callahan, John F. Introduction. *Ralph Ellison's "Invisible Man": A Casebook*. Ed. John F. Callahan. New York: Oxford UP, 2004. 3–19.

Ellison, Ralph. Preface. *Invisible Man*. New York: Vintage, 1989.

Ellison, Ralph, and Albert Murray. *Trading Twelves: The Selected Letters of Ralph Ellison and Albert Murray*. Eds. Albert Murray and John F. Callahan. New York: Vintage, 2001.

Foley, Barbara. "Ralph Ellison as Proletarian Journalist." *Science and Society* 62 (1997): 24 pars. Aug. 1, 2007 <http://victorian.fortunecity.com/holbein/439/bf/foleyreleft2.html>.

Graham, Maryemma, and Jeffrey Dwayne Mack. "Ralph Ellison, 1913–1994: A Brief Biography." *A Historical Guide to Ralph Ellison*. Ed. Stephen C. Tracy. New York: Oxford UP, 2004. 19–55.

Jackson, Lawrence. *Ralph Ellison: Emergence of Genius*. New York: Wiley, 2002.

Murray, Albert. *South to a Very Old Place*. 1971. New York: Vintage, 1991.

O'Meally, Robert G. *The Craft of Ralph Ellison*. Cambridge: Harvard UP, 1980.

Posnock, Ross, ed. *The Cambridge Companion to Ralph Ellison*. Cambridge: Cambridge UP, 2005.

Rampersad, Arnold. *Ralph Ellison: A Biography*. New York: Knopf, 2007.

Sundquist, Eric J., ed. *Cultural Contexts for Ralph Ellison's "Invisible Man."* Boston: St. Martin's Press, 1995.

West, Hollie. "Growing Up Black in Frontier Oklahoma...From an Ellison Perspective." 1973. *Speaking for You: The Vision of Ralph Ellison*. Ed. Kimberly W. Benston. Washington, DC: Howard UP, 1987. 11–14.

Woolf, Virginia. *A Room of One's Own*. 1929. San Diego: Harcourt Brace Jovanovich, 1989.

Wright, John S. *Shadowing Ralph Ellison*. Jackson: UP of Mississippi, 2006.

Chapter 1

CONTENT

As Ellison struggled through the early moments of composing *Invisible Man,* he wrote to Richard Wright:

> It isn't the prose, per se, that worries me; it's the form, the learning how to organize my material in order to take the maximum advantage of those psychological and emotional currents within myself and in the reader which endows prose with meaning; and which, in the writer, releases that upsurge of emotion which jells with conceptions and makes prose magical. (RWP Aug. 5, 1945)

His ruminations on form reveal the intimate connection he anticipates between the content of his work and its structure. He greatly admired rhetorical theorist Kenneth Burke, who argues that in literary works form and content enjoy a pragmatic relationship such that "at every point, the content is functional—hence, statements about a poem's 'subject,'...will be also statements about the poem's form" (102). As Ellison wrestled with the content of his novel, he pondered deeply how its organization could most powerfully tap into the deepest reservoirs of the reader while also achieving the polished arrangement he felt distinguished great literature.

Understanding his conception of how narrative form and content interrelate vaults a review of *Invisible Man*'s content from mundane summary to the first step of determining its meaning. Similar to blues and jazz music, Ellison insisted that the literature of black Americans best captures the complexity of black existence by giving form to chaos. The pain, agony, and perseverance coloring their cultural past endow minority writers with the opportunity to present American experience with new depth and truth; for Ellison, the form of such an endeavor naturally returns to Burke's model for tragedy. Ellison explains that his novel reflects a "three-part division," in which each part represents the "narrator's movement from...purpose to passion to perception. These three major sections are built up of smaller units of three which mark the course of the action" (*Collected Essays* 218). With this form in mind, he crafts a linear narrative made simultaneously circular by the repetition of the mini-evolutions charting his protagonist's movement from personal and social naiveté to enlightenment.

The Burkean tragedic paradigm organizing the narrative proper is embedded within the frame of the prologue and epilogue. These framing portions establish the purpose of the narrative and reveal Ellison's desire to draw on black vernacular tradition. The frame forces readers to remain highly conscious of the narrator as a *teller* and writer of his tale and provides a foundation for understanding the unifying thread of the episodic story. *Invisible Man* begins with the narrator's the dramatic pronouncement, "I am an invisible man" (3). He clarifies that although he is invisible, he is not like one of Edgar Allen Poe's spooks or a Hollywood creation, thereby establishing his position in America's ever-evolving popular narrative forms. Contrary to popular belief, he asserts that he possesses a mind, a discovery he will return to in the epilogue to emphasize the circular nature of his story, and he insists that he is invisible only because others decline to see him. To illustrate the consequences of this optical problem, he recounts his altercation with a blond man. When the narrator accidentally bumps into the man and hears the man curse him, he demands that the stranger apologize and violently beats him when he refuses. The narrator only halts his frenzied violence when the humor of the situation strikes him; the man is being beaten by a phantom of his own imagination.

Discoveries like this, the narrator suggests, grant him a richer appreciation of his position in society and dictate new rules for his conduct. Since the general population refuses his humanity, he no longer abides by society's rules. His successful theft of energy from Monopolated Light & Power to light his rent-free basement abode offers a case in point. His battle reaffirms his "vital aliveness" and enables him to power the 1,369 lights illuminating his "hole," a forgotten section of a basement under a whites-only building in the border region of Harlem (7). He declares that light allows him to see his form and verify his reality; consequently, he is in the midst of covering his walls with lights and plans to turn to the floor when he finishes. Considering the ingenuity of his strategy, the narrator claims his position in the tradition of American tinkers. He is a "thinker-tinker" (7).

Ellison introduces the generative nature of jazz through the narrator's reflection on Louis Armstrong. Recalling an experience of listening to "What Did I Do to Be so Black and Blue" while high on reefer, he discovers he can enter the music and compares his experience to a fight he witnessed between a yokel and a prizefighter. The yokel beats the scientifically superior fighter by stepping inside his sense of time. Like the yokel, the narrator enters Armstrong's song and "descends" its levels "like Dante." In this italicized portion of the text, the italicization representing deep or subconscious thought, he describes seeing an ivory-colored girl pleading before slaveowners bidding for her naked body, and on a lower level he hears a sermon on the "Blackness of Blackness" (9). Turning his attention to the old singer of spirituals, he acknowledges his acquaintance with ambivalence, one of the central emotional states he struggles to comprehend throughout the framed narrative. When she divulges that although she both loved and hated her master who gave her several sons, she loved freedom more, he suggests that "freedom lies in hating" (11). She disagrees, insisting that freedom lies in loving. When he presses her to refine her idea of freedom, she concludes, "I guess now it ain't nothing but knowing how to say what I got up in my head" (11). His additional questions distress her, and one of her sons repays him for his insensitivity by striking him and commanding, "Next time you got questions like that, ask yourself!" (13). As the music beats faster, the narrator begins to yearn desperately for tranquility and slowly emerges from the depths of the music to hear Armstrong ask, "What did I do to be so black and blue," a question that he feels demands action (12).

The narrator concludes his prefatory remarks by proclaiming that "hibernation is a covert preparation for a more overt action" (13). He wonders whether his urge to capture invisibility in words, or his desire to become a writer, is really an urge to make music visible. Before launching into his retrospective narrative he admits that he is irresponsible, and in a tone smacking of Dostoyevsky's *Notes from the Underground* (1864) protagonist, insists that he cannot be held accountable since "responsibility rests upon recognition" (14). Submitting his altercation with the blond man as proof, he decides that all dreamers and sleepwalkers share a responsibility to society, and he implies that his tale will in some way pay his debt. His focus on responsibility and writing rounds out the prologue with a nod to what the framed portion should accomplish: a presentation of individual experiences that yield personal insight useful for a broad audience. In other words, the narrator undertakes the task of the American novelist.

PURPOSE

In Burke's structure for tragedy, purpose constitutes the illusion of being able to act, an apt description for much of the narrator's early experiences. He begins his narrative by noting that it goes back some 20 years and details his struggle to define his identity in spite of the constellation of forces aligned against him. Notwithstanding the boldness of his current proclamation, "I am nobody but myself," he admits his former shame regarding himself and his heritage (15). His grandparents had been slaves until 85 years prior to the penning of his story and the narrator reveals that he is believed to have taken after his grandfather. On his deathbed the old man summoned enough strength to enjoin the narrator's father "to keep up the good fight" because "life is a war" and he has been a traitor all his life. Instead of viewing meekness as merely conciliatory, he directs his son to live with his head "in the lion's mouth" and "overcome 'em with yeses, undermine 'em with grins, agree 'em to death and destructions, let 'em swoller you till they vomit or bust wide open" (16). The dying man then commanded his son to share this vital counsel with the children, but the narrator's parents order him to forget the old man's words.

Despite his parent's admonition, the grandfather's words color all the young protagonist does and thinks, and his repeated contemplation of the old man's advice underscores the circular nature of his tale. When he is invited to give his graduation speech at a function for the most powerful white men in town, he worries that despite his honest desire to please those in authority he is carrying out his grandfather's polemical advice. His personal policing of such a devious mentality obliges him to acquiesce when the men demand that he participate in a battle royal before delivering his speech. Feelings of discomfort only arise from his sense of superiority over the other black boys taking part: he worries associating with them may detract from his speech. We quickly perceive the narrator's small-minded naiveté when he expresses shock at observing the prominent white men, not his black peers, behaving with drunken abandon. To make matters worse, the riotous men force him and the other boys to join their lascivious enjoyment of a blonde dancer performing completely naked. The narrator's description of the blonde signifies one of his earliest experiences with contradictory feelings. In subconscious recognition of his inherent connection to her, he silently declares, "I wanted at one and the same time to run from the room, to sink through the floor, or go to her and cover her from my eyes and the eyes of the others with my body; to feel the soft thighs, to caress her and destroy her, to love her and murder her" (19).

Tellingly, his obsession over the purpose he imagines accounts for his presence at the gathering blinds him to the demeaning position the white men impose on him. He observes the men's animalistic attitude but remains oblivious to the invisible social constructs authorizing the scene. When the men cover his eyes with bands of white cloth, the irony of his lament that he "was unused to darkness," richly imparts the severity of his cultural blindness (21). Throughout the violence and chaos of the fight he practices his speech and hopes it will be effective. Even when the men expose their sadism by directing the boys to collect their prize money from an electrified carpet, the narrator remains focused on his speech. He is only slightly sidetracked by his yearning to obtain the most money. Forgetting his bruised and battered body, he proclaims his intention to "get the gold and the bills," "use both hands," and throw his "body against the boys...to block them from the gold" (26). This willful sacrifice of his already broken body for monetary gain, in addition to a white man's designation of him as "Sambo," establishes his tendency to act the part of this derogatory symbol and anticipates a later scene involving an old-fashioned Sambo-like figurine bank (319).

The night culminates with the physically broken narrator delivering the first of several speeches in his narrative. As he struggles through the blood and saliva choking him, he confuses the words of his valedictory oration and mistakenly says "social equality" while trying to say "social responsibility" (31). His anxious correction of this blunder signals his desperate attempt to abide by Booker T. Washington's philosophy—he parrots the former college president's 1895 Atlanta Exposition address—as well as his fear of angering whites. Satisfied with his performance, the school superintendent gives him a leather briefcase containing a scholarship to the local Negro college. The dribble of bloody saliva he unintentionally drools onto his prize metaphorically forecasts the violence and chaos awaiting him on the path the scholarship commences, but the narrator obliviously runs home overjoyed by his good news. He looks triumphantly at his grandfather's photograph, but that evening he dreams of the enigmatic old man who directs him to open his briefcase. Inside he finds a letter that says, "Keep This Nigger-Boy Running" (33). So begins his long journey to enlightenment.

The narrator renders his college memories in a naturalistic style that reflects both his frame of mind during that time in his life as well as the image the college projects. He describes the campus grounds as if they are something out of a pastoral and pauses to contemplate the statue of the founder. The bulk of his school memories surround his experience with Mr. Norton, a rich, white trustee whom he is charged with driving around campus. As the ride begins the protagonist is quickly caught up in trying to decipher Norton's vague description of his commitment to the college. The trustee explains that he is a Northerner, recommends Emerson to the narrator, and divulges that his philanthropic mission derives from a commitment to his beautiful daughter who passed away unexpectedly. The sexual undertones of his description of his daughter, combined with his erotic portrayal of the founder's work as turning "barren clay into fertile soil," connect him to the sexually deviate men of the battle royal, but once again the protagonist fails to penetrate this meaning (45). Lost in his own thoughts, the narrator stumbles upon Jim Trueblood's cabin and unwittingly discloses that the sharecropper has impregnated both his wife and daughter. Norton demands to talk to the farmer, and upon facing Trueblood he indignantly proclaims, "You have looked upon chaos and are not destroyed!" (51). To the narrator's horror, the sharecropper agrees to the trustee's request that he share his story.

Trueblood is a gifted performer and clearly enjoys his dubious fame. He begins his account by relating how the college officials tried to run him away when his predicament first became known, gloating over how the powerful whites protected him and repeatedly listened to his tale, wanting to hear "about the gal lots of times" (53). As he launches into the heart of his saga, the narrator notes that Trueblood's voice assumes a "deep, incantatory quality, as though he had told the story many, many times" (54). He details how he mistakenly had sexual intercourse with his daughter whom he was forced to sleep beside because of his family's dire economic circumstances. The particulars he shares as he leads up to the all important dream, as well as in the dream itself, highlight the strong sexuality pervading his cabin. Trueblood recollects smelling the "fat meat" in the cold night and thinks of how his daughter looks like his wife when she was young before he begins reminiscing of lovers from his past (54). He transforms sites of the country into erotic and suggestive images that anticipate his transgression. Piling metaphor on metaphor he compares listening to the boats in Mobile to seeing watermelons "split wide open a-layin' all spread out and cool and sweet on top of all the striped green ones like it's waitin' just for you, so you can see how red and ripe and juicy it is and all the shiny black seeds it's got and all" (56). This picture leads seamlessly to thoughts of girls in red dresses and specifically to his old girlfriend who whispered "Daddy" in the night in much the same manner that his daughter Matty Lou does.

The sharecropper suggests that Matty Lou's untimely murmur forces him back to the present and sets him speculating over whether his daughter and the boy hanging around her have become physically involved. As he angrily mulls over this possibility he drops into a dream that commences with his search for fat meat, a repeated detail indicating the artful nature of his tale. His dream search leads him to the home of his white boss, Mr. Broadnax, and he enters the house by the front door. Once inside he finds the interior appointed with shiny furniture and numerous pictures until he finds himself in a white bedroom, a foreshadowing of the mystery woman's apartment where the narrator later finds himself trapped. When a white lady steps out of the clock and grabs his neck, Trueblood tries to escape her hold, and they fall onto the white bed. Through the terror engulfing him, he hears Mr. Broadnax say, "They just nigguhs, leave 'em do it" (58). At this point Trueblood escapes into the clock where he runs down a long dark tunnel which ends with a burst of electric light that scalds him as he drowns in a lake of water. He then awakes to find himself atop Matty Lou and he vainly attempts to extricate himself without moving because moving "would be a sin" (59). When his wife awakes to this sight she begins hurling any object she can find ignoring Trueblood's contention that he has only committed a "dream-sin" (62). When he fails to get off of her child, apparently waiting until Matty Lou climaxes before he moves, Kate levels a gun at her husband before she settles for an ax, brutally cutting his face. After her wrath finally subsides, Trueblood does not know where to turn and begins singing a church song but ends up singing the blues, determining, "I ain't nobody but myself" (66). With this conclusion Norton gives him a $100 bill and weakly tells the narrator that he needs a stimulant.

The narrator decides to take the trustee to a local brothel, the Golden Day, its name based on the title of Lewis Mumford's critical classic *The Golden Day* (1926). As he steers the car toward the bar, he recognizes the familiar sight of the veterans who are mental patients in a nearby asylum. Although Norton is barely conscious in the back seat, when the narrator explains who the vets are, the trustee notes that they should have "an attendant" reflecting both his characteristic belief in order as well as his subconscious perception of the immediate danger of impending chaos (73). The protagonist reflects inwardly that although the vets have been labeled crazy, he wonders whether they simply engage in a subtle game he cannot understand. When he arrives to the bar, Halley, the owner, refuses to allow him to take whiskey outside of the bar for fear that he will get in trouble with the school officials. Halley's additional quip that they "don't Jimcrow nobody" at the Golden Day subtly anticipates the inverted racial power dynamic existing inside his tavern (76).

At his wit's end, the narrator returns to the car to retrieve Norton and finds him unconscious with his open mouth revealing "amazingly animal-like teeth" (76). Two vets help him transfer Norton into the Golden Day with one pausing to declare the trustee Thomas Jefferson and therefore his grandfather. Inside the saloon other patients proclaim him John D. Rockefeller and the Messiah, suggesting the mythic stature white men assume in unstable black minds. Supercargo, the vets' giant attendant, appears in his boxer shorts and attempts to reassert order, but without his starched white uniform and straightjacket, metaphors for white power and brutality, the men balk at his commands. Thus both symbols of white authority, Norton and Supercargo, lose control of their positions as the vets begin to beat Supercargo brutally in the frenzied intoxication of newfound freedom. One vet directs the narrator to observe him kicking the felled attendant, admitting "sometimes I get so afraid of him I feel that he's inside my head" (84). The double images of white dominance intimate that the vets are not insane; instead, they are victims of the emotional trauma white power and control systematically wreak on black minds.

As the narrator's panic rises to a fever pitch amid the chaos, a seemingly sound vet directs him and Mr. Norton to a private room where the trustee can recover. To the narrator's ever escalating horror, when they arrive in the room, a prostitute begins to expound upon the sexual vigor and bestiality of white men. She supports her assertions by describing the parallel between their social and sexual desires: white men "want to have the whole world" (88). Sarcastically building on her observations, the vet attending Norton declares him a "trustee of consciousness" (89). The narrator misses the implications of their statements and sees only Norton's status and the immediate impact that incurring his displeasure might have on his future. When Norton revives, the vet speaks openly about his past and eventually causes the narrator as much discomfort as Trueblood. He recounts how American racism forced him to surrender his dream of gaining dignity through his profession as a surgeon, and he mockingly listens to Norton's assertion that the college is his destiny. The vet's tirade reaches a fever pitch when he describes the narrator as "invisible" and orders both men away, commanding them to "descend...into chaos" (94, 95).

This initial confrontation with the idea of invisibility makes virtually no impact on the narrator. He shakily drives Norton back to the idyllic campus, which now appears threatening as he imagines the consequences awaiting him. Bledsoe, the college president, worriedly greets his return and berates him for allowing the trustee to direct their drive. The narrator is shocked by the president's admonition that contradicts everything Bledsoe preaches in public. He is even more surprised to witness the president masterfully mask his emotions before speaking to Mr. Norton. Erasing his angry exterior, when he arrives before the trustee, Bledsoe croons over Norton's slight injury like a grandmother and promises him that the narrator will be disciplined. Although Norton assures Bledsoe that the protagonist is not at fault, his inscrutable manner and assertion that he will not "be needing the machine" leave the narrator apprehensive about his appointed meeting with Bledsoe (108).

Before he reports to the president, the narrator must attend chapel, and as he observes other students approaching the space of worship, he notices their acute sense of being on display. Even natural elements such as the moon transform into a "white man's bloodshot eye" under the auspices of the surveillance-oriented campus (110). The students mechanically perform spirituals for the millionaires' pleasure, and the narrator recalls his own previous performances upon the stage. His orations had been elocutionary triumphs rather than meaningful discourses, and he ironically recreates a former address which plays on musical reference, traditional black sermonic turns, and verbal charisma—all replacements for substance. These memories of his own oratorical artifice segue into Reverend Homer A. Barbee's sermon. When the preacher stands from his seat beside Bledsoe, the narrator reflects that it seems as if part of the college president had stood and moved forward while the other part remained seated, intimating the unnerving connection between Bledsoe and Barbee.

Barbee's homily artfully recounts the history of the founder. Much like Booker T. Washington's autobiography, *Up from Slavery* (1901), Barbee's account includes key details that play on Frederick Douglass's archetypal slave narrative and seek to cement the founder's authority in black cultural history. Barbee's oration also imbues the founder with qualities that liken him to Aristotle, Moses, and Jesus. Using call and response as well as masterful rhetoric, Barbee impresses upon the narrator the treachery of any act that endangers the school and its legacy, for the college. more than just an institution of higher learning, is an integral part of black spiritual and cultural heritage. The preacher's sermon, filled with vivid visual images, emphasizes Bledsoe's position as the founder's heir, a designation overlaid with religious imagery, and demands that the narrator view his transgression in an equally spiritual manner. Under the spell of the reverend's words, the narrator admits, "old Barbee had made me both feel my guilt and accept it" (134). Unable to contain his emotion, he stumbles out of the chapel certain that leaving the hallowed grounds of the college would be like the "parting of flesh" (133).

Bledsoe's office, the scene of the narrator's judgment, epitomizes the school's function as a space for wielding and displaying power. The president questions the narrator harshly, disbelieving his answers and proclaiming, "Nigger, this isn't the time to lie" (139). In stunned disbelief, the narrator endures his interrogation while desperately hanging onto his old understanding of the world. Bledsoe's announcement of his intention to expel the narrator enrages the younger man, and the narrator impulsively threatens to tell everyone of the president's duplicity. His menace only elicits laughter from Bledsoe who proceeds to lecture the naïve student on the nature of power, his own path to authority, and his dedication to maintaining his station at all costs. Bledsoe concludes his rant with a promise to assuage the narrator's embarrassment over being expelled by sending him to New York where he can work for the summer and earn enough money to pay his tuition the coming year. The president counsels him to keep his eyes open, and as he fingers the slave shackle that he calls a symbol of black progress, he directs his gullible listener not to open the sealed letters that will serve as his introduction to powerful friends of the school who might employ him. Topping off the first two pieces of paper the narrator has received—his high school diploma and dream letter from his grandfather—Bledsoe's sealed epistles represent the repetitive nature of the narrator's reconception of his purpose.

When the protagonist boards the bus to New York, he finds the vet seated on it, too. He has no choice but to sit beside the talkative vet since blacks are only permitted to occupy the back of the bus in the Jim Crow South, but he internally yearns to distance himself from all reminders of past unpleasant experiences. Rather than attempting to learn from the traumatic episodes, he tries to bury them. The vet is undeterred by the narrator's inhospitable manner and teasingly describes the many possibilities that await him in New York. He encourages the narrator to "learn to look beneath the surface" and to be his "own father," and he mockingly tantalizes him by discussing the prospect of interacting freely with white women (153, 156). As if to validate the premonitory quality of the vet's words, the narrator's first unnerving experience in New York involves riding pressed close to a white woman on the subway. He is shocked by the sights of blacks in New York filling roles not allowed in the South, but he remains focused on patterning himself after Dr. Bledsoe.

His monomaniacal commitment to this narrow idea of success reflects his dedication to his purpose as he imagines it. As he confidently delivers his letters to the men of power the envelopes name, he dismisses the quizzical looks he receives from secretaries. He only becomes concerned after a week passes and none of the offices have contacted him. To guard against the possibility that the secretaries have tampered with his previous letters, he requests an appointment with Mr. Emerson and is elated when his petition is granted.

On the morning that he is scheduled to meet Mr. Emerson, the narrator encounters a man pushing a cart down the street and singing a blues song. The man introduces himself as Peter Wheatstraw, but to the narrator his strange song and perplexing questions link him to the Golden Day vets. Wheatstraw explains that his cart is filled with blueprints for all sorts of things which were never built because people changed their plans. Hearing this, the narrator confidently responds that it is best to remain committed to a plan of action prompting Wheatstraw to observe, "You kinda young, daddy-o" (175). As the narrator leaves the cart man, he wonders about the contradictory nature of Wheatstraw's song, a song that subtly foreshadows the unveiling of Bledsoe's letter in Emerson's office.

The Wall Street space reminds the narrator of a museum and dazzles him beyond anything he has seen at college. Still eager to inhabit a realm where power is displayed ostentatiously, he divulges to the young man who takes his letter his hopes to become Bledsoe's assistant. The young man's attempts to dissuade him from returning to the South, in addition to his talk of abstract ideas and the unjust nature of the world, distress and confuse the narrator, who accuses the white youth of attempting to thwart his ambitions. Realizing his mistake, the young man reveals that Emerson is his father and shows Bledsoe's letter to the protagonist who reads it in disbelief. Bledsoe's letter clearly asserts that the narrator will never be readmitted to the school and exposes the malicious nature of the president's plan. Stunned beyond belief, the narrator mechanically rejects young Emerson's invitation to a party, job offer to be his valet, and advice about for a job at Liberty Paints. As he rides on a bus back to Harlem, he recognizes the tune a man hums in front of him and intones the words, "*Well, they picked poor Robin clean*" (193). The meaning of Bledsoe's treachery removes his blinders to his cultural past, and he feels intimately connected to the subject of the folk song. He realizes that he will never be the same and is filled with a desire for revenge, but he first decides to look into the job at Liberty Paints. Thus ends the first incarnation of his sense of purpose.

PASSION

Burke describes passion as the predicament of being acted upon and suffering, the circumstance of working tirelessly only to find self-sacrifice on the other end. The narrator initiates this new phase of his journey by seeking a job at Liberty Paints. The factory is located on Long Island and its sign emerges out of the fog to read "Keep America Pure With Liberty Paints" (196). This logo, along with its emblem of a screaming eagle, signals the metaphorical implications of the narrator's coming experience. He is assigned to work in a section of the factory where the company's most renowned product, "Optic White" paint, is produced by adding ten drops of a black substance to white paint. The factory touts the flagship color as the purest white paint ever prompting the narrator to wonder if Optic White covers the buildings on the college campus. His boss informs him that the batch he is working on is destined for a national monument and orders him to follow his directions but not to think, an order the narrator scorns. When he runs out of the black substance responsible for making the paint so white, he mistakenly refills his dropper with concentrated remover. His paint samples go from being smooth and white to sticky and diffused with gray. His boss, furious upon discovering his mistake, allows him to finish the job even though the corrected samples remain tinged with gray. When the buckets are ready for delivery, he releases him.

The narrator is then sent to work for Lucius Brockway in the basement of a factory building. The small, elderly black man suspiciously assesses the narrator and inquires about his education and skills. Although the narrator can tell that Brockway is not educated, he guesses that like other black men he has known, Brockway probably performs the work of an engineer by virtue of his on the job training and long tenure at the company. Similar to the black drops added to the company's most profitable white paint, Brockway symbolizes blacks' roles as the foundation for great American structures. The old man brags about his indispensable position in the factory and explains that although he cannot even read a blueprint, his ability to mix the base for all the paint produced by Liberty Paints cannot be duplicated, declaring *"we the machines inside the machine"* (217). He brags that he even helped create the slogan for Optic White, "If It's Optic White, It's the Right White" (217). The narrator silently derides Brockway's reverence for the factory, so similar to his own past feelings about the college, and even connects the Optic White slogan to the childhood chant "white is right," which he inexplicably forgets that both the vet and Bledsoe suggested he, too, believed. Filled with his new sense of knowing, he decides that he dislikes Brockway, who reminds him of the old black men that he has been counseled all his life to respect.

When the narrator retrieves his lunch from the factory locker room, he happens upon a union meeting. The members violently attack his admission that Brockway is his foreman and declare him a fink without allowing him to defend himself. They vote on whether to allow him to join the union before he can even express interest, capping off his sense of denied agency. He returns to the basement only to meet Brockway's fury when he tells the old man that he was held up by the union meeting. The old man's frenzied vow to kill the narrator, an additional ironic parallel to the narrator's recent declaration to kill Bledsoe, kindles the narrator's wrath, and the younger man throws himself into fighting his elder. He only stops when Brockway begs for mercy. Trusting the old man's agreement to call a truce, he realizes too late that his conniving supervisor has something up his sleeve. As the machines begin to hiss, Brockway orders him to turn the white knob, which triggers a massive explosion that the foreman laughingly escapes.

The narrator awakes in the factory hospital where he hears voices diagnose him as "merely stunned" before they state that he will be kept for observational purposes (231). He is placed inside a kind of glass machine where he receives brutal electrical shocks, and throughout this experience he hears various kinds of music that remind him of his childhood and build on the folk tunes he recalls after reading Bledsoe's letter. In stark contrast to these tunes, the doctors discuss his treatment in cold, scientific terms that thinly veil their barbarity. When the electrotherapy resumes, the shocks fill the narrator's mouth with blood while the doctors quip, "Look, he's dancing" and jeer "Get hot, boy!" (237). The gratuitous violence of the scene recalls the battle royal, and the entire hospital experience suggests a kind of rebirth. Yearning for freedom from the machine, he thinks "When I discover who I am, I'll be free" (243). He recoils when the nurses cut the cord attached to his stomach, again signaling the pain associated with rebirth, and when the director informs him that he will be released but will no longer work at the factory, he enigmatically inquires whether the man knows Norton. He leaves the hospital realizing that he is no longer afraid and notes that his mind and body are no longer getting around in the same circles; this discovery indicates an existential theme in the text.

Notwithstanding his new sense of freedom, as his "infant eyes" focus on the city around him, he faints (251). A passerby named Mary Rambo observes his weakened state and insists that he come home with her where she can nurse him until he recovers. He submits to her hospitality and only returns to the Men's House, his old abode, after he is well rested. Upon entering his residence, the narrator looks at the men gathered in the lobby through new, knowing eyes. He feels free and scorns the illusions that they operate under. In a burst of fury he mistakes a well-known preacher for Bledsoe and covers him with the contents of a spittoon. His rash act bars him from returning to the Men's House so he goes back to Mary's where he continues his struggle with the new "contradictory voice" in him (259).

The narrator yearns for inner peace, and in an effort to calm his roiling emotions, he plunges into the Harlem streets that have been transformed by new fallen snow. As he passes local shop windows, their paradoxical displays uncover the identity confusion that plagues the black community and keep his emotions boiling. He decides to buy a baked yam from a street vendor in an effort to reclaim the personal authenticity and frankness he long ago abandoned. Declaring "I yam what I am," the narrator vows to begin thinking for himself again and basks in a feeling of freedom reclaimed (266). His triumphant mood receives a jolt when he stumbles upon an eviction. The old woman being forced from her home seems to speak directly to him when she decries her predicament, and the marshal's command to "Shake it up" echoes the white men's calls to "Mix it up" during the battle royal, linking the experiences and emphasizing the narrator's new state of mind (268, 22). The history he observes through the mélange of objects reminds him of his own familial past, and before he realizes what he is doing, he finds himself making a passionate speech to the crowd. Like the speeches he recalls giving in the chapel, his words at the eviction display more emotion than thought, and eventually the crowd surges past him in violent protest. Their action again recalls his past experience as a woman kicks the downed marshal in the same way a vet at the Golden Day kicked Supercargo. His description of her face "a blank mask with hollow black eyes" denotes her similar mental state (280). The circularity of his experiences highlights the unacknowledged parallel between the North and the South and indicates the necessity for watchfulness in both regions. The narrator subconsciously recognizes this; thus, when Jack compliments his speech and offers him a job, he notes that the redheaded man seems to be "acting a part" and rejects his proposal as likely another instance in which someone was trying to use him (288).

The smell of Mary cooking cabbage impels him to reconsider Jack's proposal. He realizes how unthinkingly he has relied upon Mary's generosity and decides to find out more about Jack's offer. At a party in a building called the Chthonian, conspicuously named after the home of the underworld gods in Greek mythology, Jack informs him that his organization, the Brotherhood, would like to make him the next Booker T. Washington. The narrator is flabbergasted by their proposal and impressed and flattered by their interest in him. Notwithstanding the vague and confusing terms they use to describe the Brotherhood mission, he accepts their job offer and agrees to cut off his connections with Mary, his family, and anyone else from his past. He even accepts the new name that Jack directs his mistress, Emma, to hand him along with $300 and the promise of a handsome salary. Although the Brotherhood's manipulative tactics are clearly displayed, the narrator ignores all signs of the group's dictatorial and exploitative nature. Not even a drunken brother's request for the narrator to sing a spiritual, or "git hot," a sinister repetition of the factory doctor's sadistic jibe, clues the narrator into the organization's true essence (312). He simply laughs off the incident and returns to Mary's feeling excited and expectant.

The next morning the narrator awakes to the clamor of tenants banging their pipes to protest the loss of heat in the apartment building. In a frenzy of enlightened outrage, he strikes back at the insensitive bangers by beating a Sambo bank noisily against his pipe. When the bank shatters under the force of his wrath, he decides to give Mary enough money to cover the coins from the crushed bank rather than inform her of the mishap. His unwillingness to confront Mary as he embarks on a new path symbolizes the return of the mentality he possessed prior to his hospitalization. Tellingly, his attempts to dispose of the broken bank are thwarted at every turn, and he is forced to take the broken image with him as he begins his Brotherhood work.

For his first assignment he speaks at a rally organized to solidify Brotherhood presence in the black community. Before delivering his address the narrator realizes the venue for the rally is the same location where a black prizefighter lost his sight in a crooked fight. Startled but not deterred, he nervously awaits his turn to speak in the arena. The canvas covered platform and blinding light evoke the battle royal episode, and once again, he depends on a traditional black oratorical mode to buttress his performance. A voice from the crowd establishes a familiar call-and-response pattern, and the narrator delivers an emotionally charged speech that concludes with his tearful revelation that he feels "more human" (346). The crowd erupts in approval, but many of the brothers denounce his performance as unscientific and incorrect. He is ordered to spend time studying Brotherhood ideology with Hambro and returns to his apartment to ponder this new and exciting phase of his life.

Four months later while the two men are having a drink at the El Toro Bar, Brother Jack announces the narrator's appointment as the chief spokesman for the Harlem district, "a new instrument of the committee's authority" (363). At his first meeting in Harlem, the narrator encounters Tod Clifton, the local youth leader in Harlem and learns about Ras the Exhorter, the head of a black militant group. He and Clifton decide to take their message to the streets to challenge Ras directly, and during the narrator's first street oration, a brawl with Ras and his men erupts. In the midst of the altercation, Ras fervently exhorts Clifton to leave the Brotherhood and join his exclusively black outfit. He lectures both young men on the innate dishonesty of white people whom he insists could never value them and honestly respect their talents. Clifton and the narrator are momentarily caught up in his eloquent plea, but the narrator breaks the spell by returning to Brotherhood rhetoric and informing Ras that they will continue to spread their message in the community.

The narrator passionately throws himself into his work with great results and fancies himself somehow a latter-day Frederick Douglass. He connects the high school speech that won him his scholarship to the other speeches that have propelled him forward and sees in his success a legacy reminiscent of the great abolitionist's. His continued naiveté hints at his mistaken focus; instead of concentrating on his oral performances, he should be connecting the written documents that have defined key moments in his life, a truth driven home when he receives an unsigned note at his Brotherhood office. The handwritten message warns him against moving too fast in the Brotherhood and deeply disturbs the narrator who views the organization as a sacred space of racial and social solidarity untouched by such spitefulness. Uncertain over where to turn for assurance, he questions Brother Tarp about the Harlem district's view of his work. The old man reassures him of the community's support for his efforts and seeks to allay his fears further by placing the narrator's political work in larger historical terms. He tells the young leader of his 19 years on the chain gang and bequeaths the link he filed to escape to the bewildered but touched narrator. Although he admits that he neither wants the token nor knows what to do with it, the narrator accepts the gift and ponders its significance.

PERCEPTION

Ellison explains that each of the three major sections of the narrative "begins with a sheet of paper" that directs the narrator "through illusion to reality" (*Collected Essays* 219). The mysterious note that raises the specter of duplicity within the Brotherhood ranks and indirectly prompts Brother

Tarp's story represents the final paper incarnation of a descriptive identity note. For the rest of the narrative, the narrator works to discover the truth about Brotherhood philosophy, and his gradual perception of his cultural value occupies a pivotal place in his perception. Burke described perception as a new awareness of the forces that govern the world, and in the final portion of the novel, this is exactly what the narrator achieves.

At the next committee meeting, a black brother named Wrestrum accuses the protagonist of attempting to use the Brotherhood for his own purposes and offers the magazine picture and article as proof. Although the committee finds the article harmless, they remove the narrator from his Harlem post until the other charges can be investigated. In the meantime, he is reassigned to speak on the Women Question. His anger over his predicament quickly subsides as he decides that his reassignment demonstrates the Brotherhood's belief in his ability to address all aspects of their ideology. At his first lecture on the Woman Question, a female from the audience invites him to her house to clarify aspects of Brotherhood philosophy. The narrator's description of her apartment, a richly decorated space that surprises him, recalls Trueblood's dream, particularly her white bedroom. Despite this premonitory scenery, he is unable to extricate himself from the situation, even when the woman confesses that she finds his speeches laced with something primitive and hears tom-toms in his voice. His feelings are conflicted, in much the same way that he felt as a boy watching the nude dancer at the start of the book, and he thinks fleetingly of stories of the historical reality of black men sexually exploited by white women. He ultimately gives in to her advances and awakes to find her husband looking down at him in a disturbing, yet unconcerned manner.

The narrator leaves the apartment horrified by his failure to withstand temptation and worried that the committee will learn of his transgression. Instead, he hears that Brother Clifton is missing and he is being moved back to Harlem to locate the vanished youth leader. When he returns uptown he finds the people disillusioned and antagonistic toward the Brotherhood. He discovers the district offices largely deserted and notes the disappearance of even Brother Tarp and the Douglass portrait that he had given the protagonist. After attempting to contact the committee leaders in vain, he decides to shop for new shoes so that the brothers will not be able to locate him when they do call. As he walks along the hot New York streets, he comes upon Clifton selling Sambo dolls. Clifton's spiel begins with "Shake it up," the same words the marshal at the eviction bellowed and an echo of the "Mix it up" the white men at the smoker commanded, and suggests the satirical nature of Clifton's position. The protagonist cannot fathom what could have brought Clifton to this point, and the obscene dancing doll enrages him. Unable to contain his anger, he spits on the mocking image only to illicit laughter from the crowd who instinctively connect the protagonist to the stereotype he has worked so hard to avoid. The scene renews his belief that only the Brotherhood saves him from becoming such a degrading figure and makes Clifton's decision to "fall outside of history" all the more perplexing. He walks away from the scene but then chances upon Clifton refusing to be pushed around by a police officer. When Clifton hits the officer, the policeman shoots him.

Witnessing Clifton's death forces the narrator to reassess his idea of the world, and he feels as if he is awaking from a long sleep. He sees the residents of Harlem with new eyes and questions his past relationship with them. Although he does not grasp the metaphorical implications of his discovery that Clifton had been making the paper doll dance by pulling an invisible black thread, the narrator senses that he must infuse greater meaning into his friend's death and absolve himself of any possible culpability. He resolves to organize a community-wide funeral for Clifton that will also protest police brutality and stages the funeral in the park to encourage the greatest participation. The funeral turns into a march complete with singing of old songs and speeches, but the protagonist feels unable to make it properly scientific and political. Instead, he gives a speech emphasizing Clifton's individuality and humanity. He feels his address is a failure, but when he looks into the crowd after he finishes, for the first time he sees not an undifferentiated mass, but the "set faces of individual men and women" (459).

When the Brotherhood leaders condemn the narrator for organizing a public funeral for Clifton, he explains that he tried to contact the committee for guidance, but when they failed to respond he was forced to act on his "personal responsibility" (463). In yet another circular move emphasizing the interrelationships between the narrator's experiences, his phrasing here echoes the words that he stumbled over in his battle royal speech. At the smoker he accidentally substitutes "social equality" for "social responsibility," but when the white men draw his attention to his mix-up, he quickly retracts his inadvertent words. His refusal to back away from his claim that his personal responsibility led him to spearhead Clifton's funeral starkly contrasts his previous commitment to pleasing the white men in power. Instead of buckling in the face of their anger, he challenges their assumptions about the black community and contends that their narrow ideas blind them to the complex humanity that Clifton embodies and Harlem embraces. For the first time in his life, the narrator accepts and celebrates the contradictions that his friend represents. He mocks Brother Tobitt, who suggests that marriage to a black woman provides him with intimate knowledge of black American life, and maintains that he knows about the consciousness of Harlem's black residents. In an angry outburst, Jack reminds the protagonist that he was "not hired to think" (469). Jack declares that the Brotherhood does not operate according to the childish ideas of the Harlemites; rather, they tell them what to think. The narrator's responding question as to whether Jack is their "great white father" or "Marse Jack" infuriates Jack to the point that his fake eye pops out and falls into a glass of water (473). The narrator correlates the physical blindness that the missing eye symbolizes to Jack's social blindness and realizes that his faith in the Brotherhood will never be the same.

As he makes his way to Hambro's home, Ras's men attack him ostensibly for the Brotherhood's failure to intensify their protest of Clifton's murder. The narrator decides that he needs a disguise to avoid their aggression, so he purchases dark green glasses and a wide hat. Everything looks different through the green shades in a way strangely reminiscent of his view of the other fighters through his blindfold at the battle royal. When a number of people mistake him for someone named Rinehart, he ponders the fluidity of identity and how his disguise makes him both highly visible and invisible. The more he is confused with Rinehart, the more the narrator realizes that endless possibilities exist for personal creation. Rinehart is a runner, a gambler, a briber, a pimp, a preacher, and probably fills a host of other identities. This knowledge shakes the foundation of the narrator's worldview, and he quickly discovers that brothers like Hambro are too narrowly logical to make sense of such human volatility. As Hambro lectures him on the necessity of sacrificing the Harlem community for the greater good of the Brotherhood, the narrator silently demands, "Look at me!," repeating an exclamation he first uttered in his initial Brotherhood speech (505, 345). Whereas he originally employs the words to direct the crowd's eyes to his blackness in affirmation of the Brotherhood's belief in the common man, his plea to Hambro reflects his new realization that the brothers are blind to his individuality. He leaves Hambro's apartment understanding his own complexity, accepting his past, and valuing his experiences. Instead of continuing to accept the reality that others have defined for him, he resolves to explore his invisibility and vows to sabotage the Brotherhood's work in Harlem. He thinks his plan reflects his grandfather's advice to "agree them to death and destruction," and he decides that in order to carry it out he will need a woman to inform him of the Brotherhood's real intentions.

He chooses a Brotherhood big shot's wife, Sybil, to mine for informa-tion. She is a middle-aged woman filled with stereotypical sexual fanta-sies about black men, and instead of uncovering the secret plans of the organization, the narrator finds himself participating in Sybil's perverted imaginative dramas. She begs him to pretend to rape her, and as they both become drunk, he impulsively scribbles "Sybil, you were raped by Santa Clause, surprise" on her stomach with her lipstick (522). He realizes that for her, and for the Brotherhood, he is no more than a mythical figure, and he sadly accepts this reality before falling asleep. He awakes to a frantic call from the district asking him to come to headquarters, and impulsively grabbing his prize briefcase, he coaxes Sybil out of his apartment and into a cab. When he crosses under the bridge into Harlem, a flock of birds shower him with defecation in a gesture of welcome to the boiling uptown streets.

The narrator enters the fray of the riot in a bewildered state and is promptly nicked by a bullet from a police gun. While the physical as-sault on his head is not fatal, it metaphorically represents the violence of his disillusionment. A man named Scofield generously suggests that the protagonist stick with them until he gains his bearings. The group of men that Scofield accompanies is not only stocking up on various kinds of merchandise from looted stores but also planning to burn down the ramshackle tenement in which they live. Fascinated by their commitment to their plan and its audaciousness, the narrator tags along and groggily takes in the sights of the riot. He assists the men in setting fire to their apartment building and celebrates their success, which he thinks signals a victory over the Brotherhood's dim view of their ability to take charge of their lives. Yet when someone describes the night as a "race riot," he real-izes that the events of the night do not signal victory or suicide but mur-der planned by the Brotherhood. Even his decision to feign agreement to the organization's philosophy contributed to the current destruction of the community. Seeing the white dummies hanging from light posts, he thinks of Sybil and wonders what is real and what is not, his feelings summariz-ing the larger state of confusion engulfing him. When he runs into Ras, sit-ting atop a horse and decked out in the garb of an ancient warrior complete with a spear, the Exhorter turned Destroyer is too much to bear. The narra-tor tries to explain that they have both been duped by the Brotherhood, but Ras commands his followers to hang the narrator like the dummies. The absurdity of the night descends upon the protagonist, and he realizes the futility of reasoning with Ras. He impulsively throws Ras's spear at him, catching the Destroyer through his cheeks, and flees the scene in a desper-ate and confused attempt to return to Mary's house.

He finds himself in a residential area listening to men discussing Ras's antics, and when he starts back down the street, two white men ask him what is in his briefcase. He darts away and, in his haste, falls into a manhole which someone has left uncovered. As the two men shout down at him, he realizes that he is no longer afraid. He mockingly replies to the men's demands as to what he has in his briefcase. Cursing him and dropping a few matches into the hole, they recover the manhole and leave him alone in the darkness. When he awakes he realizes that he will have to create a torch to light his way out of the hole, and since he cannot find any paper in the coal cellar where he has landed, he is forced to light his way out using the paper inside his briefcase. He first burns his high school diploma, next Clifton's Sambo doll which burns slowly and stubbornly, and then the anonymous letter warning him against moving too fast in the Brotherhood. The note burns so quickly that he takes out the paper on which Jack wrote his new Brotherhood identity to burn, too, and in the light of the fire he sees that the handwriting on the two papers is the same. Rocked by his discovery, he falls into a fit of rage to know that he had been named and sent running by the same pen. When he awakes from his fit, he has lost all sense of time and drifts back into a dream state. He dreams that Jack, old Emerson, Bledsoe, Norton, Ras, his high school superintendent, and others relieve him of all illusions by castrating him. With a sense of immense pain, he watches his generations wasting upon the air and water. Then he begins to laugh explaining that the death of his seed also represents the loss of their world, for he now sees that his presence in American society is inexorably tied to the country's success. He awakes to discover he is whole and decides to stay underground to think things out. He surmises, "The end was in the beginning" (571).

The narrator ends his story with the epilogue, a closing framing device. He confesses that his reflections constitute a lesson of his own life and notes that he has been trying to be honest in recounting his experiences. His "hibernation" has given him an opportunity to understand his invisible status, but he now realizes that he cannot remain hidden away because "there's the mind, the *mind*" (573). Returning to his grandfather's advice, he decides that the old man must have been counseling him to affirm the democratic ideal America was founded upon while he rejected the men who corrupted it. As he learned from his final dream, the joke in their perversity is that blacks are a *"part of them"* (575). Now that he understands this, he has been trying to figure out what he wants and who he wants to be, and his inability to answer these questions have kept him in his hole. Yet his effort to write his experiences down has shown him that much of his problem lies within him, and his acknowledgement of this implicitly returns to the old slave woman of the prologue who claimed that freedom is *"nothing but knowing how to say what [you] got up in [your] head."* Thinking over the horrors of history throughout the world, he asserts that he now possesses a better understanding of his relation to the world and wonders why so many people yearn for conformity when the real greatness of America comes from its diversity.

He knows now that few people truly understand this truth and therefore fail to comprehend the future of the country. As a case in point, he describes seeing Norton in the subway station. The old man is literally in need of guidance as to what train to take, but the narrator now realizes the trustee's cultural confusion. Again returning to the slave woman's words, he confesses that he knows now that he loves despite all that has happened to him and that trying to write all of this down has forced him to admit that he must end his hibernation. His narrative has attempted "to give pattern to the chaos which lives within the pattern" of life, but he vows to never lose sight of the chaos (580–581). This, he has learned, is the essence of a vibrant life. He closes with the question, "Who knows but that, on the lower frequencies, I speak for you?" (581). His final query proclaims his new conception of himself as well as those around him who imagine no connection to his life. Thus, the purpose that he originally imagines for his life and the misguided passion for action that lead him down a path of further self compromise finally give way to his perception of American society. This journey to tragic enlightenment reveals the success of the venture that he describes in the epilogue: he uses literary expression to transform his chaotic life into a means of illuminating the human condition. In much the same way that Ellison celebrates the blues as the most generative critical register for exploring black American existence, his narrator discovers via writing a method for achieving self-knowledge. Put simply, the content of the narrative he crafts gives birth to the narrator's *and* Ellison's form.

WORKS CITED

Burke, Kenneth. *The Philosophy of Literary Form: Studies in Symbolic Action.* 1941. Berkeley: U of California P, 1973.

Ellison, Ralph. *The Collected Essays of Ralph Ellison.* Ed. John Callahan. New York: Modern Library, 1995.

———. *Invisible Man.* 1952. New York: Vintage, 1980.

Richard Wright Papers. James Weldon Johnson Collection. Yale Beinecke Library.

Chapter 2

TEXTS

In the summer of 1945, Ellison secluded himself in a Vermont barn to explore the fictional consciousness of a black American pilot imprisoned in a Nazi war camp. As he wrestled with his prose, a voice proclaiming an invisible existence interrupted his thoughts. Ellison recalls this incident in the introduction to the thirtieth anniversary edition of *Invisible Man.* He describes the voice as possessing a down-home laughter and knowing irony that fused a constellation of experiences into one interconnected picture. Ideas as diverse as the nation's racial tensions and memories of children's games mingled naturally under the supervision of the raucous intonation. The blues timbre pervading the voice as well as its demands for a more experimental narrative struck Ellison as both akin to and distinct from the modernist literary legacy that he admired, and the novelist eagerly delved into the possibilities of such an approach. His method felt intoxicatingly genuine for probing black American existence and appropriately complex for presenting his artistic vision. Putting uncertainties of his success aside, he felt confident that the core notions his fiction sought to examine, as well as his narrative technique, contained value. He declared to Richard Wright in August 1945, "The only stable thing I have in all this sea of un-certainty is the raft of concepts on which I lie as I paddle my way toward shore. These I think are valid; and even though I fail they will be useful and will overlap with those being treated by anyone who truly writes of our time" (RWP). Similarly, seven years later when he had completed the page proofs of the novel, he reflected to his friend Albert Murray who was also in the throes of composition, "One thing both of us can be sure of is that whether our books are miscarriages or what not, this kind of labor of love is never lost... because just the effort to do what has never been done before, to define in terms of the novel that which has never been defined before is never completely lost" (Ellison and Murray 25).

These statements serve as bookends for the creative process that generated *Invisible Man*. While Ellison hedged his assessment of whether his novel would be successful, he unequivocally endorsed his maturing sense of artistry. In an interview three years after he published the novel, he described the odyssey behind it as providing him "the possibility of contributing not only to the growth of literature but to the shaping of [U.S.] culture" as he would like it to be (*Collected Essays* 224). He repeats this claim in several essays, and his words reveal the logic behind his creative philosophy. According to his writerly creed, American fiction should always aim to make a lasting and serious impression upon American culture, and he knew that this formed the very foundation of his artistic endeavor. He strove to answer the question of what comprised the "specific *forms* of [Negro humanity]," and in doing so, he felt that he moved closer to providing a more complete assessment of American identity (*Collected Essays* 213). In the end, he dedicated five years of his life to a novel that tackles this task with wit and verve, and in many ways, his success validates the artistic objective his novel celebrates.

TEXTUAL HISTORY

The first excerpt of *Invisible Man* Ellison shared with the public appeared in 1947 as a short story in the British literary periodical *Horizon*. Although the piece became known as the battle royal scene, he initially titled it "The Invisible Man" and was greatly encouraged by the reviews. In January of 1952, two months before the publication of the complete novel, he published the prologue in *Partisan Review* and again received a largely positive critical response. By the time the novel appeared in March, Ellison had immersed himself in a second novel to stave off the creeping depression he felt over having finished his initial tome. He also was returning to the critical writing that would ultimately comprise a significant portion of his artistic legacy. Despite these efforts to spring ahead, the phenomenal success of the novel reclaimed his attention. During the months immediately following its release, *Invisible Man* was widely hailed a landmark success, and Ellison was described as a leading black American author and invited to give countless talks and interviews. The novel won the National Book

Award in 1953 and began being translated for foreign language editions the same year. After it appeared in Great Britain in 1953, it was published in no less than 13 languages, sometimes in multiple editions.

Since its initial 1952 publication by Random House, numerous other editions of the text have appeared. In 1980 Franklin Library published two editions of the novel as a part of its Signed Editions series and 100 Greatest Books of American Literature series. Both books are handsome volumes with dark red leather-bound hard covers embossed in gold and include several illustrations throughout the text. The signed edition is illustrated by Will Harmuth and contains a special message to subscribers while the other edition features illustrations by Steven Stroud but lacks Ellison's signature and prefatory note. Harmuth's images depict several notable scenes. He portrays the narrator listening to music in his underground dwelling, the pregnant Kate and Matty Lou, the narrator accepting Bledsoe's reprimand, the old woman being evicted, Brother Tarp escaping the chain gang, the interior of Rinehart's church, and Ras attired for the riot. Stroud's pictures assume an even stronger semblance to portraits. He renders Trueblood telling his story to Norton, Bledsoe looking furious behind his desk, Lucius Brockway in the basement of Liberty Paints, Brother Jack eating cheesecake, Ras holding a knife with an anguished expression, Clifton manipulating a Sambo doll, and the narrator disguised as Rinehart.

The illustrations in both editions emerge as straightforward, sterile interpretations of the scenes they represent and largely substantiate Ellison's skepticism about translating his literary ideas into visual pictures. He originally asked John Groth to illustrate the edition and was dismayed when his friend described the terms of Franklin Library's commission for the work. Writing to Groth in October 1979, Fanny suggests that since the publishers seemed to be rescinding their offer of allowing Ellison to select the artist, he might "propose very definitely that the book not be illustrated at all" (REP Box 154). Although the editions clearly proceeded to be published with illustrations, the end result undoubtedly reminded Ellison of the difficulty such a task entailed. Even in projects he collaborated on with artists he knew well and greatly respected, such as the August 1952 *Life* photo essay he completed with Gordon Parks, he characterizes the work as ineffective due to the "tremendous difficulty of translating such intensified and heightened prose images into those of photography" (RWP Jan. 21, 1953). What is more, he refused countless proposals to make his novel into a film, turning down producers from Sydney Lumet to Roy Campanella, Jr., in the process. He told one hopeful producer he preferred his novel "be read rather than transposed into a form for which it was not written," and he goes on to outline the difficulties of adapting nuanced literary episodes into cinematic form (REP Box 153). He also rejected opera proposals from names like Gunther Schuller and a proposal by *Marvel Comic* to include *Invisible Man* in a new line of graphic adaptations of great twentieth-century books.

Ellison's ambivalence regarding the translation of his prose into pictures makes the Franklin Library editions intriguing exceptions. The "Special Message" in the signed edition also warrants attention as a kind of dry run for Ellison's much discussed introduction to the novel's thirtieth anniversary edition published in 1982. He worked hard on the short piece for the Franklin Library, and after numerous drafts he continued to express concern over its usefulness. Two years later Ellison revisited the strategy of his Franklin Library prefatory remarks and developed them into a valuable reassessment of his work. His introduction, reprinted in the 1992 Modern Library edition as well as the 1995 second Vintage International edition, retraces his thoughts during the creation of his novel and describes the larger issues permeating his conception of the work. In fact, notwithstanding his stated reservations about Henry James's famous prefaces, Ellison's introduction offers a Jamesian reframing of his text that is an important piece for readers to review.

The 1994 Modern Library edition also merits a brief mention for its preface by Charles Johnson. Although his celebratory remarks focus less on the intricacies of the narrative than on general thematic strokes, his words helpfully contextualize the novel as it was received in the 1960s. Taken together, all of these editions of the novel along with Ellison's introduction and prefatory remarks constitute an invaluable picture of *Invisible Man's* textual history. Yet nothing reveals more about the genesis of his novel than the manuscript drafts housed at the Library of Congress. Acquired between 1995 and 1997 from his wife, Fanny McConnell, the collection as a whole consists of 46,100 items divided into various boxes. The drafts and typescripts of *Invisible Man* fill 11 boxes plus one oversized box. The papers related to the composition of *Invisible Man* remain arranged by episode rather than chronological order to reflect Ellison's personal style of organization, and they reveal the meticulous and laborious nature of Ellison's creative method. He reworked numerous scenes several times and placed the typed and long-hand drafts in folders labeled by episode. For example, 12 folders bear the "Brotherhood" designation, and several others include pages pertinent to these scenes. Some folders boast 200 pages of manuscript including scraps of paper with scrawled sentences in the exact form they take in the 1952 text.

While this organization makes it difficult to determine the chronological order of Ellison's composition of these episodes, especially since he often uses different colors of paper randomly, his papers disclose the relentless nature of his revisions. The manuscript drafts incorporate a number of scenes not included in the published novel, and the original and final typescripts demonstrate how late in the compositional process Ellison implemented certain changes. He initially crafted a novel well over 800 pages in length, but before the serious editing began, he told friends he had cut 200 pages to get "it down to 606" pages (Ellison and Murray 19–21). His narrative technique aided him in reshaping his plot without compromising the essence of his text. Throughout the penning of his narrative he created countless outlines ranging from a 10-page typed scheme that sketches out the entire novel to countless mini-outlines for episodes, small scenes, and larger structural ideas. His skeletal plans helped him maintain control over his unruly narrative ideas with even snippets of paper displaying outlines with ideas numbered from 1 to 23. Typed drafts are often interrupted by narrative notes detailing the intended shape and goal of particular scenes and overarching ideas. Such examples show that Ellison left little to chance.

NOVEL GENESIS

To gain a solid sense of the novel's evolution, this chapter focuses on the most significant narrative differences between the manuscript drafts and the published work. Barbara Foley's article "From Communism to Brotherhood: The Drafts of *Invisible Man*" (2003) remains one of the only scholarly pieces to consider the manuscript drafts. Her targeted analysis concentrates on Ellison's evolving attitude toward communism and his depiction of the Brotherhood but does not present a picture of the manuscript in its entirety. This chapter adds to Foley's central and insightful claim that the manuscript reveals a greater interest in the portrayal of Harlem. In addition to considering the finer points of Ellison's extended contemplation of Harlem, it ponders episodes that reveal a fuller image of the narrator's romantic interests, the details of his Brotherhood work, major changes in the depiction of his college experience, and an array of interesting scenes completely deleted from the 1952 text. These narrative divergences reflect the dramatic evolution of the novel and the flexibility of Ellison's creative eye.

Ellison originally imagined depicting in rich detail the exigencies of black folk living in urban spaces, and he charged the character Mary with achieving this. He shares part of his original plan for her role in his short story "Out of the Hospital and Under the Bar" published in *Soon, One Morning* in May 1963. In the note preceding this piece, he laments the necessity for reducing Mary's role and asserts that the selected excerpt shows his narrator's inability to reconcile himself to his folk past. This difficulty is patently clear in the voluminous manuscript drafts that Ellison generates to explore Mary's life. The archive contains no less than eight folders dedicated to Mary, not including folders concentrating on individual boarders, and these drafts present her as a fully developed personality. Like the 1963 story, most of Ellison's drafts cast Mary as a cleaning woman in the hospital where the narrator undergoes painful scientific experiments. She not only helps him by unlocking the lid to a machine and nourishing him with her mother's secret potion to fortify his weakened body, but she also gives him her address and encourages him to find her if he successfully escapes. Mary elects herself his rock of strength and refuge, and as such, the earlier versions of her character more conspicuously present the black folk heritage in religious terms.

These manuscript accounts depict the narrator's escape dramatically. He is kept naked in the machine, and when he makes his way to the New York streets, he is completely nude. In one version, he flees through the hospital, is chased out of the basement of a bar, climbs up a manhole to the street, and receives clothes from young men who attribute his nakedness to a secret rendezvous gone awry. When he finally reaches Mary's block, a blind man requests his assistance in crossing the street and eerily echoes his grandfather's haunting words. This encounter, topping off his harried getaway, disturbs the narrator who arrives at Mary's house dripping wet and shaken. Her boardinghouse is filled with energetic boarders and teems with life. The tenants include a young black man called Portwood, a jazz trumpeter named Bouché, Mrs. Garfield, who was previously married to a black man involved in union politics, and an attractive young black woman named Cleo. After drying off and calming down, the narrator joins the other tenants who listen to Mary recount her first experiences in the North. She regales them with stories that subtly advocate black pride and perseverance.

She recalls how in the early days of her Northern residence, her niece, Lurlene, took her to a fancy building to see a movie. While her niece studiously avoids appearing "countrified," Mary stares at everything. Before she knows it, she finds herself face to face with a naked statue and is so surprised she falls down the stairs. Lurlene, horrified by Mary's bumpkin behavior, pretends not to know her aunt, but Mary confesses, "I felt shame for her afterwards, but shucks I had to see. That's what I come there for, to see, and so did the other folks. They didn't have no time to pay attention to what I was doing and I sho didn't care what they thought about me" (REP Box 142). In a different episode, Mary reminisces over a time when she and her daughter witness a car accident and see a big bag fly out of the car window. When they find the bag filled with something heavy and clanking, they secretly smuggle it into their apartment and commence to dreaming of how they will spend what they believe is a fortune of money in the bag. Mary eventually discovers that the bag contains nothing but old car chains. Both of her tales exemplify her growth through experience, her solid sense of self, and her understanding of society. The narrator, of course, misses the deeper meaning of her anecdotes.

Besides listening to Mary's proverbial tales, the boarders dance to music, discuss politics, and share their own past experiences. When the narrator joins them at Mary's table, he thinks that they are gathered there for a funeral because there is a black wreath on Mary's door; thus, he is confused by their animated behavior. Mary tells him that they are not grieving but celebrating life, notwithstanding the sad news that a past boarder, Leroy, has died at sea. The boarders speak of the lost sailor admiringly, and Cleo grieves as a lover. In most drafts of the scene, a white sailor named Treadwell interrupts their dinner to deliver a portrait Leroy has left to Mary. Mary's invites him to join them, and Treadwell stays and reminisces over his friendship with Leroy, especially their provocative conversations. He confesses that Leroy forced him to see the world in new and uncomfortable ways, uprooting his "most deeply seated prejudices" (REP Box 142). As he falls deeper into the philosophical nature of his discussions with Leroy, Mary draws him back to the present by reminding him of the painting.

The boarders express amused surprise when Treadwell unveils the painting. It is an abstract portrait of Leroy, and Treadwell explains that a cubist painter created it in hopes that "by breaking up the details of Leroy's figure and rearranging them ... he would give a stronger impression of Leroy's personality" (REP Box 142). Ellison reworks several versions of this scene to introduce Leroy vividly and distinguish his worldview, as well as that of the other boarders, from the narrator's shallow intellectualism and extreme naiveté. Treadwell's memories of Leroy assume visual form in the radically abstract portrait, and the tenants' candid analysis of the painting hints at urban blacks' ability to use their mother-wit for interpreting modern society. Mary, the character most deeply attuned to her folk heritage, reads meaning in the strange shapes and colors of the picture, astonishing Treadwell, whose interpretations are distinctly academic. By contrast, the narrator remains more concerned with appearing knowledgeable than with seeking real understanding. He resents the painting for highlighting his ignorance and dislikes Leroy for his apparent intelligence.

Ellison's notes suggest that Leroy functions as a kind of complex guide for the narrator. In a number of drafts, the protagonist lives in Leroy's old room at Mary's where he peruses Leroy's scholarly array of books and his provocative journal. These drafts catalog long, single-spaced entries from Leroy's journal that express his sophisticated ruminations on American culture and politics. The narrator takes the journal with him when he leaves Mary's and scrutinizes the entries as he reflects on his own experiences. Given the length of the journal entries (over a seven page stretch the single spaced accounts occupy almost the entirety of every typed page) and the broad scope of their topics, Leroy's diary makes explicit much of the philosophical meaning underpinning the narrator's journey and provides a more biting assessment of U.S. culture than the published novel submits. Ellison seems to have excised this heavy-handed character device at the suggestion of someone with the initials "HF," in all likelihood Harry Ford, the editor of Knopf and one of Ellison's good friends. "HF's" notes advocate dropping Leroy's diary "entirely" since the entries are "prolix, didactic and inimical to the narrative—a crutch for the narrator which never entirely works." He goes on to suggest the character be cut entirely, and surmises that in this scheme "Mary has no reason for being, and all passages relevant should be deleted" which would result in "an invaluable tightening of the narrative" (REP Box 151). Although Ellison opts to keep Mary in a radically reduced capacity, he clearly agreed that Leroy and his diary shouldered too much of the interpretive burden for both the reader and his fledgling protagonist. What's more, his friend's suggestions respond to a manuscript still at least 868 pages long, and Ellison was surely looking for ways to cut pages.

His reduction of Mary's role creates a domino effect on the narrative and key aspects of the narrator's character. Most significantly, his interaction with women and the Brotherhood are greatly diminished. Critics have long mused over the narrator's conspicuous disinterest in women, and although Ellison claims a love affair "would have been inconsistent" with his narrator's personality, he originally conceives of two romantic relationships for his narrator to pursue (*Collected Essays* 221). In the drafts the narrator engages in a sexual relationship with Cleo, the young black woman at Mary's house who had been Leroy's lover. Although she initially seduces the protagonist, slipping into his room and joining him in bed, after their first kiss his own arousal drives him forward. The sexually explicit scenes

Ellison crafts around their encounters build on the narrator's competitive feelings toward Leroy. Cleo begs him to take her virginity, a difficult task because of her unusually taut hymen, and although he initially thinks that he falls short, he later sees purple stains on his hands and realizes that he has succeeded where Leroy failed. Drafts of these scenes trouble a number of critical readings by revealing Ellison's serious contemplation of a sexual relationship between the narrator and a black woman. In a strange twist that Ellison clearly understood, Mary's reduction produces this dramatic streamlining of the narrator's identity exploration. His abrupt departure from her boarding house after he accepts his Brotherhood job (in the drafts he continues living there for an unspecified time while working for the Brotherhood) denies him the opportunity to experience Harlem with the same depth.

In the drafts the narrator's more intimate knowledge of Harlem shapes his Brotherhood work. Ellison devotes entire folders to fleshing out individual Harlem Brotherhood members like Hattie and Julius Franklin who are committed to the organization and treat the narrator like family. The attention these characters receive personalizes the Brotherhood and presents the narrator as a part of the black community. His close relationships transform moments when he depends solely on himself in the published novel into shared occasions in the drafts. For instance, when he learns of the confounding existence of Rinehart, he turns to Julius for information. Ironically, Julius's reply elicits the narrative nugget responsible for the posthumously published *Juneteenth* (1999). He tells the narrator that Rinehart had been a boy preacher, and the protagonist recalls "another boy preacher who had grown up and passed for white and become…a reactionary writer on politics—with no one except a few negroes the wiser" (REP Box 146). This line directly precedes the narrator's feeling of being removed from a "plaster cast," the moment in the published text where he begins to sense the chaotic nature of black American existence (499). Not surprisingly, Ellison originally planned to introduce his next major character interest through the prodding of the common black man.

A different Brotherhood draft episode documents the narrator's effort to expand the organization's presence in Harlem. After listening to Brother Tarp's story of how blacks during his youth barbecued everything "from chickens to bears," the narrator resolves to use a bear to advertise a Brotherhood barbecue in Harlem. He finally locates a bear that can be flown in from Alaska and displayed in a local restaurant's refrigerated display case. To his disappointment, the bear arrives already skinned and when they stand him in the window holding a sign that reads, "YOU HAVE A DATE WITH

JACK THE BROTHERHOOD BARBECUE BEAR, FREE," the Harlem-
ites stare incredulously at the carcass and wonder whether it is a man or a
bear (REP Box 143). Like the episode with Julius Franklin, the bear incident
focuses attention on the narrator's dependence on Harlem residents' earthy
knowledge as he performs his Brotherhood work. In a different Brotherhood scene that Ellison incessantly reworks, the narrator agrees to join the
Brotherhood only after witnessing a huge march sparked by his eviction
speech. The young Harlem boys' transformation of a political chant about
dispossession into the familiar sounds of the Southern dozens fascinates
him. Taken as a whole, the drafts tie his relationship to the Brotherhood
directly to his interactions with and respect for the people of Harlem.

In spite of this, the narrator's impetus for learning more about the Brotherhood is his attraction for a white female member, Louise. Even while he
listens to the folksy chanting of the young boys at the march, he remains
focused on finding the white girl that he encountered at the eviction. He
reflects, "I wanted to see her again if only for a little while, long enough to
recapture the memory of her face in the darkened frame of the doorway"
(REP Box 142). In numerous drafts of this scene, the party at the Chthonian follows the march, and there, Jack formerly introduces the narrator
to Louise. As they talk he finds himself increasingly attracted to her and
vows inwardly, "You'll be my Liberty and Democracy ... the justification
for manhood ... for you I'll make myself into this new name they've given
me and I'll believe that Brother Jack and the others mean what they say
about creating a world in which even men like me can be free" (REP Box
143). The narrator tops off his bizarre proclamations by flirting brashly
with Louise who returns his overtures in good-spirited fun. The two eventually leave the party in her convertible Lincoln, and she drives him to the
subway. As they part, the black station porter suggestively congratulates
the narrator who in turn denies the young man's sexual insinuations. He
considers their budding romance above such crass generalization. Ellison
contemplated retaining the character Louise as late as the original type-
script where the protagonist mentions her name in what appears to be the
prologue. Some drafts even identify Louise as the wife of Brother Clifton.
Like Cleo, her inclusion, and Ellison's early commitment to her character,
troubles critical interpretations that cast broad explanatory nets to explain
the role of women in the novel. Louise, even more so than Cleo, emerges
as a fully conceived character not relegated to the narrow stereotypes that
critics often say undermine both black and white females in the novel. The
drafts recast the surface characterizations of women in the published text as
a function of editing rather than a result of Ellison's creative disposition.

In comparison to Ellison's long evolving ideas concerning the representation of the narrator's northern experiences, the early portions of the narrative set in the South appear largely unaltered. The publication of the battle royal scene in 1947 offers a key example of this trend. His penciled corrections highlight how small word changes magnify the connection between the position of the blonde and the boys, but the overall structure and sequence of this and his other Southern encounters remain virtually unchanged from his drafts to the 1952 text. The major exception to this tendency appears in Ellison's composition of the protagonist's time at college. In the drafts, a professor named Woodridge emerges as a developed character, and Ellison's notes suggest that he symbolizes the tension surrounding black educators. On a page of Fanny Ellison's memo paper, he scribbles "the Negro teacher, the true teacher is a threat to the whole Southern system. On the level of ideas this act is the equivalent of a crime, in that all acts which enlighten the Negro student are against the state and on the biological level this might merge with the homosexual. i.e. idea without action" (REP Box 151). In the published novel, the narrator only mentions the professor's name in passing as he reflects on his first Brotherhood speech and wonders whether his claim of feeling "more human" stems from "something that Woodridge had said in the literature class back at college" (354). Yet the episode drafts include several versions of two conversations the protagonist shares with his teacher and deepen the nefarious picture of the black college's Washingtonian philosophy.

In one draft of the scene, after hearing Reverend Barbee's guilt-inflicting sermon, the narrator seeks out Woodridge in a desperate attempt to make sense of the mess that his drive with Norton has created. He finds the literature professor drinking whiskey in his beautifully decorated room and wearing a woman's stocking over his head to maintain his hairstyle. Woodridge alludes repeatedly to rumors of his homosexuality and teases his young student for having the courage to visit him in his room. Sidestepping the narrator's dilemma relating to Mr. Norton, Woodridge dwells on his sexuality asserting that even if the rumors are true it should not surprise anyone if they accept sociological claims labeling the Negro the lady of the races. Falling into a rage he advises the narrator to "forget the books, literature, oratory" because in the reality of their society, such niceties mean nothing (REP Box 144). After exhausting himself with a profanity-laced tirade, Woodridge describes a recurring dream in which he gouges out the eyes of his students who obliviously allow him to execute his gruesome task. As he drops the bleeding eyeballs into a cotton sack chained around his neck, he wishes that at least one of them would feel the pain. By way of explaining his nightmare, he drunkenly declares the protagonist's willful belief in surface meanings a recipe for living without feeling. He then orders his baffled student to leave his rooms.

The professor's tone and language echo the vet's outburst at the Golden Day suggesting that Ellison considered using the professor, another black professional pushed toward insanity, to articulate the narrator's invisible existence. Woodridge apologizes to the narrator the next morning and explains in less dramatic terms the danger of the college's philosophy. He encourages his student to "discover adequate" books and the narrator notices a quote of the final lines of Joyce's *A Portrait of the Artist as a Young Man* (1916) written on the board behind him. Stephen's final proclamation, "Welcome, O life! I go to encounter for the millionth time the reality of experience and to forge in the smithy of my soul the uncreated conscience of my race," represents his decision to forgo the traditional route to success and power in favor of accepting the responsibility of the artist in an effort to aide his culture (REP Box 144). The protagonist, however, fails to understand the implication of the quote and its connection to his professor's words. He leaves the campus with his narrow idea of life and success in tact.

A few other episodes included in the drafts but excised from the finished novel seem worth noting given the compositional energy that Ellison devoted to their creation. All of these scenes comprise parts of the narrator's New York experiences and receive at least a few full-fledged revisions. Ellison takes up the "Priest Scene" repeatedly. In one version directly after having cheesecake with Brother Jack (in letters to Richard Wright, Ellison labels liberal ideology "cheesecake optimism"), the narrator comes upon the scene of a car accident. A truck driver has hit an old man who lies dying in the street. In a panic, the white truck driver demands that the protagonist act as a priest to fulfill the old man's final wish to talk to a religious father. The narrator unwillingly succumbs to the burly driver's command and shockingly discovers that the dying man never recognizes his race. As he fumbles over the Latin phrases he assembles from the trucker's slim memory of Catholic rites and his own musical knowledge, he finds himself crying real tears in a sudden burst of emotion. In a different version of the scene, the protagonist recalls the incident as a touch point for deciding how to proceed with Pemberton, an alumnus of his college staying at the Men's House. Pemberton remains committed to the surface appearance of success the narrator has come to scorn, but as the narrator recalls the priest incident, he decides there is no more reason to disabuse Pemberton of his hopeless illusions than there was to deny the dying white man of his last wish, even if the young black man is ultimately the victim of a charade.

In two other eliminated scenes Ellison further explores the narrator's reaction to people's willful embrace of complicated illusions. Since the prologue was one of the last sections Ellison composed, these episodes seem formulated to accomplish the narrative goals the published prologue elegantly achieves. In much the same way that the latter priest scene results in the protagonist leaving Pemberton's delusions intact, these episodes revolve around the narrator's cultural awakening at the Men's House. The first scene originally followed the protagonist's discovery of Bledsoe's duplicity. After his fateful meeting with young Emerson, he spends his time sulking in the Men's House lobby over his jobless predicament and brooding over Leroy's diary. He accepts a job as a dishwasher at a charity dinner given by a wheelchair-bound philanthropic woman, and he approaches his assignment with antipathy wondering whether his employer has ties to his old college. His night of work is long and arduous, and he receives only a dollar and a half as pay, an amount so paltry he laughs in disgust. When the crippled hostess overhears him and good naturedly inquires about the source of his happiness, the narrator sarcastically refers to his meager wages and impulsively pushes her wheelchair off her grounds and down the hill of a busy street. Instead of becoming angry, the woman apologizes for her insensitivity and muses that her physical disability has not made her as sympathetic to the plight of black Americans as she assumed. Her conciliatory attempt sends the narrator into another fit, and he fumes at the parallel she draws between race and her injury. He shouts, "So you think it's no more than a crippled leg!" before accusing her of being a fraud. In a final dramatic rage, he forces her out of her wheelchair to prove her deceitfulness, and she miraculously discovers that she can walk (REP Box 146).

The melodramatic scene illustrates the narrator's volatile response to his forced plunge beneath the surface of life and his desire to impose the same fate on others. To amplify this theme, Ellison originally composed an additional scene to follow the "Wheelchair" episode. In this instance the narrator, worried that he might be sought by the police for his irrational behavior with the crippled woman, avoids the Men's House lobby and rarely leaves his room at Mary's where he peruses Leroy's books. His self-sequestration gives him a good deal of time to think, and he reminisces about a favorite relative, Uncle Charles, who was a waiter and promised to teach him the tricks of the trade so he could earn good money over the summers when he returned home from college. Since he had always admired his uncle's polished appearance and elegant style, the narrator approvingly follows Uncle Charles's lead. They are assigned to attend a large party hosted by a young white man who grew up around Uncle Charles and is home visiting from his northern college. As the night wears on, the protagonist appallingly observes his uncle assuming a Sambo-like demeanor in an effort to attain a higher tip. Instead of appreciating this self-deprecating behavior, the young white man reprimands Uncle Charles for giving his northern friends the impression that he's "an unreconstructed slave-driver." To the narrator's dismay, even this embarrassing rebuke only serves to make his uncle wonder how going north could "spoil a good southern boy like that" (REP Box 146). Reflecting back over the episode, the narrator decides that although he originally focused his anger on his uncle, the white man had humiliated him most by failing to acknowledge his existence.

Both episodes trace the protagonist's immature grasp of his invisibility, and the relatively high page numbers typed on the scenes (they number from pages 508–547) suggest Ellison intended them to portray his narrator's first efforts to confront the reality of his black American status. Without the prologue, individual scenes assumed a greater burden in explaining the narrator's tumultuous embrace of invisibility. As Ellison crafted his two framing devices, he felt increasingly comfortable dispensing with these episodes. In the 1952 text, digressive scenes give way to the modernist prologue where the narrator's artful ruminations preview his journey towards invisibility. The final prologue and epilogue's ability to perform the work of hundreds of expunged pages and achieve similar narrative results highlights the brilliance of their constructions and the success of Ellison's revisions.

More generally, the impetus behind major narrative changes seems to be Ellison's growing confidence in, or demand for, his reader's interpretive dexterity. Other dramatic episodes he appears fascinated with, like "Revenge in Mt. Morris Park," a scene where disaffected Harlemites attempt to murder the narrator for misleading their community, or experimental sketches like "Blues" and "Something About Blues" in which the speaker carries on an extended conversation with "Blues," provide a picture of Ellison's developing narrative style and enthusiasm for experimentation. He clearly hoped his narrator's journey toward self understanding would lead readers on a parallel excursion through innovative narrative structure. To achieve this final result, he also relied on documents from the world around him. His copious clippings and thematically ordered subject folders uncover this aspect of his creative method. A newspaper article depicting a 1946 Battle Royal in Nassau, as well as a 1948 piece featuring a man living in a deserted basement beneath a New Orleans police station where he and other hobos "tapped police power lines for lights, police water pipes for water and the station heating system for heat," verify Ellison's imaginative amalgamation of narrative material. He even saved a business card printed for a Reverend J. H. Tompkins that proclaims "BEHOLD THE INVISIBLE" as it touts the experience of this "spiritual holiness expert" (REP Box 151). Other clippings ironically support Ellison's contentions that real life often follows fiction. Letters such as one from a "Mark Trueblood," who in 1966 expressed dismay that Ellison affixed his family surname to a character as reprehensible as Jim Trueblood, amused Ellison as much as an April 1952 newspaper article titled "Whitest Paint Available Used on White House" (REP Box 154, 145). The creation of art observed few boundaries.

As ambitious and impressive as *Invisible Man* is, Ellison's compositional strategy uncovers an even grander imagination behind it. In a manner reminiscent of his work as a sculptor where he modeled clay into shapely forms, he molds and sculpts his prose into a form best suited for achieving his narrative goals. The meticulous nature of his creative process gives birth to a novel as dense as it is enjoyable, and its evolution reveals Ellison's maturing philosophy about the work of the black American novelist. His numerous drafts and incessant revisions attest to his commitment to producing a novel worthy of presenting the complexity of black American life. His consistent reappraisal of the structure and content of scenes, devised to foreground the contemplation of a range of issues and ideas, highlights the seriousness with which he approaches his task. In essence, the transformation of his manuscript uncovers an important moment for the transformation of African American literature.

WORKS CITED

Ellison, Ralph. *The Collected Essays of Ralph Ellison*. Edited by John Callahan. New York: Modern Library, 1995.

————. *Invisible Man*. 1952. New York: Vintage, 1980.

Ellison, Ralph, and Albert Murray. *Trading Twelves: The Selected Letters of Ralph Ellison and Albert Murray*. Eds. Albert Murray and John F. Callahan. New York: Vintage, 2001.

Foley, Barbara. "From Communism to Brotherhood: The Drafts of *Invisible Man*." *Left of the Color Line: Race, Radicalism, and Twentieth-Century Literature of the United States*. Chapel Hill: U of North Carolina P, 2003.

Ralph Ellison Papers. Manuscript Division. Library of Congress.

Richard Wright Papers. James Weldon Johnson Collection. Yale Beinecke Library.

Chapter 3

CONTEXTS

Anyone trying to appreciate the rich contexts of *Invisible Man* empathizes with the observer who squints at a kaleidoscope. For both symmetrical vistas are discernible, yet full perception remains elusive. Admitting the peril involved in the task, this chapter presents the background of Ralph Ellison's first novel. It explains the book's allusions as well as the social atmosphere surrounding its composition. While exhaustive accounts are not undertaken, the chapter does afford a detailed glance into the world of *Invisible Man*. In particular it shows the interplay between that world and the one that Ellison inhabited. Understanding this relationship is always a crucial part of analyzing literature, but for Ellison's readers, it distinguishes casual engagement from deep comprehension. *Invisible Man*'s premises are intimately tied to distinguishing peculiarities of American culture. By making these sometimes subterranean dimensions conspicuous, this chapter prepares readers for a more rewarding trek through the text. Such preparation tightens one's grasp of the novel and clarifies the exuberance that makes Ellison so central to the American literary canon.

Invisible Man's chronology reflects amazing ingenuity. At base the book spans about 20 years from 1928 to 1948, but references to figures like Frederick Douglass and Booker T. Washington take prior African American experience and make it an active participant. Post-1948 events receive similar treatment. For example the Civil Rights Era was still nascent in 1950; nevertheless, the protagonist's underground musings anticipate that period's focus on the stakes of integration. By stretching his narrative's historical boundaries, Ellison achieves an epic tone and emphasizes the inescapable tie that binds the past, the present, and the future. Acknowledging his design and the purposes behind it, this chapter examines *Invisible Man*'s contexts by dividing them into three periods. These periods roughly correlate to the historical epochs of slavery, segregation, and nascent integration. While these categories suggest relevant chronological parameters, they do not convey the precise significance of each period to Ellison's project; therefore, the chapter uses section headings: "Crucibles of Consciousness: Precursors to Segregation," "Jim Crow: An Incubator of Twentieth-Century Blackness," and "Free Minds: Scaffoldings of an Integrated Mentality."

"Crucibles of Consciousness" limns black American experience before 1896. Identifying Ellison's implicit attentions to slavery, Reconstruction, and nineteenth-century sociopolitical ideologies, it identifies the features that make the protagonist's Southern rural adolescence so significant. In "Jim Crow," the physical and mental reality of segregated America receives treatment. Aside from discussing *Plessy v. Ferguson* (1896) and the protocols of racial separation, this section also looks at military service, the Great Migration, the Harlem Renaissance, and the Great Depression. Revealing Jack the Bear's exemplification of the angst of separate-but-equal society, this segment shows why his confusion carries such powerful implications.[1] "Free Minds" pulls themes from the protagonist's Harlem existence. Including commentary on communism and oration, this part also looks at World War II, modern technology, and the atomic age. As these descriptions imply, this chapter's contents, while sequential, range across a variegated landscape. In one sense the variety indicates America's unruly legacy, but a clearer estimate recognizes these heterogeneous strands as an index of Ralph Ellison's brilliance. Peering through the lens that they form produces a more insightful view of his often daunting fiction.

CRUCIBLES OF CONSCIOUSNESS: PRECURSORS TO SEGREGATION

In America chattel slavery was legal until 1863. While the material facets of this peculiar institution were debilitating, its psychic consequences are equally intense and perhaps more enduring. Ellison only shows passing interest in the former, but *Invisible Man* serves as an extended meditation on the latter. One recurrent example of this is the novel's varied depiction of racial stereotyping. The battle royal while set in the 1920s evokes some conventions of blackface minstrelsy, an entertainment that flourished in the early nineteenth century.[2] Specifically the battle royal's emphasis on the comedic spectacle of black intellectualism relates to Zip Coon, a popular minstrel character. Drawn as a fop who affects high-flown syntax and discriminating tastes, Zip Coon according to David Pilgrim "thought he was as smart as White people; however, his frequent malapropisms and distorted logic suggested that his attempt to compete intellectually with Whites was pathetic" (par. 8). Since Ellison portrays his protagonist's ambitions as a perverse, if naïve recapitulation of white prescriptions, Jack the Bear in an ironic inversion of the racist motives behind Zip Coon illustrates the results of African Americans who unquestioningly pursue the refinements of the mainstream culture. The novelist's penchant for density would not leave the portrayal thus undeveloped. If the protagonist, a valedictorian of his class, acquires Zip Coon's comic aura because he does not sense the degree to which the white town fathers are using him to justify and to engineer their own contorted perceptions about blacks and social progress, then likewise the white male town fathers do not understand how their own appetites goad the boy on a quest that carries him through dissimulation towards an appreciation of the complexities of identity. Just as the Zip Coon figure begins in a fixed intent of deprecation and evolves to a more troublesome reflection of a national negotiation regarding class, race, and commerce, Ellison suggests that Jack the Bear is never comfortably a victim or a victor. If the battle royal illuminates one pole of *Invisible Man*'s focus on stereotyping, then the Trueblood episode reveals another equally complicated aspect.

Jim Trueblood's incestuous encounter with his daughter conjures the rhetoric of black male hypersexuality and generic racial depravity; rhetoric that slavery apologists both before and after the Civil War exploited as they stressed the benevolent consequences of bondage and the abiding need to civilize black populations. Ellison injects Trueblood's dilemma with elements of this discourse, but utilizing Freudian notions of taboo and repression, he makes the myth of black male sexuality a talismanic projection of white male desire. Thus, Norton's reaction to Trueblood initially appears paternalistic, still his zeal and the shadings of subsequent portrayals suggest that his fascination with the sharecropper is less reparative and more voyeuristic. These respective depictions of minstrelsy and incest not only show Ellison's interest in stereotyping, one that persists throughout *Invisible Man,* but also they suggest his fundamental belief in a dynamic process of identity acquisition. In sketching Jack the Bear, he consistently rejects the totalizing notion that the oppressions of slavery inherently determine the black personality, yet at the same moment he relentlessly asserts that the cauldron of consciousness contains a conditioning awareness of prior experiences. It is this insistence on complexity that guides Ellison's look into the psychological character of bondage. In this regard his evocation of Frederick Douglass is illustrative.

Born in 1818, Douglass spends his early years between the Eastern Shore of Maryland and Baltimore. He witnesses and experiences the cruelties of slavery, and his 1845 book, *Narrative of the Life of Frederick Douglass,* expresses the agony that his condition inspires. In particular, Douglass articulates the effects of literacy and self-consciousness on the captive individual. He confesses, "I would at times feel that learning to read and write had been a curse rather than a blessing. It had given me a view of my wretched condition, without the remedy" (67). Douglass's mental state resembles that of *Invisible Man*'s protagonist. Alternately distinguished and frustrated by his intellect, he, like Ellison's character, struggles for an answer to the riddle of self-definition. When Douglass's later life is examined, this comparison gains more texture.

Douglass escaped from slavery in 1838, and by 1841, he worked as a lecturer for the Massachusetts Anti-Slavery Society. There, he met the legendary abolitionist, William Lloyd Garrison. Initially, Garrison impressed Douglass, but as American race relations evolved, the black man found the white one ideological and impractical. Ultimately, they parted ways. Brother Jack and the protagonist occupy a different historical moment; nevertheless, their focus on black liberty and their divergence regarding its attainment intersect tellingly with the Garrison-Douglass situation. One final observation about Douglass illustrates the extent of Ellison's interest in him. Aside from the *Narrative,* Douglass completed two other autobiographies, *My Bondage, My Freedom* (1855) and *The Life and Times of Frederick Douglass* (1881). These volumes simultaneously reveal his anxiety regarding his legacy and his belief that writing allows him to fix his identity. *Invisible Man*'s protagonist produces a single text, but his underground work reflects convictions similar to those held by Douglass. He believes that his experiences are revelatory, yet he knows the volatility inherent in self-expression. As Henry Louis Gates, Jr., has suggested, Douglass is "The Representative Colored Man of the United States" during the nineteenth century (99). He voices black concerns, and because his life spans the signature transition from slavery to freedom, he embodies one generation's struggle for dignity. Brother Tarp places Douglass's portrait in the protagonist's Brotherhood office to suggest a racial lineage. Excavating the unspoken tensions both in Douglass's life and in broader black experience, Ellison makes this gesture ironic. Understanding this irony requires a look at miscegenation.

Sex between white masters and black female slaves produced in Earl V. Thorpe's estimation "a brood of over one-half million mulattoes by 1860" (5). While Thorpe's figure may partake some of jest, his point is clear. Lust, psychology, and commerce made master/slave commingling inevitable. Since by law, black children inherited the status of their mothers, impregnating a slave not only relieved sexual tension, but also enriched the labor pool. This development appealed to the planter class, but fallout from it settled across a substantial landscape. For the wives of slaveholders, their husband's antics produced shame, insecurity, and resentment. To soothe their hurts, these ladies sometimes singled out slave mistresses and their mulatto children for whippings, arduous chores, or resale. These reactions conveyed white female anxiety, but black women evinced equally complex responses. Harriet Jacobs, in her book *Incidents in the Life of a Slave Girl* (1861), described the lechery of her master, Dr. Flint. Convinced that she could resist him only by becoming pregnant, she mothered two children for another white man, Mr. Sands. This scenario shows how bondswomen tried to control their choices even under abject subjugation, and from another perspective, it illuminates the ambivalence of the nameless mother in *Invisible Man*'s prologue. That mother loves and hates her master, who is also the father of her sons. Though the circumstances are not identical, her emotions resemble those of Jacobs towards Sands. On one level, the claim that this man exercises is innately repulsive. Despite this his role in her motherhood provokes undeniable intimacy. This struggle surfaces literally in the mixed race of the children. The mother's blackness coexists with the father's whiteness, and reactions to that mixture betray confused allegiance. For instance, the father's death prompts moans from the mother; however, the sons laugh about the event. If this divergence centers on an isolated case, then the broader idea of colliding racial differences becomes a recurrent theme for *Invisible Man*'s protagonist. Nowhere is this more evident than in the text's subtle attention to the War Between the States.

The Civil War (1861–1865) had many complicated causes, but its close association with slavery makes it a vital touch point in black experience. While the novel includes no explicit references to the conflict, John S. Wright has suggested that it is "one of the great understated themes of *Invisible Man*" (104). The odyssey of the book's protagonist definitely mirrors two of the war's major features. For instance the division between the North and the South constitutes a fault line in the protagonist's thinking and experience. His periodic bouts with violence stem from a frustrated inability to resolve the worldviews of these two regions. This is true not only in his interracial disagreements with Brother Jack, but also in

his intraracial skirmishes with Ras. By linking a signature national crisis
to one individual's anguish, Ellison invests his depictions with immense
allegorical potential. Ironically, the deepest meaning emerges when dis-
sonance coexists with reconciliation. The immediate aftermath of slavery
features alternating advocacy and repression in black-white relations. As
African Americans define themselves, they sort through these oscillations
and discover the nation's posture toward their existence. *Invisible Man's*
protagonist initially stumbles in this complex process; however, his encounters with paradox ultimately sharpen his focus on reality.

The Emancipation Proclamation (1863) and the Thirteenth Amendment
(1865) heralded slavery's end, yet attitudes and circumstances from the
earlier era persisted. Ellison dramatizes this reality in a detail from the
eviction scene. When an elderly couple is thrown out of their apartment,
the protagonist glimpses the old man's "free papers." This document notes
that John Samuels liberated Primus Provo in 1859. Just as this manumis-
sion commemorates personal freedom, racial liberty seems tied to Abraham
Lincoln's order and Congress' legislation. In the wake of emancipation,
optimism rose; nonetheless, the Provos's dilemma circa 1933 suggests that
slavery's legacy is tenacious. The protagonist feels that bondage should be
a more distant event, but in the scene's action, he recognizes its imprints.
Before he catapults his readers into an urban Depression Era setting, Ellison
explores that extraordinary nineteenth-century enigma, Reconstruction.

The Civil War was an embittered contest for America's soul; in the postbellum moment, Reconstruction (1865–1877) signaled pursuit of healing.
August in name and intent, this controversial program attempted to ease
the Confederacy's passing and to determine the shape of black civic life.
Its seeds blossomed unevenly. The election of black officials demonstrated
the immediate effect of enfranchisement. In Mississippi, before the war,
blacks were a nonexistent voting bloc. During Reconstruction, they help
send the first black men, Hiram Revels and Blanche K. Bruce, to the United
States Senate. The height of these men's achievement is extraordinary, but
the fact of their election is not. By the end of Reconstruction, hundreds of
black legislators had served mostly in state assemblies. These individuals
galvanized racial pride, and forming coalitions with white Republicans,
they pressed for expanded civil rights and widespread public education.
Their efforts benefited from the support of the Freedman's Bureau, a federal agency that oversaw Reconstruction. Although the Bureau, solidified
by Congressional support in 1866, provided numerous services from food
rationing to employment mediation, its administration of schooling was a
crowning achievement. Not only were disadvantaged children introduced

to learning, but also teacher-training institutions like Fisk, Hampton, and Howard accelerated their work. The faith in education that prompted these actions was not confined to government entities; Northern philanthropists also invested in all levels of black instruction. Since this class received a nuanced portrayal in *Invisible Man,* pausing to consider its exemplary actors seems appropriate.

George Peabody was among the earliest contributors to Southern schools. By 1870, his Peabody Education Fund had devoted close to a million dollars to the effort. While his interests included black institutions, they were not his exclusive beneficiaries. Around the turn of the century, John F. Slater and Anna T. Jeanes endowed eponymous funds that primarily supported black secondary schools. In particular, these organizations promoted the training of black teachers, preparing them to enter rural districts. John D. Rockefeller and Julius Rosenwald founded funds that nurtured American higher education. Consistent with these aims, they made substantial contributions to African American colleges and universities. Though none of these individuals prompted Ellison's depiction of Mr. Norton, a white trustee, several generic similarities exist. Like Norton, these benefactors came from Northern families who amassed fortunes in mercantile industries. Also, they tended to view philanthropy as an intimate part of their personal missions. Rockefeller explained, "I believe the power to make money is a gift from God... Having been endowed with the gift I possess, I believe it is my duty to make money and still more money and to use the money I make for the good of my fellow man according to the dictates of my conscience" (Platt 229). Rockefeller's rhetoric differs significantly from Norton's; nevertheless, they both believe that their fellow man's destiny is somehow tied to their own. Most of these figures emerged after the end of Reconstruction; despite this, their convictions owed much to the recuperative impulses of the post–Civil War era. The attempt to unify the nation sparked profound questions about social responsibility. On one side, attitudes of charity proliferated; at the same moment, the age gave rise to eloquent doctrines of self-help. No black voice on that topic carried further than Booker T. Washington's.

Washington enrolled at Hampton Institute in 1872, nearly six years into Reconstruction, but even then, attitudes were percolating that would undermine black civil liberties. As early as 1875, statutes restricting access to public places were passed; by 1881 when he started Tuskegee, federal anti-discrimination laws were under attack. The end of Reconstruction meant that governance in the South transferred from reform-minded Republicans to embittered Democrats. Facing this reality, Washington plotted a course of appeasement. Instead of demanding suffrage, he convinced Southern leaders that black labor was reliable and indispensable. To vivify his point, he molded an obscure Alabama school into a potent symbol of industry, decorum, and acculturation. Tuskegee was largely a self-sufficient enterprise. It received aid from outside sources; however, students and staff did everything from cultivate food to construct dormitories. Stressing hygiene, vocational training, and social conformity, the college exemplified Washington's ideas about improving life for African Americans. In 1895, his status along with the school's reputation increased considerably.

To show off the postbellum South's advanced industrial capabilities, Atlanta hosted the Cotton States and International Exposition. As part of the program, Booker T. Washington was invited to address the Board of Directors and the broader assembly. The invitation itself provoked apprehension. Some planners wondered whether a black man should take center stage at such a prestigious event. They feared that he was going to embarrass the region in front of an international audience. If misgivings afflicted a few folks before Washington's remarks, they disappeared afterward. In a speech, later ironically called the "Atlanta Compromise," he stressed blacks' willingness to play a role in traditional Southern life. Using phrasing that boomerangs through history, Washington argued that "in all things that are purely social [blacks and whites] can be as separate as the fingers, yet one as the hand in all things essential to mutual progress" (222). These sentiments prompted a robust handshake from Rufus B. Bullock, a former Georgia governor, and following Frederick Douglass's death by about seven months, this speech sealed Washington's position as one of, if not the most powerful black man in America. He was the new symbol of an age.

The protagonist of *Invisible Man* refers to Washington's Atlanta Exposition speech during his valedictory address. While the allusion intimates reverence, Ellison's portrayal exposes hilarious incongruity. Graduation's pomp and circumstance laud the valedictorian, but the bedlam of the battle royal episode makes his speech a mockery. Before he can demonstrate his eloquence, he must submit to a humiliating boxing match and a painful turn on an electric rug. After all this, the white audience perceives his statements as a sort of polysyllabic minstrelsy. Ellison links the protagonist's unwitting performance to Booker T. Washington. While the President of the United States, Grover Cleveland, wrote Washington a congratulatory note, a vocal segment of the black elite viewed the Atlanta Exposition address as a betrayal. By bending to white expectation and avoiding agitation for political rights, he, in their minds, sold his birthright for a mess of pottage. Ellison acknowledges this contingent, and in his portrayal of the protagonist's development, he challenges the durability of Washington's approach. In particular, his depictions of the college question the perpetuation of the Tuskegee Wizard's ideas in post–World War I America.

JIM CROW: AN INCUBATOR OF TWENTIETH-CENTURY BLACKNESS

When tentative steps toward disfranchisement matured, and racial segregation hardened, blacks in the South endured what historian Rayford W. Logan in *The Negro in American Life and Thought* (1954) terms "the nadir" of their post-slavery existence (52). A crucial landmark along the road to despair was the *Plessy v. Ferguson* case. Homer Plessy, a 30-year-old black shoemaker, believed that his first class ticket entitled him to accommodations in the first class car, a white car. When a Louisiana circuit court ruled against him, Plessy, in 1896, appealed to the Louisiana supreme court, and then to the United States Supreme Court. The Supreme Court's decision in this case generated the phrase "separate but equal," a label designating a system of apartheid that shaped American life for nearly 60 years. Explaining the decision, Justice Henry Brown observed, "A statute which implies merely a legal distinction between the white and colored races—a distinction which is founded in the color of the two races, and which must always exist so long as white men are distinguished from the other race by color—has no tendency to destroy the legal equality of the two races" (Martin 78). *Plessy* enshrined an ideology that draws its strength from racist assumptions, and it paved the way for a web of laws that forcefully separated blacks and whites. These Jim Crow laws began with marriage, public accommodations, and education, and they expanded to cover the entire social intercourse between the races. *Invisible Man* begins in the Jim Crow South, and the early part of the novel considers the protagonist's experiences at a segregated school. While those experiences ostensibly center on the classroom, Ellison points us to extracurricular events that require an understanding of sharecropping, W.E.B. Du Bois, and black military service.

The postbellum South remained an agrarian society, and devoid of other opportunities, many blacks made their living off of the land. Some were able to purchase property, but most obtained access via tenant farming and sharecropping (Barbeau and Barbeau 8–10). The former was the less onerous arrangement. In it, a tenant secured land from the owner and agreed to pay a set rent. Outside of this rent, all proceeds from the crop belonged to him. Sharecropping involved a more complicated process and resulted in greater abuses. A sharecropper cultivated part of his landlord's crop with the promise that when the harvest was sold, he would receive a percentage of the profits. While theoretically fair, this system produced peonage. Small farmers borrowed against their earnings to buy food, clothing, and supplies; when these expenses were deducted from their share, they invariably were deeper in debt. Because of mounting debt, sharecroppers rarely severed their ties to the landlord. Thus, dreams of saving and buying their own acreage disappeared. Throughout the South, sharecropping persisted well into the twentieth century, and its appearance in the 1928 section of *Invisible Man* not only presents the region's anachronistic economic development, but also the intraracial tensions produced by class divisions. The novel's protagonist describes Jim Trueblood as "a sharecropper who had brought disgrace upon the black community" (46). While Trueblood's ostensible transgression is fathering a child by his daughter, he also symbolizes what the protagonist calls "the black belt people, the 'peasants'" (47). These individuals embody lifestyles and habits that the refined collegians find repulsive. This tension symbolizes the struggle between folk experience and the progressive ethos of racial uplift; Ellison uses it to show the anxiety and the snobbery that afflicts the aspiring black middle class. A consideration of W.E.B. Du Bois's ideas offers greater insight into this phenomenon.

If Booker T. Washington was the preeminent black leader until World War I, then W.E.B. Du Bois reigned as his ubiquitous foil. Favoring a liberal arts curriculum, Harvard-educated Du Bois spurned Washington's vocational emphases. He also renounced Washington's patient approach to political liberty. In 1905 Du Bois helped form the Niagara Movement, an organization whose manifesto demanded immediate suffrage for black men. These divergences predictably positioned Washington and Du Bois at opposite ends of the spectrum; nevertheless, Du Bois's contentious notion of a "Talented Tenth" harmonized with certain facets of Washington's plan for black society. Explaining the concept in 1903, he writes, "The Negro Race, like all races, will be saved by its exceptional men. The problem of education, then, among Negroes...is the problem of developing the best of [the] race that they may guide the Mass away from the contamination and the death of the Worst" (373–374). *Invisible Man* never explicitly alludes to Du Bois, but the protagonist's vision of his destiny relies on Du Boisian assumptions. Throughout the novel, he casts himself as an aspiring savior of his people. That he receives his instruction at the college, a Tuskegee-like entity, does not temper these ambitions. Ellison suggests that notwithstanding their philosophical differences, these two extremes of black leadership both depend on an enlightened class to shepherd masses to an identity. This prescription is imperiled because as the protagonist learns, the erstwhile leaders frequently lack a clear picture of themselves or their constituencies. The fortunes of black soldiers illuminate this point.

During the Civil War, Frederick Douglass and Monroe Trotter, a prominent newspaper editor, aggressively recruited blacks for the Union Army. Portraying military service as a marker of loyalty both to the race and the republic, their appeals inspired enthusiastic response. The 54th Massachusetts, one of the first Northern regiments, assembled in February of 1863; by July of that year, their performance in the attack on Fort Wagner proved their valor. Colonel T. W. Higginson averred that his First Regiment South Carolina Volunteers manifested "a personal purpose" in battle. He stated, "It would have been madness to attempt, with the bravest white troops what I have successfully accomplished with the black ones" (*The War of the Rebellion* 198). By 1867, 14 black soldiers received the Congressional Medal of Honor. These achievements occurred against a backdrop of unbounded optimism. The Civil War, in black minds, existed as a contest for liberty. When the nineteenth-century South drifted toward racial segregation and the nation refused to intervene, military service acquired a more complicated cast. Most black units disbanded as Reconstruction ended. The soldiers, who were crucial to the Union victory, quickly became an unwanted surplus. This development disenchanted many young black men; however, it did not stop them from embracing the opportunities for adventure, livelihood, and bravery that the armed services offered. Evidence of this can be seen in their participation in the Spanish-American War.

In 1898, America committed troops to Cuba's fight for independence from Spain. Support for Cuban liberation grew steadily throughout the 1880s, and the explosion of the U.S.S. *Maine,* an American battleship, led to a formal declaration of war. Of the regiments that participated in the conflict, four of them were all black. Describing two divisions that rescued his unit, no less a personality than Theodore Roosevelt stated, "I don't think that any Rough Rider will ever forget the tie that binds us to the 9th and 10th Calvary" (qtd. in Buckley 139). The Supreme Court, via the *Plessy* decision, gave imprimatur to second class status for African Americans, yet not two years later, black soldiers continued to sacrifice their lives. Ellison knew this paradox intimately since his father, Lewis, enlisted in 1898. Lewis Ellison missed the Cuban based battles of the Spanish-American War, but he saw action in the Philippines when Emilio

Aguinaldo established a government in that country (Jackson 6–9). Although Ellison was not alive during his father's military career, he heard vivid stories from his mother, Ida. These stories made indelible impressions on a young boy, and when the adult artist scrutinized the episodes, he detected rich ambivalence in the situation. Military service and military actions remained for Ellison one of the costs of democracy; nevertheless, as his portrayal of World War I veterans suggests, he senses for the African American a unique perspective on what cultural commentators often term the war within the war. At the same moment as blacks from the Revolutionary War forward volunteered to defend the possibility of a free United States of America, they also battled domestically fomented racial prejudices that threatened to undermine national solidarity. By the end of the nineteenth century, the pressures of such a bifurcated reality were felt not only in armies, but also throughout a South that in economic and cultural terms was becoming almost untenably inhospitable.

Until the mid-twentieth century, the bulk of America's black population resided in its Southern reaches.[3] Slavery and the brief optimism of Reconstruction conspired to reinforce this geographical reality, but the last decades of the nineteenth century and the opening ones of the twentieth brought circumstances that increasingly convinced a significant number of African Americans to leave the South. The promise of economic opportunity prompted many blacks to move north and west, vanguards of a growing mass that would be labeled The Great Migration. Destined for cities like Chicago, Philadelphia, New York, and Detroit, these travelers not only sought higher wages and greater job security, but also relief from racial harassment and intimidation. The most chilling index of this persecution could be seen in the statistics regarding lynching. During the 30-year period from 1884 to 1914, more than 3,500 blacks died via this heinous ritual (Franklin and Moss 282). The majority of these victims were killed in deep-South states like Mississippi, Alabama, Georgia, and Louisiana. The vulnerability that these events symbolized registered starkly in the minds of African Americans who were growing disenchanted with many aspects of Southern existence. Before they committed themselves wholeheartedly to departure, segments of the black Southern population registered their discontent via public unrest that presaged more intense demonstrations later in the twentieth century. Riots in Wilmington, North Carolina, (1898) and Atlanta (1906) indicated both the extent to which racial animosity prevailed and the consequences that violent action carried. Witnessing this growing combustibility, a distinct segment of the black community decided to seek their fortunes outside of the South. Ralph Ellison understood this

impulse firsthand since it manifested itself in his parent's ultimate reloca-
tion to Oklahoma. Like many migrants, the reality of their new homes
proved a distinctly mixed bag. Social freedoms often carried the taint of
circumscribed possibility and volatile duration. No event exemplified the
paradox of this conditional liberty more dramatically than World War I.

Over 350,000 African American soldiers participated in World War I
(1914–1918). Following a trend set during earlier armed conflicts, many
soldiers viewed their service as a double blow, one for national security
and one for the cause of racial equality. As a black speaker expressed it,
African Americans enlisted with the hope that once they had proven themselves "worthy to…fight and die for" America, then "a grateful nation"
would grant them "the rights and privileges of true and loyal citizens"
(Barbeau and Barbeau 7). The soldier's optimism spurred them to participation; nonetheless, from the outset the nation's reaction revealed ironic
shifts. Although the war had begun in Europe during the summer of 1914,
the United States did not enter the fray until early in 1917. Once the nation
committed itself, black soldiers immediately volunteered for duty. Initially
their eagerness was ignored. Gerald Astor in *The Right to Fight* (1998)
suggests that "there was little inclination of whites to have blacks stand
shoulder to shoulder with them" (108). This disinclination at first manifested itself bureaucratically in white draft boards' denials of black applications. After the Selective Service Act (1917) invalidated this practice,
draft boards changed tactics and began admitting African Americans at an
accelerated rate. This acceleration did not reflect a change of heart regarding the suitability of the black soldier; rather, it suggested a determination
to administer the draft almost punitively. If blacks wanted to serve, they
would be allowed to do so, yet they would do so in segregated units that
reinforced humiliating social mores.

Ralph Ellison's awareness of World War I black veterans' absurd dilemmas emerges prominently in *Invisible Man*'s Golden Day episode. There,
the protagonist's attempt to bolster Norton, the white trustee stupefied
by Trueblood's storytelling, propels both he and his erstwhile "destiny"-
maker into a maelstrom replete with metaphorical importance. The novel's
burlesque adds considerable nuance to this episode's focus on the inter-
penetrating realities of American race relations, and at base its message
is a simple one, namely the denial of a linked destiny results in a dangerous insanity. The bedlam unleashed in Norton's presence becomes analogous to the chaotic responses of mainstream American society to black
patriotism. World War I African American soldiers who emblematize the
simultaneously segregated, yet enmeshed state of the nation are early in

the twentieth century an inconvenient marker of national hypocrisy. As such, their status in *Invisible Man* reflects not only the psychic disorientation that experiments in racial equality hazard, but also the shameful reactions on the parts of both blacks and whites to spectacular failures. The race riots that occurred throughout America in the aftermath of World War I could be Ellison's macrocosmic model for his portrayal of microcosmic chaos.

In 1919 the large scale relocations labeled The Great Migration were occurring at a steady clip, and coincident with this exodus, the end of World War I caused a tapering off of wartime's massive industrial demands. This development, along with the return of soldiers to the work force, created a highly competitive employment situation. When blacks and whites vied for the same positions, racial antipathy often morphed from seething resentment to overt hostility. The latter half of 1919 saw a string of race riots that touched cities both large and small in every geographic section of the nation. Although tense economic factors were not the motivation for all of these conflicts, cultural chasms were widened by the perception that the sustenance of individuals and families was being compromised via prejudicial racial judgments. This was especially rankling to black soldiers who often felt that their enthusiastic patriotism did not translate into practical advances. For all of the North and the West's promises of greater freedom, riots in Detroit, Chicago, and Omaha in addition to those in Knoxville belied any belief in utopian urbanity. Ralph Ellison, born into this coalescing reality, later understood this transitional moment as a vital one in the creation of modern African American consciousness. In fact, he makes the journey from the South to the North a metaphor of the protagonist's attempt to fashion a healthy identity. Doing so requires a confrontation with innumerable agents who would prescribe for Jack the Bear a particular role. One of these agents, Ras, evokes Marcus Garvey, the celebrated leader of the Universal Negro Improvement Association (UNIA).

Entering the world on August 17, 1887, Marcus Moziah Garvey initially lived in St. Ann's Bay, Jamaica. Garvey's formal schooling would end in 1903, but through travels and associations with influential thinkers, he acquired a robust understanding of the psychology and the economics of colonialism. After spending time in Central America and England during 1910 and 1912 respectively, Garvey returned to Jamaica in 1914. Within months of this homecoming, he started the UNIA, an organization designed to put his ambitions for black people into action. Adolph Edwards describing Garvey's brainchild offers the following synopsis: "The purpose of the [UNIA] was to unite 'all the negro peoples of the world into one great body to establish a country and government absolutely their own'" (qtd. in Clarke 9). After cultivating the Jamaica branch of the UNIA for two years, Garvey, in 1916, traveled to Harlem and began his U.S. activities. Street-corner, soapbox oratory afforded Garvey access to New York's black masses, and during the spring of 1916, it allowed him to perfect the rhetorical phrases, "One God!, One aim! One destiny!" and "Africa for Africans," that would attract millions of followers. From a modest start as a sidewalk haranguer, Garvey grew into one of the most magnetic black leaders of the early 1920s. Assessing his success and his appeal, John Henrick Clarke observes, "The Garvey Movement was perfectly timed. The broken promises of the post-war period had produced widespread cynicism in the Black population," and here was a man who, in the words of Adam Clayton Powell, Jr., "brought to the Negro people for the first time a sense of pride in being Black" (9; qtd. in Clarke 9). The way that that pride was delivered was one of the more arresting facets of Garvey's legacy.

A master manipulator of ritual and pageantry, Marcus Garvey frequently staged elaborate parades. Filled with uniformed men and regal women, these processions indelibly impressed spectators of all ages. Frances Warner describes the atmosphere: "Every window that you looked at, people's heads were out, to see the Marcus Garvey parade. Most of them wanted to see Marcus Garvey and he was very well decorated, his hats, and the feathers, but he drove always in his automobile, sitting back." Charles Mills expresses the thrill that seeing his father dress for the parade inspired: "As a young boy to see my father in the parade was one of the greatest things in the world. I would be right there to see him put on his tunic and I loved to see that sword that he carried. It really made me feel very proud of him."[4] Ellison captures Garvey's rhetoric and his ethnic legacy in his depiction of Ras, but he also suggests the extent to which Garvey penetrated the vocabulary of black spectacle when he talks about his protagonist's organization of the Eviction parade protest and The People's Hot Foot Squad. These activities carry analogues in mainstream American culture; nevertheless, Ellison realizes that the black masses respond to particular refinements both in the structure and the symbolism of these events. Here, his refraction of Garvey's influence is perhaps most cannily presented. Garvey's approach depends simultaneously on an exclusionary ideology and on an appeal to the hybrid essence of Western culture. Where Ellison senses the need to embrace such hybridity, he casts Ras, a stand in for Garvey-esque misperception, as the propagator of a specious racial purity. Just as the novel judges Ras harshly, so to does Garvey's precipitous decline reflect intriguingly on his personality and his program.

In August of 1920, Garvey was presiding over the first international conference of the UNIA. By February of 1925, he was on his way to federal prison, convicted of mail fraud. Eventually, Calvin Coolidge would pardon him paving the way for his release in 1928. Despite this reprieve, Garvey never again commanded the imagination of as large a following. He passed away in 1940, a poor inconsequential denizen of London. Garvey's odyssey clearly informs what some critics have seen as *Invisible Man*'s sustained meditation on "the problem of the hero and black leadership" (Wright 89). In fact, some commentators like A. F. Elmes have attributed to Garvey the status of "a prophet" (qtd. in Clarke 123). Despite this access to a quasi-divine calling, Garvey, in Ellison's mind, along with many other post–World War I black leaders, exemplifies the profundity of the widespread confusion about black identity. To appreciate the range and the complexity of this dilemma, one must look at the NAACP, the Urban League, the YMCA, and the way that the black public mind appeared in the days before the Great Depression.

Flowering in part from the seeds of the Du Bois-spearheaded Niagara Movement, the National Association for the Advancement of Colored People was formed in 1910. Associated with luminaries like Jane Addams, John Dewey, and Ida B. Wells, the NAACP always existed as a symbol of interracial cooperation. Initially the organization proclaimed interests in economic expansion and social justice. Over time its efforts on behalf of the latter superseded its attentions to the former. From the moment of its formation up to the early 1920s, the NAACP grew at a prodigious rate. Its first branch, in Chicago, spawned over 400 nationwide agencies in just over a decade (Franklin and Moss 288). These branches were crucial both for gathering the statistical data necessary to document the facts of racial inequality and as a sign of broad-based black dissatisfaction with that inequality. The harvest of both of these functions is perhaps best observed in the longstanding, yet ever metastasizing legal interventions of the NAACP. Although much scholarship identifies Charles Hamilton Houston's 1935 special legal counsel appointment and Thurgood Marshall's steadily growing role as pivotal moments in the NAACP's courtroom efforts, Susan Carle examining the early roots of the organization's posture towards litigation-based racial reform sees other intriguing facets. In her article, "Race, Class, and Legal Ethics in the Early NAACP (1910–1920)," Carle argues that while "many of the lawyers who were pioneering creative public impact litigation techniques in civil rights cases…were African-Americans," these black attorneys, in the early days, were not invited to join the NAACP legal committee (113). She asserts that the organization, even after a 1913 expansion of the committee, "was not seeking African-American civil rights lawyer-activists to direct its legal strategy"; rather, Carle believes that the NAACP via its white upper crust, well-credentialed committee members sought "to signal the elite professional status of… [its] representatives" (115). Given the immediate successes achieved in residential segregation and murder cases, the NAACP's strategy indisputably paid dividends; nevertheless, the organization's integrated origins and its perceived class snobbery quickly and persistently aroused detractors. In fact Marcus Garvey, who often sarcastically said that the acronym NAACP stood for National Association for the Advancement of Certain People, targeted the organization and its leaders for some of his most bitter accusations of black self-hatred. While Ellison does not appear to level his pen at the NAACP in *Invisible Man,* his portrayals of the idealistic young Emerson, the great white father Norton, and for that matter the Liberty Paints factory do emphasize the unrelenting challenge of accurately determining the role of whiteness in blackness and vice versa. If this challenge is subtly, yet profoundly at work in the NAACP's activities, then two institutions that seem directly relevant to Ellison's depiction of his protagonist are the National Urban League and the YMCA.

George Edmund Haynes and Ruth Standish Bowles Baldwin played distinctly different yet equally prominent roles in establishing the National Urban League. In 1908, Haynes was a graduate student in the doctoral program at Columbia University. Pursuing his interest in the difficulties of blacks who were migrating from the South, he compiled a dissertation which was published as *The Negro at Work in New York City* (1913). Haynes's research suggested that employment discrimination, inadequate schools, and unsanitary lodging were among the most pervasive challenges that black migrants faced. Inspired by his findings, other committees that had been studying the conditions of blacks in New York decided to collaborate. The ultimate result of their cooperation was the establishment in 1911 of the National Urban League (Weiss 29–46). Although Haynes's study provided guidance for the organization's philosophical values, it was the financial support and the liberal mindset of benefactors like Ruth Baldwin that enabled its implementation of practical reforms. Ruth Baldwin was married to the president of the Long Island Railroad, William H. Baldwin, Jr. In addition to running the railroad, William also oversaw the National Child Labor Committee and interestingly served as a trustee of Tuskegee Institute. Some speculate that Ruth Baldwin's involvement with the Urban

League reflected Booker T. Washington's megalomaniacal aims, but there is no evidence to support this contention. In fact, Mrs. Baldwin's involvement with the labor movement indicates that she had her own social agenda. That this agenda would include the plight of African American migrants is a telling sign both of how social change occurs and of just how intensely Ralph Ellison studied the processes of such transformation.

Ruth Baldwin's participation in the National Urban League not only shows, as the organization's present Web site avers, that "the interracial character of the League's board was set from its first days," but also it exemplifies a theme sounded often in *Invisible Man,* namely the profound relationship between white philanthropy and black self-definition (par. 7). In the case of the National Urban League, this interplay prevails as African Americans increasingly inhabit urban as opposed to rural spaces. If World War I's expanded industrial opportunities make the economic interventions of the National Urban League noteworthy, then its social actions amid the volatile postwar mixture of decadent consumption and escalating racial strife forecast both the seductiveness and the inadequacy of certain facets of its idealism. The YMCA, another institution that early in the twentieth century showed renewed interest in black urbanites, revealed other dimensions of this conundrum. While YMCAs serving blacks had existed since the middle of the nineteenth century, the segregated status of those institutions underscored a troubling incongruity that would linger almost until the end of World War II. From one perspective, the simultaneous benevolence and exclusion inherent in this arrangement become a leitmotif of Ellison's exploration of his protagonist's and the American national psyche. As the oscillations of the 1920s began, the inchoate Harlem Renaissance dramatized the literary proclivities that made *Invisible Man*'s depictions of the domestic identity crisis so startlingly original.

If one harvest of World War I was riots and other signs of heightened racial animosity, then another one, paradoxically, was the Harlem Renaissance, a cultural movement that like the NAACP, the National Urban League, and the YMCA, heralded the complicated possibilities of interracial cooperation. Stirrings of the Renaissance's ultimate bounty emerged as early as 1918 when Benjamin Brawley published his controversial study, *The Negro in Literature and Art.* While Brawley is not often acknowledged as an architect of the Harlem Renaissance, his early declarations on the place of blacks in American artistic production become intriguing complements to the movement's evolution. In the preface to *The Negro in Literature and Art,* Brawley asserts that "so far as we can at present judge, the Negro, with all his manual labor, is destined to reach his greatest heights in the field of the artistic" (8). This claim, framed as it was by Brawley's discussion of peculiar racial "genius," raised serious questions related to essentialism; nevertheless, it opened an avenue of thought that several leading Harlem Renaissance representatives exploited. Consider, for example, James Weldon Johnson's oft-cited remark in his preface to the 1922 classic, *The Book of American Negro Poetry:*

> A people may become great through many means, but there is only one measure by which its greatness is recognized and acknowledged. The final measure of the greatness of all peoples is the amount and standard of the literature and art they have produced. The world does not know that a people is great until that people produces great literature and art. No people that has produced great literature and art has ever been looked upon by the world as distinctly inferior. (861)

With similar assumptions, Alain Locke, in a 1925 issue of the magazine *Survey Graphic* that became the heart of his magnum opus, *The New Negro,* wrote,

> Negro genius today relies upon the race-gift as a vast spiritual endowment from which our best developments have come and must come. Racial expression as a conscious motive, it is true, is fading out of our latest art, but just as surely the age of truer, finer group expression is coming in for race expression does not need to be deliberate to be vital. (659)

Brawley, Johnson, and Locke differ in their beliefs about what techniques will lead to great African American art, but all agree that art is the sphere where blacks will distinguish themselves. To the extent that they accord African Americans any distinct racial genius, at the start of the 1920s, each man believes that such genius inheres in artistic production. This kind of consensus optimism fueled the variegated creative achievements of the following decade.

By any measure, the artistic output of African Americans during the Harlem Renaissance (1919–1929) was voluminous. Encompassing literary genres as diverse as poetry, drama, essays, short stories, and novels, the outpouring also featured significant contributions from painters, sculptors, dancers, and musicians. The accomplishments of these artists manifested incredible variety. For example, Jean Toomer's masterpiece *Cane* (1923) merged poetry and loosely connected fictional vignettes creating an experimental form that was somewhere between a novella and a tone poem. Countee Cullen, in an alternate vein, offered Romantic-inspired verse in the traditional forms of the sonnet and the ballad. His collection *Color* (1925) not only garnered an award from *Crisis,* but also it cemented his position as one of the darlings of the more conservative brokers of the Harlem Renaissance. If Cullen represented the restraint and the respectability that many black leaders felt would advance the cause of racial equality, then Claude McKay and Langston Hughes, while equally vibrant and certainly more prolific, exemplified a more radical Harlem Renaissance strain. Both men would be associated with leftist politics, and in their respective arts, both would at times portray a grittier side of black urban experience. Hughes, in his 1926 manifesto "The Negro Artist and the Racial Mountain," offered one of the more eloquent defenses of these kinds of depictions. Commenting on the artistic priorities of the new vanguard, he asserted:

> We younger Negro artists who create now intend to express our individual dark-skinned selves without fear or shame. If white people are pleased we are glad. If they are not, it doesn't matter...If colored people are pleased we are glad. If they are not, their displeasure doesn't matter either. We build our temples for tomorrow, strong as we know how, and we stand on top of the mountain, free within ourselves. (1271)

The difference in content and technique that typify Cullen, McKay, and Hughes finds an analogue in many other areas of artistic production. Jessie Fauset's novels of middle-class domestic life and Wallace Thurman's charged racial satires tilled soil quite remote from the agrarian meditations of Zora Neale Hurston. Likewise, in music, a dizzying array of distinctly talented individuals was maturing.

Edward Kennedy Ellington, known to posterity as Duke, left his native Washington, DC, and headed for New York City in 1922 (Schuller 319). After a misstep on that first trip, he returned the following year and began a climb that would make him arguably the most illustrious black composer of the twentieth century. Ellington and his band initially worked at the Hollywood Club, yet it was their playing at the world-famous Cotton Club that launched them into permanent success. Possessed of an elegant formality that infused not only his compositions but also his orchestra, Duke emanated the sort of style that Ralph Ellison alluded to in describing the impact of Jimmy Rushing, Charlie Christian, and other performers from his youth. If Ellington's implacable dignity defined one pole of Harlem Renaissance musical taste, then Louis Armstrong's exuberant showmanship occupied the other. Louis Daniel Armstrong cut his musical teeth in the rough and tumble world of good-timing New Orleans. After moving to Chicago in 1922, he joined King Oliver's band. New York and its rich musical treasures soon beckoned, and in 1924 he briefly moved to the city. While in the Big Apple, Armstrong joined Fletcher Henderson's Orchestra and according to Jeffrey Magee "taught the band—and the rest of the world—to swing" (1). Though Armstrong's ties to the Harlem Renaissance were tenuous at best, his career nevertheless embodied several of its central dilemmas. A recent migrant from the South, Armstrong artistically and culturally brought with him strong tendencies that many, among them his second wife Lil Hardin, felt were out of step with the cosmopolitan demands of big cities. Armstrong acknowledged that his hardscrabble upbringing had curtailed his view of many facets of refined living and listened when Hardin and others suggested that he expand his musical horizons. Despite this, as his neighbor Selma Heraldo later attested, he never accepted the necessity of "putting on airs" (qtd. in Hentoff 142). Determining the value of this simultaneity, holding onto crucial anchoring antecedents and embracing alternate possibilities, is what vexes Harlem Renaissance culture brokers, and it is at a later moment the question that Ellison takes up in his portrayal of *Invisible Man*'s protagonist. Greater texture emerges when one considers other developments in music.

Jazz and the blues provided one arena for the expression of black musical talent, but it could be argued that African American classical musicians most aptly exemplified the ideology of New Negro architects. While Ellington, Armstrong, and Henderson provided a swinging soundtrack for Jazz Age revels, Nathaniel Dett, Roland Hayes, and Marian Anderson plied their trade domestically and internationally, showing the nation and the world that blacks could master and contribute to Western musical idioms. Neither Dett nor Hayes was based in Harlem during the Renaissance; however, their preoccupations echoed those of Renaissance commentators. Dett, commenting on early African American classical composers, believed that emulation of white models was an inevitable byproduct of slavery and its attendant effect on black musical training. Still, he felt that true innovation would come when a black classical writer "who is thoroughly alive to and appreciative of the traditions of his race" exploits the rich potential of the "musical language of his fathers" (qtd. in Spencer 138). This sentiment echoes the search for anchored invention that Armstrong embarked on, but the rarified atmosphere and the already esteemed tradition in which Hayes and Anderson performed suggests subtle, yet profound distinctions in how their achievements were viewed. When Roland Hayes performed at prestigious houses like Symphony Hall (Boston), Carnegie Hall (New

York), and Wigmore Hall (London), his mere presence implicitly pled the case of black worthiness. Likewise, Marian Anderson's triumphant debut with the New York Philharmonic (1925) not only burnished her musical skill but also it, through the agency of widely dispersed newspaper accounts, thrust the defiant reality of her expertise on a sometimes skeptical spectatorship. Hayes and Anderson's accomplishments in traditionally European art forms, at least as Renaissance thinkers rationalized them, placed these artists and by extension African Americans unassailably in the mainstream of American cultural excellence. Such centrality was the precise aim of men like Alain Locke and W.E.B. Du Bois, especially the latter, for they felt that if artists could make the case as it were for racial equality, then it would advance the sociopolitical struggle immeasurably. The untimely ravages of the Great Depression unleashed variables that would drastically defer the results of New Negro experiments.

As the Harlem Renaissance signaled the buoyant fortunes of African American artistry in the 1920s, so too did the meteoric prosperity spawned by the stock market influence key facets of Anglo-American life. The incredible carnage of World War I had poignantly affected the mentality of the young soldiers who fought, and as they returned home, many were determined to balance the civic obligations that had sent them abroad with a more energetic indulgence of their individual desires. These determinations not only led to the relaxation of traditional signs of morality but also to a holistic embrace of the culture of indulgence. Spurred by access to unprecedented financial resources, the young adults of what came to be termed "The Jazz Age" pursued decadence as a salve for their unremittingly intense disillusionment. In this context, cities like Chicago and New York became playgrounds, especially for the social elite. F. Scott Fitzgerald's 1920 novel *The Great Gatsby* vividly captured the New York flavor of these developments, and that book's protagonist Jay Gatsby a.k.a. James Gatz exemplified for Ellison the moral hazards of what he deemed the Lost Generation's indulgent malaise. This malaise, in Ellison's opinion, was a sort of abdication not only of the artist's responsibility, but also of the social courage which ennobles democracy. If mere disenchantment seemed insubstantial in the context of a thriving economy in the 1920s, then the Great Depression of the 1930s clarified some of the reasons why.

For the bulk of the three Presidential administrations after World War I, those of Warren G. Harding (1921–1923), Calvin Coolidge (1923–1929), and Herbert Hoover (1929–1933), the United States enjoyed spectacular financial success. Spurred in part by the savvy of Andrew Mellon, the corporate titan who served as Secretary of the Treasury for Harding, Coolidge, and Hoover, this prosperity, though it may have inspired grumblings about materialism, indisputably relieved the nation of a substantial portion of the debt that it had incurred during World War I. Mellon's attentive coaxing of industrial development prompted explosive growth, and his approach to taxation freed the wealthy to pursue maximum profitability without a fear of the government dipping deeply into their tills. From his appointment in 1921 up until 1929, Mellon's policies operated efficiently, yet in the latter year, an unraveling of epic proportions occurred. The causes of the Great Depression are still debated hotly with certain scholars blaming the economic catastrophe on the federal government's problematic monetary policy while others point to the spending habits of individual consumers (Friedman and Schwartz xi-xii; McElvaine 28). Regardless of what prompted it, the Great Depression's consequences were portentous not only materially, but also culturally.

FREE MINDS: SCAFFOLDINGS OF
AN INTEGRATED MENTALITY

Invisible Man's protagonist arrives in Harlem during the Great Depression, and his urgent, yet fruitless search for employment reflects both Bledsoe's direct sabotage of his prospects and the more pervasive difficulties that a widespread recession creates. Ellison's sensitivity to the former may have been somewhat metaphoric, but his experience of the latter, especially after his mother's funeral, was palpably robust. In a 1982 interview with Walter Lowe, Ellison revealed that his 1938 experience of sleeping on the benches in St. Nicholas Park still resonated (42; Jackson 199). His remark about this interlude revealed his thoughts regarding individual destiny and governmental policy. When Lowe asks Ellison about Ronald Reagan, the novelist responds that the President was "dismantling many of the processes and structures" that Franklin D. Roosevelt's New Deal implemented (42). In Ellison's mind, such actions were glib and myopic because he believed that Roosevelt's interventions had helped take him from destitution to success as a writer. Although Jack the Bear's odyssey does not parallel Ellison's exactly, it does reveal the extent to which Depression Era complications are an intimate part of the protagonist's quest for consciousness. In particular, his interactions with the Brotherhood illuminate his and Ellison's complex courtship with leftist politics, a courtship that many budding intellectuals both black and white find alluring in the face of the Depression's havoc.

Splintering off from the Socialist Party of America, the American Communist Party was formed in 1919. Though it sponsored activities in many regions of the country, for its first 10 years, the party and its leadership was most active in New York City (Klehr and Haynes 20–58). Its slow, but steady growth in popularity not only coincided with the opulent wealth of the post–World War I period, but also with the arrival of many black migrants from the south, a contingent that would eventually become agitated by a lack of jobs and by exploitative housing arrangements. This cluster of circumstances almost insured that some African Americans would wade into the waters troubled by Communist ideology; nevertheless, Communism was not the only leftist movement that aroused black attention. As early as 1917, A. Philip Randolph and Chandler Owen were circulating Socialist views via their magazine *The Messenger.* Randolph and Owen pursued several ventures related to black labor unions, but their signature work was the organization in 1925 of the Brotherhood of Sleeping Car Porters. Notwithstanding the gradual, if sometimes grudging acceptance of interracial cooperation in leftist and radical organizations, the tenacity of racism like that Randolph encountered when negotiating with the American Federation of Labor often made blacks wary of participating in integrated groups. Despite this wariness, the sense as Randolph termed it that "exacting justice, both from the white labor unions and from the capitalists or employers" requires that "Negro workers" seek "a new leadership... of uncompromising manhood" prevailed over traditional inhibitions and the broader integration of radical American institutions quickened (12). Ralph Ellison's place in that quickening is now more clearly understood.

Barbara Foley, most passionately in her article "Ralph Ellison as Proletarian Journalist" (1997), objects to the elision of Ellison's radical tutelage from the overall consideration of his odyssey as an artist. Illuminating her reasoning, she writes, "There exists... considerable anecdotal evidence showing that Ellison was a more committed fellow-traveler than he subsequently admitted; when the Ellison papers become available... further indications of his involvement with the left may well be discovered" (par. 6). In considering the two biographies that have been written about Ellison, it becomes clear that her objections were not baseless. Not only did Ellison meet Communists and learn "the broad ideological strokes of the political parties" but also his social circulation among leftists bespoke an attraction to their "reputation for revelry," a factor not to be dismissed in the life of a 24-year-old college dropout (Jackson 170, 172). The slippery skein of Ellison's relationship to Communist causes cannot be held firmly; nonetheless, his portrayal of the Brotherhood and for that matter

Ras's proto-black-nationalist movement clearly alludes to the complex landscape that existed in 1930s America. Such complexity reflected not only the precise disorientation unleashed by the Great Depression, but also the frenetic pace of American postwar social and intellectual evolution. Standing astride that maelstrom and seeking via one of the most spectacular feats of social engineering to tame it was the only President in United States history who served more than two consecutive terms, Franklin Delano Roosevelt (FDR).

FDR tried to accelerate the nation's economic recovery via several different government-funded agencies; however, none of them bolstered the careers of more fledgling authors than the Federal Writers' Project (FWP). Started as a way to extend the Works Progress Administration's relief efforts into the ranks of creative artists and scholars, the FWP, as William Stott's *Documentary Expression and Thirties America* (1986) has shown, quickly became more than it was officially intended to be. Charged with assembling a series of guides that detailed prominent features of states as well as select cities, the FWP also compiled extensive oral histories, ethnographies, and some children's literature. Ellison's job with the New York branch of the FWP gave him a firsthand glimpse both of how the agency operated and what it could provide for a struggling wordsmith. It also clarified the proximity between Communist ideals and the cures prescribed by Roosevelt's administration. As Lawrence Jackson explains it, "The New Deal welfare state remedies of [FDR] coordinated, oddly enough, with the Popular Front rubric of the Communist Party. Ellison joined the [FWP] at a period of relative harmony, when it was not quite a contradiction for a vanguard revolutionary artist to be employed by the capitalist state" (199). In acknowledging the allure of radicalism, Ellison not only expressed his own evolving posture towards existence, but also he reflected an attitude that increasingly held sway among 1930s American intellectuals. A look at the career of Edmund Wilson is illustrative.

Paul Johnson avers that for most of American history, the country's "men of ideas and letters" have been in tune with the nation's prevailing spirit. In his opinion this changes in the wake of the Great Depression. Johnson observes, "From the early Thirties...the intellectuals, carrying with them a predominant part of academia and workers in the media, moved into a position of criticism and hostility towards the structural ideas of American consensus, the free market, capitalism, individualism, enterprise, independence, and personal responsibility" (743). No one, to Johnson's thinking, exemplifies this development more emphatically than Edmund Wilson. Born in Red Bank, New Jersey, and educated at Princeton, Wilson became by most accounts one of the foremost literary critics of his day. He reflected on the mood of the 1930s in his essay, "The Literary Consequences of the Crash." There he wrote that "the age of influence was now dawning for American writers, especially the younger ones who had grown up in the Big Business era and had always resented its barbarism, its crowding out of everything they cared about." For Wilson, the prospect of change even when yoked to penury could not inspire pessimism; in his mind the 1930s "were not depressing but stimulating. One couldn't help being exhilarated at the sudden unexpected collapse of the stupid gigantic fraud. It gave us a new sense of freedom; and it gave us a new sense of power" (qtd. in Johnson, 743). Wilson's outlook synched with that of later thinkers like Kenneth Burke and Stanley Edgar Hyman, all men who either directly or indirectly influenced Ralph Ellison's artistic apprenticeship.[5] If their sense of leftist potential hit a high point in the 1930s, then the premonitions of World War II brought with them another set of ideological adjustments. The plight of Ellison's erstwhile mentor Richard Wright gives a clear sense of this trajectory.

Richard Wright's prominence as a Communist Party operative allowed him to be a tremendous ally for Ralph Ellison, and in many ways he was responsible not only for Ellison's earliest writing assignment, a 1937 book review of Waters Turpin's *These Low Grounds,* but also for the younger writer's entrée into the clannish world of radical politics. Wright's authority in the Harlem *Daily Worker*'s bureau signals his visible, if tenuous integration into the Communist hierarchy, but his departure from the party a mere five years after meeting Ellison suggests the chafing that he felt personally and the limits of the institution's viability for any artist with avant-garde aspirations. Langston Hughes, the elder statesman who had so eloquently declared artistic independence during the Harlem Renaissance, retained his status as a latent black artist radical well beyond World War II, but for Wright and a few other African American artists, the Communist Party specifically and leftist politics in general lost its luster. In part this disenchantment stemmed from a belief that the party's early commitment to racial equality was too readily abandoned when it became politically expedient. Harold Cruse evaluating this breach in *The Crisis of the Negro Intellectual* (1967) argued that the "unwillingness or inability of the Communists to come to grips with Negro national group realities" fundamentally thwarts their usefulness in the pursuit of black liberation (150). While Mark Solomon's *The Cry Was Unity* (1998) strenuously refutes Cruse's broad accusations of indifference and duplicity, he does acknowledge the failure of the Communist Party to convince "a steadfast white working-class majority" that the cause of black liberty deserved their support (307). World War II dramatized the kinds of vicissitudes that these commentators later detected, and it also sparked a move away from symbolic demands to the more complex pursuit of practical redress.

In 1935 Harlem experienced widespread violence after rumors circulated that a black youth accused of stealing had been murdered by white police.[6] Almost 10 years later, a white officer's wounding of a black soldier prompted unprecedented racial hostilities that resulted in six fatalities and more than 200 injuries (Capeci 99–100, xi). These events, the latter covered by Ralph Ellison for the *New York Post,* suggest an intractable discontent, and falling as they do before and after the United States' entry into World War II, they show that the international fight against fascism did little to alleviate domestic discomfiture regarding race relations. If anything the Second World War even as it held the promise of accelerating integration convinced African Americans that a healthy skepticism was in order regarding the resolution of longstanding inequalities. This skepticism applied equally to leftist organizations, who while active in isolated endeavors, could not mount a national campaign to shift the status of blacks and to the federal government, which counted among its inner circle a tireless advocate like First Lady, Eleanor Roosevelt. Ultimately, the urgent calls for freedom and justice globally struck a hypocritical note in many black ears. It was not that African Americans supported Hitler or Mussolini; the latter's aggression against Ethiopia and the former's attempts to humiliate Jesse Owens were abundant signs that they were not allies. Rather, they again contemplated the vexing dilemma of how to rationalize fighting abroad for a dignity that they did not receive either at home or even in the throes of combat. In this conflict, the chorus taken up by black leaders would differ from earlier verses.

Franklin Roosevelt's popularity with the American people grew in no small part because he reassured them that "the only thing we have to fear is fear itself" and that economic recovery was not only possible but likely (Parks and Parks 146). Through creative policies and a conditional alliance with the powerful Southern Democrats in the Congress, he made headway, gradually putting significant sections of the country back to work. African Americans were not insensitive to Roosevelt's programs, and for many he became a much beloved figure. Despite this admiration, African Americans still felt that the march towards integration was progressing too slowly. When black leaders like A. Philip Randolph, Mary McLeod Bethune, and Walter White met with Roosevelt, they lobbied him to address employment discrimination, inadequate funding for black schools, and police brutality. Although Roosevelt frequently made promises, as in the case of his discussion regarding the desegregation of the armed forces, he at crucial moments overlooked those obligations often citing the fragile alliance with Dixiecrats without whose help he argued no reform would be possible. African Americans listened to these excuses, and as they listened they concluded that their place in the nation was taken for granted. Such treatment, in the face of widespread mobilization for World War II, acquired a peculiarly poignant irony. While the nation's Congressional leaders decried the inhumanity of Nazism, they sent black soldiers, who were organized in separate-but-equal units, to secure world peace. Such hypocrisy did not confine itself to the military.

In Murray Rothbard's view, "more than any other single period, World War I was the critical watershed for the American business system." He uses the term "war collectivism" to describe the blend of "big-business interests" and central governance that thrived then and suggests that it is "the model, the precedent, and the inspiration for state corporate capitalism for the remainder of the twentieth century" (66). This model led to unprecedented productivity, and its success hinged on a large workforce and the widespread implementation of scientific management and new technology solutions. These innovations greatly enhanced the efficiency of factories, and as the demands of World War II mounted, their legacies gave rise to further refinements. The activities of Henry Kaiser offer a glimpse into the era's leading traits. Initially associated with a road paving business, Kaiser during World War II made a name for himself as a ship builder. The father of the famous "Liberty Ships," modestly sized aircraft carriers, he revolutionized production techniques, and from an initial turnaround time of "196 days," Kaiser Shipyard evolved until in 1943, they were finishing a new ship "every 10.3 hours" (Johnson 781). This kind of resourcefulness enabled America to construct what FDR called "the arsenal of democracy," yet as *Invisible Man*'s Liberty Paints episode makes clear, crucial racial realities were concealed beneath the gently humming industrial surface (Parks and Parks 220). Chester Himes, in the novel *If He Hollers Let Him Go* (1945), creates a stark counterpoint to the serene triumph of Kaiser's California shipbuilding. Telling the story of Bob Jones, a black man who is almost destroyed by the prejudice of the Los Angeles shipyard where he works, Himes shows that African Americans who were cogs in the machine of America's World War II efforts sometimes incurred debilitating psychological wounds. The plights of black war workers in Detroit provide an authentic analogue for this fictional account.

The *Chicago Bee,* noting area YWCA's efforts, offered this view of providing lodging for laborers, especially single women, during wartime: Giving "a home to a war worker [is not] just a business proposition—it

[is] a patriotic service" (qtd. in Kimble 428). While the newspaper's perspective may have held some sway in Chicago, black laborers in Detroit encountered a more vexed sentiment. Led by Charles Diggs and other members of the Coordinating Committee on Housing, African American war workers had been agitating for expanded and improved conditions since 1940. As their efforts intensified, the Detroit Housing Commission and the federal government promised in 1941 that a new housing project would be constructed. Located close to the predominantly Polish neighborhood of Hamtramck, the Sojourner Truth Housing Project immediately became a source of controversy. White residents and local real estate agents objected to black residency in the housing project. Concerned that such a constituency would ruin property values, they lobbied local congressmen and complained to the mayor. Once the housing project was built, Diggs's Committee was absorbed into a larger group, the Sojourner Truth Citizens Committee. This group specifically advocated for the right of black workers to reside in the buildings, but growing media attention suggested that this conflict was a microcosm of a wider, more combustible racial animosity. Eventually, black workers were allowed to move into the Sojourner Truth Housing Project; still, within a year Detroit and the Sojourner Truth area were embroiled in one of the most destructive riots of the war years.

Ellison's portrayal of the narrator's interactions with Lucius Brockway explore the metaphorical position of blacks in the American industrial consciousness, but it additionally considers the lethal consequences of not acknowledging in sociopolitical terms what is already true in psychocultural ones, namely that the United States is already an integrated nation. When circumstances like those in Detroit take place, it is, to Ellison, doubly absurd because it reveals not only the material costs of a profound national denial, but also the zeal with which the citizenry will fight to maintain a shuttered vision. That all of this takes place in the context of a fight against fascism is transcendently ironic. Add to that the complexity of Pearl Harbor and the opening of the Pacific Theater, and one senses more urgently than ever the forces that motivate Ellison to his eccentric meditation on national identity. If the European theater features a uniformly despicable personality who galvanizes a global coalition, the major plot item in the Pacific war may be the Atomic bomb and how its deployment impacts views of science and civilization.

Commenced in 1939 after Albert Einstein notified FDR that the Germans had begun their own efforts to purify uranium, the Manhattan Project headed by Robert Oppenheimer symbolized both the delirious potential and the pernicious possibilities of scientific cooperation. Galvanizing the knowledge of specialists from over a half dozen disciplines, the project represented a sort of supercharged parallel to the efficiency-hungry industrial exploits of individuals like Kaiser. Nevertheless, its result, the atomic bomb, gave rise even in its creators to emotional paradoxes that some of them never completely escaped. The collision between patriotic duty and the reality of Hiroshima and Nagasaki's utter destruction removed the Manhattan Project from the abstract realm of wartime research cheerleading to the practical sphere of human management of immensely destructive potential. That such transitions were undertaken in the shadows of internment camps and an escalating agitation for civil rights reinforces the inextricable links of national existence, a theme that Ellison uses as the most basic unifier within *Invisible Man.*

The hospital scene in *Invisible Man* provides the best glimpse of Ellison's playful evocation of the mad scientist. The localized efforts of the factory doctors place them at a far remove from vast international endeavors like the Manhattan Project; nevertheless, the benefits of vigorously interrogating one's motives emerges in each case. The doctors abandon medical ethics and acquire an egomaniacal voyeurism that morphs into perverse exploitation. They perform experiments on the protagonist merely because they can, and with no curb on their curiosity, their transgressions seem boundless. Likewise the potential benevolence of the Manhattan Project collides with the complicated facts of a real world use of the technology. What is the creator's relationship to her product? Can one be held accountable for improper uses of one's creations? These questions arise in the aftermath of World War II, but for Ellison they are not just the questions of a nation managing atomic capabilities, they are also the fundamental queries of American democratic pluralism. The time between the end of World War II (1945) and the publication of *Invisible Man* (1952) arouse within the writer a cautious optimism.

FDR, in 1941, created the Fair Employment Practices Committee (FEPC). Designed to "protect the civil rights of minorities" by "enforc[ing] nondiscrimination in defense contracts," the FEPC tried valiantly, yet only fitfully fulfilled its purpose (Graham 53). In many ways it is indicative of the 15-year span from the outbreak of World War II until the landmark Supreme Court decision in *Brown v. Board.* Indisputable progress took place. Enough of it in fact to recall once skeptical spectators like Ralph Ellison back into a tough-minded engagement with democratic hope. This hope was spawned not just by the victories of the NAACP Legal Defense Fund in cases like *Shelley v. Kraemer* (1948) and *Sweat v. Painter* (1950) or by Harry S. Truman's "moral courage and political recklessness"

(Gardner 3), but also by Ellison's conviction that the Robert Park and Gunnar Myrdal schools of black victimization needed to be confronted. Perhaps Ellison's stubborn pride pushed him through over a half decade of composition just so that he could present his side of the story. Whether that is true or not, what cannot be denied is Eric Sundquist's remark about "the extraordinary wealth and vitality of Ellison's historical imagination." He argues that Ellison's "capacity to rewrite African American history in the experiences of a single hero" is an act of recovery. The writer seeks to exhume "for future readers those materials of black culture... that threatened to become lost from view" (27–28). If this chapter clarifies the energy of his exhumations, it has done its work.

NOTES

1. Throughout the lengthy record of his existence in critical literature, the protagonist of *Invisible Man* has been called by many names. Following the narrator's request in the prologue and for purposes of variety, the moniker, Jack the Bear, will be used alongside the already established labels, protagonist and narrator (6).

2. Beginning in the 1830s, blackface minstrelsy evolves into a highly conventional, incredibly popular mainstream ritual, and by the middle of the nineteenth century, it is well established as a mass entertainment. Before the Civil War, the form was largely confined to white actors who "blacked up" to offer their portrayals of black characters. The postbellum period saw a number of black performers participating in this spectacle. See Dakle Cockrell's *Demons of Disorder: Early Blackface Minstrels and Their World* (1997) and William J. Mahar's *Behind the Burnt Cork Mask: Early Blackface Minstrelsy and Antebellum American Popular Culture* (1998) for more expansive discussions.

3. According to *The African-American Mosaic: The Library of Congress Resource Guide for the Study of Black History and Culture,* in 1900, "approximately 90 percent of all African-Americans still resided in the South." That majority would hold until the 1970s when the black population would become predominantly a "northern, urban one" (par. 1, par. 2).

4. The quotations from Warner and Mills are taken from the transcript for the PBS documentary *Marcus Garvey: Look for Me in the Whirlwind.* The transcript is reprinted on the Web site for the documentary at <http://www.pbs.org/wgbh/amex/garvey/filmmore/pt.html>.

5. John S. Wright, relying heavily on Lawrence Jackson's research, argues that Edmund Wilson, through the books *Axel's Castle* (1931) and *The Wound and the Bow* (1941)*,* "made a singular impress on Ellison's developing literary sensibilities" (132). The "Texts" chapter of this guide makes clear the extent to which Kenneth Burke touched Ellison's thinking. According to Ted Weiss, a longtime

friend of Ralph Ellison's, one could rightly view Hyman as a crucial editor of *Invisible Man,* an editor whose absence might be partly responsible for Ellison's failure to tame the thronging pages of his final novel (Rampersad 538).

6. Lorrin Thomas offers an intriguing account of the textures of this event in his article, "'They See Us as Black Americans': Puerto Rican Migrants and the Politics of Citizenship in Depression-era New York City." There, he writes that the "1935 Harlem riots in New York" were "several days of upheaval inspired by the arrest of a Puerto Rican boy," a youth who ironically "was immediately identified, by the media and by the mostly African American participants in the riots, as simply 'Negro'" (par. 24). This appropriation of ethnic grievance did not arise from any overwhelming sense of solidarity; rather, as many have noted, it probably reflected the general combustibility of Harlem, and its readiness to erupt over any perception of a racially tinged affront.

WORKS CITED

The African-American Mosaic: The Library of Congress Resource Guide for the Study of Black History and Culture. July 5, 2005. Lib. of Congress, Washington. 8 pars. July 25, 2007 <http://www.loc.gov/exhibits/african/afam008.html>.

Astor, Gerald. *The Right to Fight: A History of African Americans in the Military.* Novato: Presidio, 1998.

Barbeau, Arthur E., and Florette Henri Barbeau. *The Unknown Soldier: African American Troops in World War I.* 1974. New York: Da Capo, 1996.

Brawley, Benjamin. *The Negro in Literature and Art.* 1918. Kila: Kessinger Publishing, 2005.

Buckley, Gail. *American Patriots: The Story of Blacks in the Military from the Revolution to Desert Storm.* New York: Random House, 2001.

Capeci, Dominic J. *The Harlem Riot of 1943.* Philadelphia: Temple UP, 1977.

Carle, Susan. "Race, Class, and Legal Ethics in the Early NAACP (1910–1920)." *Law and History Review* 20 (2002): 97–146.

Clarke, John Henrik, ed. *Marcus Garvey and the Vision of Africa.* New York: Vintage, 1974.

Cruse, Harold. *The Crisis of the Negro Intellectual.* New York: Morrow, 1969.

Douglass, Frederick. *Narrative of the Life of Frederick Douglass An American Slave Written by Himself.* 1845. Ed. Benjamin Quarles. Cambridge: Harvard-Belknap, 1993.

Du Bois, W.E.B. "The Talented Tenth." 1903. *The American Reader: Words That Moved A Nation.* Rev. 2nd ed. Ed. Diane Ravitch. New York: HarperCollins, 2000. 373–376.

Ellison, Ralph. *Invisible Man.* 1952. New York: Vintage, 1989.

Foley, Barbara. "Ralph Ellison as Proletarian Journalist." *Science and Society* 62 (1997): 24 pars. Aug. 1, 2007 <http://victorian.fortunecity.com/holbein/439/bf/foleyreleft2.html>.

Franklin, John Hope, and Alfred A. Moss, Jr. *From Slavery to Freedom: A History of Negro Americans.* Sixth ed. New York: McGraw-Hill, 1988.

Friedman, Milton, and Anna Jacobson Schwartz. *The Great Contraction 1929– 1933.* Princeton: Princeton UP, 1965.

Gardner, Michael R. *Harry Truman and Civil Rights: Moral Courage and Political Risks.* Carbondale: Southern Illinois UP, 2002.

Gates, Henry Louis, Jr. *Figures in Black: Words, Signs, and the "Racial" Self.* New York: Oxford UP, 1987.

Graham, Hugh Davis. "The Origins of Affirmative Action: Civil Rights and the Regulatory State." *Annals of the American Academy of Political and Social Science* 523.1 (1992): 50–62.

Hentoff, Nat. "Armstrong House, Alive and Well." *Jazztimes* Dec. 2003: 142.

History of the National Urban League. 2006. National Urban League, New York. 24 pars. July 25, 2007 <http://www.nul.org/history.html>.

Hughes, Langston. "The Negro Artist and the Racial Mountain." 1926. *Norton Anthology of African American Literature.* Eds. Henry Louis Gates, Jr. and Nellie Y. McKay. New York: Norton, 1997. 1267–1271.

Jackson, Lawrence. *Ralph Ellison: Emergence of Genius.* New York: Wiley, 2002.

Johnson, James Weldon. "Preface from *The Book of American Negro Poetry.*" 1922. *Norton Anthology of African American Literature.* Eds. Henry Louis Gates, Jr. and Nellie Y. McKay. New York: Norton, 1997. 861–884.

Johnson, Paul. *A History of the American People.* New York: HarperCollins, 1997.

Kimble, Lionel, Jr. "I Too Serve America: African American Women War Workers in Chicago, 1940–1945." *Journal of the Illinois State Historical Society* 93 (Winter 2000/2001): 415–434.

Klehr, Harvey, and John Earl Haynes. *The American Communist Movement: Storming Heaven Itself.* New York: Twayne, 1992.

Locke, Alain. "Youth Speaks." *Survey Graphic* 6 (March 1925): 659–660.

Logan, Rayford. *The Negro in American Life and Thought: The Nadir 1877–1901.* New York: Dial, 1954.

Lowe, Walter, Jr. "Book Essay: *Invisible Man* Ralph Ellison." *Playboy* Oct. 1982: 42.

Magee, Jeffrey. *The Uncrowned King of Swing: Fletcher Henderson and Big Band Jazz.* New York: Oxford UP, 2005.

Marcus Garvey: Look for Me in the Whirlwind. 1999–2000. Public Broadcasting Service, Boston. July 25, 2007 <http://www.pbs.org/wgbh/amex/garvey/filmmore/pt.html>.

Martin, Waldo E., Jr., ed. *Brown v. Board of Education: A Brief History with Documents.* Boston: Bedford-St. Martin's, 1998.

McElvaine, Robert S. *The Great Depression: America, 1929–1941.* New York: New York Times Books, 1984.

Parks, E. Taylor, and Lois F. Parks, comps. *Memorable Quotations of Franklin D. Roosevelt.* New York: Crowell, 1965.

Pilgrim, David. "The Coon Caricature." October 2000. Jim Crow Museum of Racist Memorabilia, Ferris State U. 14 pars. July 26, 2007 <http://www.ferris.edu/jimcrow/coon/>.

Platt, Suzy, ed. *Respectfully Quoted: A Dictionary of Quotations Requested from the Congressional Research Service.* Washington: LOC, 1989.

Rampersad, Arnold. *Ralph Ellison: A Biography.* New York: Knopf, 2007.

Randolph, A. Phillip. "Our Reason for Being." *Messenger* Aug. 1919: 11–12.

Rothbard, Murray N. "War Collectivism in World War I." *A New History of Leviathan: Essays on the Rise of the American Corporate State.* Eds. Ronald Radosh and Murray Rothbard. New York: Dutton, 1972. 66–110.

Schuller, Gunther. *Early Jazz: Its Roots and Musical Development.* 1968. New York: Oxford UP, 1986.

Solomon, Mark. *The Cry was Unity: Communists and African Americans, 1917–1936.* Jackson: U of Mississippi P, 1998.

Spencer, Jon Michael. "R. Nathaniel Dett's Views on the Preservation of Black Music." *The Black Perspective in Music* 10 (Fall 1982): 132–148.

Sundquist, Eric J., ed. *Cultural Contexts for Ralph Ellison's* Invisible Man. Boston: Bedford-St. Martin's, 1995.

Thomas, Lorrin. "'They See Us as Black Americans': Puerto Rican Migrants and the Politics of Citizenship in Depression-era New York City." *Delaware Review of Latin American Studies* 6.1 (June 30, 2005): 37 pars. July 25, 2007 <http://www.udel.edu/LAS/Vol6-1Thomas.html>.

Thorpe, Earl E. *Eros and Freedom in Southern Life and Thought.* Durham: Seeman Printery, 1967.

The War of the Rebellion: A Compilation of the Official Records of the Union and Confederate Armies. Ed. Robert N. Scott. Ser. 1. Vol. 15. Washington: GPO, 1885.

Washington, Booker T. *Up From Slavery.* 1901. New York: Penguin, 1986.

Weiss, Nancy J. *The National Urban League 1910–1940.* New York: Oxford UP, 1974.

Wright, John S. *Shadowing Ralph Ellison.* Jackson: UP of Mississippi, 2006.

Chapter 4

IDEAS

Invisible Man earns the widely applied moniker tour de force because the novel audaciously interrogates its narrator's multifaceted world. That world, the United States of the 1930s, provides the foundation for what Ellison believes is the American writer's project and responsibility: depicting experience in such a way that enables readers to acquire tools for grasping reality. He felt deeply that America's relative youth as a country compelled an incessant search for identity to which serious writers were obligated to contribute. Minority writers in particular assume this task, Ellison writes, "by depicting the experience of their own groups" (*Collected Essays* 99). *Invisible Man* charts its protagonist's journey toward understanding his humanity. Through a set of varied, and therefore valuable, experiences, the narrator develops the capacity to draw conclusions about his racial and national identity. The issues Ellison raises, then, become tools in this larger project, and although the novel's picaresque structure sometimes leads readers to presume the narrator's exploits are arbitrary, the episodes fit comfortably into three basic categories that are introduced in the prologue. Distilling these major topics unlocks Ellison's sometimes unwieldy work, and while readers may differ in their description of these concepts, a look at the novel's organization makes their prominence clear. The narrator's contemplation of his journey reveals three interrelated ideas that unite the events of his past and organize this chapter: inner blindness, cultural complexity, and artistic responsibility. With these themes setting the parameters for his narrator's experiences, Ellison explores mid-century American blackness.

This chapter employs three frames as lenses through which to consider and contain the numerous smaller ideas that Ellison insists we engage with. The variability and richness of his palette has made the text a favorite for critics of all stripes, a subject the "Reception" chapter elucidates, and in many instances the issues most discussed by scholars hit upon the most significant concepts that Ellison's bumbling narrator must grasp. The first section of this chapter, "Blindness and Sight: Ellison's View of American Psychology," considers how Ellison's view of race relations between white men and black men, as well as between white women and black men, unearths the necessity for black Americans' rejection of majority definitions of blackness. In place of deprecatory stereotypes, key scenes in the novel insist upon the protagonist's embrace of a self definition founded upon an honest assessment of majority behavior and black experience. "Cultural Complexity: Ellison's Concept of Black American Existence" extends the conclusion Ellison's focus on psychology yields by examining how seminal themes verify black American complexity. Scenes engaging folklore (and specifically the blues), violence, transcendentalism, and existentialism exhibit some of the ways Ellison probes black consciousness. The section "Fulfilling Artistic Responsibility: Ellison's Solution for Understanding Identity" focuses on Ellison's protagonist's engagement with political debates as tools for self-reflection; Ellison's protagonist ultimately finds the political debates to be lacking when compared to the art of writing. The protagonist's successful comprehension and integration of these ideas signal his readiness to depart his underground residence. While one chapter cannot fully analyze these and other themes that Ellison broaches, probing their contours discloses how characters and episodes represent larger concepts at the heart of Ellison's narrative agenda.

Ellison revels in demanding that his readers excavate the same issues that his protagonist confronts as he tries to understand American identity. Consequently, his narrator evades a straightforward description of the major categories that his experiences fall into; instead, his prefatory remarks subtly establish the rubric for navigating his evolving theory of invisibility. He begins by explaining that his condition stems from an unusual construction of people's "inner eyes, those eyes with which they look through their physical eyes upon reality" (3). His brawl with the blond man illustrates his point. In a tone that invites readers to question his sanity, the narrator observes that the white man sees him "perhaps because of the near darkness" and addresses him with derogatory language (4). Paradoxically, the physical darkness that typically impedes sight helps the man see what he passes during the day, an unremarkable black man. The

narrator's description of the man as a "blind fool" and his suggestion that
he is part of the vast group of "sleepwalkers" cleverly hints at the meaning
for Ellison's metaphor of blindness (5). According to the narrator's logic,
the failure to see correctly arises from psychological impenetrability rather
than physical deficiency, a truth responsible for his confused assessment
of himself and the people he meets on his journey of discovery. The blond
man cannot see past the stereotypes used to categorize black Americans,
a failure amplified by the newspaper report's confident labeling of the
incident as a mugging. Similarly, for much of the narrator's life, he is not
psychologically equipped to envision the white man's conception of him.
With this beginning, Ellison hints at the importance of overcoming inner
blindness, or psychological confusion, to understand identity.

The narrator's contemplation of Louis Armstrong's "What Did I Do
to Be so Black and Blue" introduces the second major theme that orders
his experiences, his grasp of cultural complexity. Listening to the jazz leg-
end's bluesy lyrics, the narrator admits that understanding invisibility helps
him sense deeper meanings in the song. To illustrate his insights he recounts his state of consciousness when he listened to the music while high
on reefer. Two visions play out against the backdrop of Armstrong's ironic
melody, and each refines the vital relationship between the narrator's acceptance of invisibility and his grasp of racial complexity. As he listens in both
space and time, he distinguishes a slave girl on the auction block before de-
scending still deeper to perceive a black church congregation participating
in a sermon on the "Blackness of Blackness" (9). The preacher's cadence
showcases traditional black religious call-and-response interweaved with
blues-inspired contradictions that seamlessly blend into the narrator's second image of an old slave woman relaying her divided feelings for the man
who owned her and fathered her sons. As the narrator attempts to wrap his
mind around her meaning, he acknowledges that he, too, understands ambivalence, and he endeavors to clear up her tangled emotions by suggesting
that the freedom she loved more than her master rests on a deeper feeling
of hate. Her contradictory insistence that freedom lies in loving leads her
to conclude that ultimately freedom "ain't nothing but knowing how to
say what I got up in my head" (11). This, of course, sums up what the narrator seeks to accomplish in the prologue. In struggling to articulate his
inner feelings, he must first confront and embrace the knotty truths of his
heritage. Both visions expand upon Armstrong's tongue-in-cheek question
that plays the color of bruised skin off of the emotionally bruising reality of
black American existence, which in turn outlines the contradictory feelings
swirling inside the bodies of blacks who look black and feel blue.

As the narrator closes his preliminary reflections, he acknowledges feeling called to action. The urge "to make music of invisibility" and "to put invisibility down in black and white" returns him to the problem of responsibility and slyly directs readers past his Dostoyevsky-like ranting. He clearly contemplates the obligation of the artist, whether he creates music or prose, and intimates that he struggles to move past psychological blindness and cultural confusion to accept artistic responsibility. Before he can proceed, he must straighten out "the incompatible notions" buzzing within his head and determine the most efficacious method for sharing his discoveries (14). Like the yokel whose art succeeds by interrupting his opponent's sense of time, the narrator realizes the necessity for disrupting the languid tempo of an American society at ease with its incongruous foundation. His closing question, "what did *I* do to be so blue," transforms Armstrong's lyrics into an impetus for self-exploration that promises to fulfill the artistic calling he heeds. In the vein of the old slave woman who yearns for the ability to articulate her own thoughts, the narrator accepts the challenge of transposing his experiences into the form of narrative art. To accomplish his task he crafts a story that wrestles with issues materializing from his struggle with each of the major themes his opening thoughts propose.

BLINDNESS AND SIGHT: ELLISON'S VIEW OF AMERICAN PSYCHOLOGY

Ellison's decision to relate physical sight and recognition to the mental condition of his characters displays his broader interest in black psychology as well as his recognition of the larger contemporary debate in the expanding field of psychology. His own involvement with the LaFargue Clinic, which he describes as one of the earliest institutions of psychotherapy tailored to serve the underprivileged and a representation of "an underground extension of democracy," verifies his contention regarding black American psychology (*Collected Essays* 320). Focusing on Harlem in particular, Ellison claims the city provides a striking microcosm of the larger difficulty overwhelming black Americans. Their existence in a city within the larger city of New York—a symbol of American possibility and achievement—dramatically illustrates the effect of denying the national dream to black citizens. Ellison insists:

> When Negroes are barred from participating in the main institutional life of society, they lose far more than economic privileges.... They lose one of

the bulwarks which men place between themselves and the constant threat of chaos. For whatever the assigned function of social institutions, their psychological function is to protect the citizen against the irrational, incalculable forces that hover about the edges of human life. (*Collected Essays* 324)

The denial of their just rights rather than any genetic or cultural disposition accounts for most irrational behavior by black Americans. In asserting this, Ellison acknowledges the polemical nature of his avowal and proceeds to explain "there is an argument in progress between black men and white men as to the true nature of American reality. Whites impose interpretations upon Negro experience that are not only false, but effectively deny Negro humanity" (*Collected Essays* 326). The willful blindness of white America, Ellison implies, contributes greatly to the state of black consciousness and American psychology more broadly.

We first confront white men's embrace of scapegoating, the psychological phenomenon most intriguing to Ellison, in the battle royal scene. Kenneth Burke, a philosopher Ellison greatly respected, defines the scapegoat in his discussion of literary form as the "'representative' or 'vessel' of certain unwanted evils, the sacrificial animal upon whose back the burden of these evils is ritualistically loaded" (39–40). The naïve narrator can draw no such conclusion about his position at the smoker. Instead, he is shocked to discover the town's leading men transformed from images of respect to states of animalistic stupor. Ellison provides key details to suggest a connection between the narrator and the blonde dancer, and by extension, uncovers the ridiculous nature of the men's attempt to transfer their lascivious conduct to the boys. The big shots command the young men to join their ravenous observation, refusing a boy who faints the luxury of remaining unconscious and ignoring the largest boy's plea to leave as he attempts to hide his erection. By forcing the black boys to participate in their consumption of the blonde's naked body, the white men attempt to transfer their acts of sexual barbarity to the boys who double as scapegoats and objectified bodies the men devour. Ellison makes this clear in the numerous comparisons he draws between the boys and the blonde. The men are "ringed around" both the boys and the blonde to form a kind of double frame (19); she is covered in "pearly perspiration" while they sport "anticipatory sweat" (19, 18); she dances in "smoke...like the thinnest of veils" while the boys weave "like drunken dancers" in "the smoky-blue atmosphere" (19, 23); and, they both perform under the greedy eyes of the men. Even the chaos characterizing the boys' fight and their electrifying retrieval of the coins echoes the pandemonium that engulfs her performance.

The deliberate parallel that Ellison establishes between the blonde and the black boys redirects attention to the architects of the scene. In fact, when the white blindfolds render the narrator physically unable to see, Ellison focuses attention more clearly on the men consuming the spectacle. While the narrator's naïveté obstructs his perception of principles governing the scene, the white men's deliberate denial and displacement of their sexual appetite displays a pernicious psychological sightlessness.

The narrator's interaction with Mr. Norton extends and sharpens the white male ritual introduced in the battle royal. When the white trustee confesses that his dedication to the college emanates from his love for his daughter, a beautiful young woman he directs the narrator to behold in a miniature portrait, he barely contains his incestuous desire for her or his attempt to transfer his immoral cravings to the work of the college: transforming "barren clay to fertile soil" (45). The narrator, again impeded by his belief in the myth of the Southern white gentleman, only vaguely recognizes a connection between the two episodes. Even when he notes that Norton greedily consumes Trueblood's story of incest "with something like envy and indignation," the narrator remains focused on the sharecropper's heinous act rather than Norton's depraved appetite for the details of black man's tale (51). The sharecropper relates that the white sheriff and other town leaders also composed a willing audience and "wanted to hear about the gal lots of times" (53). White educators even interview Trueblood and record his words in a book. This white male obsession with his story, like the men's wanton actions at the smoker, results in the chaos and violence that typifies mid-century race relations. Although both the battle royal and the brutality of the Golden Day exhibit black male violence, Ellison's artful construction of the scenes identifies white male psychology as the destructive foundation for both intra- and interracial conflict.

To further probe the role racial misperception plays in the narrator's journey toward invisibility Ellison depicts white women as hostages to stereotype, yet another culprit of fractured psychology. A number of critics discuss the role of women in the novel, and to a varying degree, connect Ellison's representation of them to the narrator's developing identity. Carolyn Sylvander, in one of the earliest pieces on the subject, attacks Ellison for resorting to "stereotype" to create female characters (77). Claudia Tate suggests that the women represent guides for the narrator. She contends, "Through his contact with [the female characters], he comes to understand that he is the means to another's end; he is a victim, growing evermore conscious of his victimization" (164). In some way, each of these critics engages the idea that understanding Ellison's presentation of the female character's psychology helps explain the narrator's emotional state.

As an apparent consequence of the white male attribution of vigorous sexual cravings to black men, white women perceive black men as studs available for satisfying their unfulfilled sexual needs. The narrator's interactions with white women associated with the Brotherhood portray in stark relief the unfortunate effects of their clichéd idea of black men. The mystery woman the protagonist escorts home after his first speech on the Woman Question tells him that his orations make her "afraid" because his delivery is "so primitive," his voice pulsing with the beat of "tom-toms" (413). Although the soundness of Brotherhood doctrine is questionable, the woman's inability to see beyond the racist images peddled by American society elucidates the depth of the problem for blacks attempting to contribute positively to their culture in ways not included in the approved script. Ellison hints that white men and women's persistent denial of uncomfortable aspects of their humanity begets problems in their own relationships, too. The mystery woman clearly pursues the narrator as a means for fulfilling her sexual appetite as well as getting back at a disaffected husband. Yet the indifference Hurbert manifests upon finding his wife in bed with the narrator suggests that their marriage lacks the bonds of monogamous intimacy that form the foundation of most unions. In the process of misconstruing black American sexuality, the white majority unintentionally confounds their own.

Sybil, with her absurd desire to be raped by a black man, her deplorable view of her husband, and her pitiful attempt at self-definition through an imagined sexual identity, epitomizes the mental state scapegoating and stereotyping generate. Nevertheless, her prescient surmise that she and the narrator are "kind of alike" indicates Ellison's deeper interest in the consequences of such blindness (520). Similarities between the protagonist and Sybil abound: they subject themselves to sexual exploitation, attempt unsuccessfully to redefine themselves, and hold irrational self-images at odds with society's view. In fact, much of Ellison's attention to white psychology seems calculated to expose the narrator's failure to understand his identity and to distinguish the accuracy of labels society freely applies. Sybil's ridiculous behavior echoes his own in much the same way that Norton's and young Emerson's tenuous hold on sanity, and the narrator's failure to detect their fragile mindsets, introduces the issue of his own psychological sightlessness.

Ultimately, Ellison's metaphor of blindness establishes a dichotomy contrasting characters who see versus those who do not. In his scheme, clarity of vision equals wisdom, and blindness amounts to foolish incomprehension at best and insanity at worst. This psychological branding associates many characters whom the narrator admires with mental frailty and destabilizes his notions of craziness. The narrator's quick assumptions about individuals in his community often reflect his facile acceptance of racist labels. Beginning with his grandfather's deathbed advice, which the narrator's parents mark as evidence that "the old man had gone out of his mind," the narrator regards ideas that contradict established societal codes as crazy and those which uphold such ideologies as sensible (16). As a result, he steadfastly works to behave "wisely" even if he must compromise himself to do so. Characters like the vet in the Golden Day possess greater insight into the ways of the world than any of the men the narrator esteems, but his acceptance of society's ordained labels blinds him to the ex-doctor's espousal of truth. The vet is the first character to describe him as "invisible" and "the most perfect achievement of [Norton's] dreams," a mocking depiction given Norton's bizarre behavior and inane worldview (94). In Alan Nadel's discussion of the extended and complex metaphor Ellison creates through his construction of the Golden Day episode, he suggests that Ellison uses the brothel to offer a dual comment on the similarly named historical period as well as the critical study by Lewis Mumford. In Ellison's hands, the bordello becomes a symbol of white men's insistence that blacks "provide the stimulation without revealing the truth which create[s] it" (96). When the vet meets the narrator on the bus, he tries to further dismantle his naïve understanding of society, exhorting "look beneath the surface" and "learn how *you* operate" (154). Accepting the vision of those in power, the vet contends, surrenders one's identity to the misperceptions of others committed to maintaining the veneer covering racist social interactions.

The narrator's fascination with succeeding in the world the vet describes prevents him from heeding the ex-doctor's advice. Only after he discovers the true nature of the Brotherhood, an organization he believes looks beyond the racial and economic boundaries ordering the broader American society, does the narrator begin seeing himself accurately. When he finds the youth leader, Brother Tod Clifton, selling degrading Sambo dolls on the street, his gradual transformation becomes apparent. Pondering his friend's emphatic rejection of Brotherhood philosophy, the narrator realizes that the books he previously relied upon for answers fail to account for men like Clifton and himself. The Brotherhood's narrow reliance on history and science neglects the complexities of black Americans whom the narrator realizes possess "natures too ambiguous for the most ambiguous words" and "who write no novels, histories or other books" (439). Such unrecorded ambiguity relegates blacks to a position beneath the surface of society, a place into which the narrator has hitherto refused to peer, and he suspects that Clifton's final acts reflect his reaction to the sight that greets his unsuspecting eyes. The Sambo dolls he sells represent his ironic acceptance of the image the white Brothers and U.S. society assign him, while his violent death symbolizes his refusal to dance at someone else's demand.

Witnessing Clifton's murder commences the narrator's slow journey toward accurate self vision. Unlike white proclivities for scapegoating and stereotyping, conscious endorsements of inaccurate vision, Clifton's embrace of Sambo represents his effort to compel more penetrating sight. Ellison touches upon this idea in an interview, explaining "If I used such stereotypes in fiction, I'd have to reveal their archetypical aspects because my own awareness *of,* and identification *with,* the human complexity which they deny would compel me to transform them into something more recognizably human" (*Collected Essays* 734). Clifton's Sambo characterizes the pain of society's systematic denial of his humanity, a lesson the narrator reiterates in his confrontation with the Brotherhood committee who accuses him of betraying Harlem's interests by defending Clifton's actions. After Brother Jack replaces his false eye, another example of Ellison's playful manipulation of blindness, the narrator quips that if he ever needs an oculist, he will appeal to Jack's, surmising, "then I may not-see myself as others see-me-not" (471).

Notwithstanding the narrator's angry recognition of the Brotherhood's duplicity, his hunger for power inhibits him from adopting an honest course of action. His clearer vision of the organization leaders only marginally impacts his perception of his community, and he enacts a plan that inadvertently aids the Brotherhood's goals. Even when he observes the dangerous state of Harlem, such as the sight of black boys "watching their distorted images as they danced before the jagged glass" of a broken mirror, he misses the implication of this physical representation of Harlem's fragmenting identity (513). Their ultimate performance of their fractured consciousness in the violence of the riot forces the narrator to acknowledge that his unsuccessful penetration of Harlem psychology spawns the self-destruction of the riot. In the midst of the violent night, he reflects, "I could see it now, see it clearly and in growing magnitude. It was not suicide, but murder. The committee had planned it. And I had helped, had been a tool" (553). Although he perceived the Brotherhood's misunderstanding of Clifton, he remained blind to the real implications of their blindness and his own. The complexity of Harlem consciousness escaped him, and the consequences loom large. Like white males who mask their contradictory natures and white females who embrace stereotypes, the

Brotherhood employs a generalized line of vision that rejects human complexity. In his discussion of the novel as an exploration of the American psyche, Jesse Wolfe argues that Ellison uses the Communist-like Brotherhood to represent the narrator's need to reject a worldview devoid of ambivalence, a move that amounts "to a direct assault on...Marxist/Hegelian philosophical tradition" (621). To achieve real insight into his own character as well as his culture's, the narrator must comprehend that humanity cannot be reduced to scientific formulae. In the epilogue he admits that getting to this point has been a major project of his narrative. He declares "I've been trying to look through myself" (572). His acknowledgement of invisibility validates his attainment of piercing vision not satisfied with surface appearances. His blindness, he explains, resulted from "the true darkness...within [his] own mind" (579)

CULTURAL COMPLEXITY: ELLISON'S CONCEPT OF BLACK AMERICAN EXISTENCE

Ellison's multifaceted assessment of psychological blindness not only guides his construction of the issues facing his narrator and his developing sense of invisibility, the theme also addresses a more pervasive problem Ellison attributes to American fiction. In his discussion of the role fiction plays in picturing black Americans, Ellison asserts, "Perhaps the most insidious and least understood form of segregation is that of the word" for "if the word has the potency to revive and make us free, it has also the power to blind, imprison and destroy." He continues,

> The essence of the word is its ambivalence, and in fiction it is never so effective and revealing as when both potentials are operating simultaneously, as when it mirrors both good and bad, as when it blows both hot and cold in the same breath. Thus it is unfortunate for the Negro that the most powerful formulations of American fictional words have been so slanted against him that when he approaches for a glimpse of himself he discovers an image drained of humanity. (*Collected Essays* 81–82)

His concerns reveal the relationship between two of the major themes in his text, blindness and cultural complexity, and point to the logical intertwining of the two and the issues they introduce. Characters' failure to understand themselves and others around them results largely from their inability, or unwillingness, to acknowledge the complexity of the human condition. Before the narrator can successfully understand American society and his place in it, he must concede his desire to maintain a simplistic view of humanity.

Beginning with the slave woman of the prologue, the character who establishes the centrality of ambivalence in black American existence, Ellison shows that the folk past holds the key to understanding black identity. The narrator's initial rejection of his cultural legacy signals his dislike for complexity, an attribute he deals with directly when he remembers his grandfather. In addition to inaugurating the narrator's struggle with distinguishing wisdom from insanity, his grandfather's dying words present him with the first "puzzle" of his life that initiates his fear of contradiction and ambivalence. He cannot reconcile the old man's defiant final directives with his meek life-long disposition, and he resents the dilemma his failure creates. Ellison hints at the danger inherent in this aversion to ambivalence when the narrator pauses to contemplate the correct response to a voice of power in the battle royal. When he hears a white man declare support for the narrator's opponent, he wonders "Should I try to win against the voice out there? Would not this go against my speech . . . for nonresistance?" (25). To answer his quandary, his opponent promptly knocks him out, signaling the peril of attempting to restrict oneself to an unrealistically narrow ideology.

The stakes rise at the black college where the narrator continues to pursue a governing philosophy that eschews personal and social complexity. Ellison uses the college to highlight the divergence between the implicit purpose of the educational institution and the reality of its philosophy. Instead of presenting new ideas as a means for inspiring students to challenge and revise the status quo, the college administrators perpetuate a legacy of dissimulation and hypocrisy. Ellison hints that the founder and his successor, A. Herbert Bledsoe, compromise their commitment to the scholarly enterprise in favor of accruing personal political power. Ellison, who attended Tuskegee University, remained critical of this and other aspects of historically black institutions of higher education. In letters to Murray he proclaimed flagship schools like Howard "a graveyard" and urged his friend not to allow the administration at Tuskegee to "turn [him] away from writing" just because his artistic devotion made him a "walking condemnation of everything they stand for" (Ellison and Murray 75, 85). Ellison felt that the work he demanded readers perform in his novel violated the complacency that many black colleges promoted in their classrooms.

The feckless educational philosophy that most instructors have foisted upon the narrator leave him unprepared to perceive life incisively. As he listens to Norton assuredly speak of fate, he recalls images from the school library depicting the first students to attend his institution. His recollection of the "black mob that seemed to be waiting...with blank faces" leads him to reject the heritage they represent in favor of identifying "with the rich man...on the rear seat" (39). He prefers the appearance of certainty and assurance regardless of the dubious logic undergirding such attitudes. Consequently, he mistakes Norton's quixotic musings for insight and dismisses the trustee's fascination with Trueblood as part of the mystery of white character. He extends no such generosity to the sharecropper, the first fully developed picture of the complexity of black existence. The symbolism of the farmer's name, he is "true" to his "blood" or certain about his identity, contrasts starkly with the narrator's blatant discomfort with his heritage and introduces the importance of folk culture in Ellison's portrayal of black identity.

Trueblood is arguably the most perplexing character in the novel. The narrator admits that before the sharecropper disgraced himself, the school officials regarded him as a respectable member of the community who provided for his family and entertained visiting officials with his storytelling and singing. As long as his folk ways benefit the school, Trueblood is deemed an asset, but the narrator confesses that in truth everyone at the college loathed "the black-belt people...like Trueblood" (47). When school officials learn he has impregnated his wife and his daughter, they view his actions as one more instance of black peasants validating the stereotypes that permeate American culture. The construction of the episode, however, allows no such simple assumption. Trueblood's vivid relation of his "dream sin" focuses attention on his virtuosic storytelling abilities rather than his heinous act, paradoxically highlighting his folk roots (62). His tale figuratively describes how the cold harshness of his present rural existence, the warm sensuality of his bucolic past, and the baffling ambiguity of his segregated reality combine to beget his horrific, yet unintended, act. In the face of his wife's violent and pained response, his community's ostracization, and God's apparent desertion, Trueblood finds himself with no one to turn to but himself and he confesses, "I ends up singin' the blues. I sings me some blues that night ain't never been sang before, and while I'm singin' them blues I makes up my mind that I ain't nobody but myself" (66). The narrator echoes his words in the prologue when he announces, "I am nobody but myself," yet he only arrives at this conclusion after many experiences and years of confusion (573).

Trueblood's pronouncement defines his position as an artist. His troubles turn him inward, and he overcomes his despair through his own creativity.

In his critical writing, Ellison singles out the blues and jazz as the most authentically American art forms as well as a means through which black Americans deal with the pain of life. His first serious application of his belief, an essay on Richard Wright's autobiography *Black Boy* (1945), explains that many critics misunderstand Wright's presentation of his childhood because they are unfamiliar with the place of blues in black American life. He argues that Wright's narrative form develops from his exposure to the blues: "In that culture the specific folk-art form which helped shape the writer's attitude toward his life and which embodied the impulse that contributes much to the quality and tone of his autobiography was the Negro blues" (*Collected Essays* 129). Thus, Wright's struggle to overcome his Southern heritage to become a writer represents a kind of blues-inspired accomplishment. Using a similar paradigm, Trueblood emerges as a character fortified by his natural reliance on the art of his culture. After singing his blues he returns home to his family and reasserts his manhood to his wife. In spite of his actions, he refuses a definition imposed by others and insists upon his own, thereby offering the narrator a valuable lesson in the art of identity formation. One's humanity can be determined by general opinion only if an individual consents, and Trueblood roundly rejects such a possibility. Houston Baker concludes that "the distinction between folklore and literary art evident in Ellison's critical practice collapses in his creative" rendition of Trueblood (829).

The sharecropper's abiding sense of self unsettles Norton and the narrator who both evade contradictory aspects in their natures in an attempt to maintain their understanding of the world. Norton's ridiculous discourse on fate and the narrator's overwhelming desire to please the powerful mark their inability to fit Trueblood into their conception of the world. Ellison suggests that the chaos Norton believes the sharecropper's actions should produce reflects the dearth of the trustee's cultural past. This is not to say Ellison condones incest; more accurately, he intimates that black American's cultural and creative richness equips black Americans with tools to overcome hardship and pain with their humanity intact. Kenneth Warren declares this black American trait as one of Ellison's principle interests in both his response to contemporary civil rights issues and his novel. Connecting Ellison's response to the Little Rock desegregation case to his invisible narrator, Warren notes that Ellison often sees black children as fulfilling "something ancient" in their confrontation of racism proving that they do not break from the past but "embod[y] it" (162). Thus, the narrator's confusion stems from having "forgotten things rather than having not yet learned them—remembering himself is to remember his past" (Warren 173). In a sense, his incapacity to grasp the meaning of Trueblood's blues is more egregious than Norton's. The white trustee does not have the same cultural reservoir, so he naturally fails to comprehend that Trueblood has not escaped chaos but simply gives it form. The narrator's experience with Peter Wheatstraw, the man pushing a cart of discarded blueprints in Harlem and singing "a blues," reiterates this message (173). Life necessitates a malleability and toughness not taught in school curricula. When Wheatstraw explains that his blueprints attest to people's tendency to change their plans, the narrator responds confidently, "that's a mistake. You have to stick to the plan" (175). The cart man's thoughtful reply, "You kinda young, daddy-o," speaks volumes (175). Changing "the plan" is the business of life.

As the second blues performer in the text, Wheatstraw adds to Trueblood's lesson in complexity the message that blacks in the North must retain their Southern roots. When the narrator displays confusion at Wheatstraw's inquiry about "the dog," the blues man bridles, "Now I know you from down home, how come you trying to act like you never heard that before! Hell, ain't nobody out here this morning but us colored—Why you trying to deny me?" (173). His words reveal his understanding that blacks often feign ignorance about their cultural knowledge in the presence of whites, but amongst each other they freely indulge their folk sensibilities. "The dog" he inquires about is just a black vernacular name for the constellation of forces that hinder black success, like hard times, racial injustice, and economic difficulty; thus, Wheatstraw wonders whether the narrator feels a sense of command over such invisible cultural powers. The narrator's initial confusion and eventual rejoinder exhibit his naïveté as well as his failure to preserve his racial roots.

Ellison thinks a good deal about black modern identity especially as it hinges on a collision between the rural past and the urban present; he often broaches the discussion through the presence of blues and jazz performers, characters' whose art exhibits the soulful fusion of the black American past and present. In his discussion of bebop's role in *Invisible Man,* Timothy Spaulding asserts that the narrator's journey, much like bebop, reveals itself a product of the interaction between "black folk culture and an aesthetic influenced by white mainstream culture" so that Ellison's "modernist aesthetic" is most aptly recognized by his assimilation of bebop improvisation in his narrative form (481, 491). Spaulding, as well as many other critics who explore the place of jazz in the text, seems exactly right to link the musical form to Ellison's artistic technique since the novelist repeatedly proclaims this connection. The narrator's arrival in

Harlem vividly evokes the challenges of that millions of black Americans experienced during the great migration and afterward. His interaction with blues-inspired characters indicates a prescription for survival. Fittingly, after young Emerson exposes Bledsoe's duplicity, the narrator recalls the lyrics to a bluesy tune about poor Robin. This reclamation of his cultural past signals his partial awakening to the need for retaining crucial aspects of his character. Even though the narrator subsequently scorns Brockway, the small black man at Liberty Paints who lords over his basement domain, telling details like his pork chop sandwich lunch demonstrate his new embrace of what he previously fears marked him as unrefined.

Even the white doctors of the factory hospital presume him cured, based on their terms, when they believe him incapable of understanding folk terms. The entire scene invokes the concept of rebirth, albeit by way of violent and exploitative scientific experimentation, and the doctors make their aims clear. One explains that the machine achieves "the results of a prefrontal lobotomy" resulting in a "complete change of personality" so that the patient experiences "no major conflict of motives, and...society will suffer no traumata on his account" (236). He deems cultural simplicity, or a lack of ambivalence, as a perfect state for a young black man. Ironically, his view is humane compared to his peer who favors castration. The electrotherapy they decide upon strangely recalls the electric rug of the battle royal, suggesting a kind of perverse, mental violence. Early in his treatment the narrator subconsciously recalls various folk tunes and sayings, and when he cannot remember the correct answers to questions that the doctors write on a child's slate, he reverts to playing the dozens. When the doctors directly engage him in this world, inquiring "WHO WAS BUCKEYE THE RABBIT?" and "WHO WAS BRER RABBIT?," the narrator feels both tired and sly for he remembers the identities as well as the need for keeping their meanings secret (242). His refusal to respond in kind or demonstrate understanding elicits approval from the doctors who seem "pleased" and apparently order his release (242). The narrator subconsciously realizes he has tricked the doctors and feels criminal in much the same way his grandfather described the necessity for overcoming those in power.

The dynamic Ellison creates in the hospital scene concretizes his belief that black Americans' cultural vitality represents the true consciousness of mid-century U.S. society, an alarming fact for the white majority. The ability to overcome the horrors of their race's past by depending on their rich and sustaining folk heritage offers an example for a country overwhelmed by the difficulties of modernity. In a letter to Wright he declares, "I see it this way: they have no conscience, being Americans, and the only force capable of awakening a conscience within them...are the Negroes. It is our job as Joyce put it, 'to create the uncreated conscience' of the Negroes" (RWP Aug. 1, 1945). Thus the white doctors seek to use science to erase that part of the black mind they subconsciously acknowledge as powerful. Unsurprisingly, the hospital episode leads to the narrator's transferal into the capable hands of Mary who tells him, "I'm in New York, but New York ain't in me" (255). She is the first character to proclaim the necessary relationship between urban existence and folk culture, and while the narrator lives with her, he becomes increasingly comfortable with the cultural confluence she symbolizes. His response to the eviction illustrates his dawning sense of black complexity.

The Provos' predicament signifies Ellison's nod to the socioeconomic issues dominating a good deal of his contemporary's black fiction. Although critics often cast him as wholly opposed to the kind of proletarian literature that made Richard Wright famous, Ellison articulates a more nuanced position. He clarifies his stance in one interview by insisting, "I recognize no dichotomy between art and protest," and after listing canonical works by non-black writers clearly concerned with social protest he concludes, "it seems to me that the critics could more accurately complain about [Negro's] lack of craftsmanship and their provincialism" (*Collected Essays* 212). In an interview 10 years later he reiterates, "I think style is more important than political ideologies" (*Collected Essays* 743). The eviction scene provides an illuminating example of his contention concerning how artists should address issues of protest. Following the narrator's self-affirming experience of eating a baked yam in the middle of the street, in his mind an act tantamount to throwing off all shackles of assimilationist pretension, he stumbles upon household objects strewn across the snow forming a sad picture of the evicted couple's life. In contrast to the somewhat infantile projection of self-confidence that eating the yam represents, the eviction provides a serious example of the difficulty of modern black urban existence. After rebuffing a bystander's attempt to ridicule his ignorance concerning evictions, the narrator surveys the myriad objects with new emotion. Artifacts such as knocking bones, an Ethiopian flag, a Lincoln tintype, a breast pump, a picture of Marcus Garvey, and free papers combine to articulate the multifaceted reality of the old couple's life. For the protagonist, the Provos' possessions reassert the intangible value of his heritage and elicit a depth of emotion he cannot yet process. The articles forcefully reify the complexity of black life in excessive and penetrating form against the backdrop of the socioeconomic exploitation blacks experienced in Harlem.

Ellison's exploration of the rural-urban and southern-northern dichotomies in black American existence initiates his reflection on the larger issue of how blacks should demonstrate a healthy understanding of their complexity. In Rinehart he ponders the reality of an individual's comprehension of the freedom such understanding affords, but Ellison also questions the moral implications of a life without boundaries. Rinehart's "confidencing" embodies the possibilities open to those who embrace the many parts of their character, but his apparent ruthlessness also indicates his loyalty to no idea other than himself. This attitude, Ellison suggests, perverts the American ideal in a manner that threatens the nation's future. For him, representing such truths remains the principle obligation of the novelist. He surmises, "Men stand only small doses of reality," and yet "the dark side of the novel's ability to forge images which strengthen man's will to say no to chaos and affirm him in task of humanizing himself and his world" is the art form's greatest asset (*Collected Essays* 701). The narrator's ultimate rejection of the freedom Rinehart symbolizes in preference for a larger truth rooted in the ideas of the country's founding documents effectively expands the discussion beyond the question of black identity formation. Ellison forces the white majority, the population most dedicated to denying the human complexity of black Americans in an attempt to preserve their own image of humanity, to confront their role in shaping the American mind.

White America's refusal to view their black countrymen truthfully, then, represents the other side of the coin demarcating the narrator's struggle to understand himself. The issue raises more dilemmas than the basic discussion of American racism permits, and through it, Ellison delves into the interstitial spaces of the American psyche. Correctly perceiving black American consciousness, he suggests, reverberates beyond the specifics of race relations; it is integral to the wholeness of white America, too. From the narrator's earliest reflections on this issue, he notes the danger of white America's negligence. He intimates that the newspaper's characterization of his violent altercation with the blond man as a "mugging," a convenient term their readers associate with black men interacting with whites, demonstrates their preference for stereotype over introspection. Their acceptance of a surface explanation could promote more such incidents, the price for protecting the right to sleep through the most serious issue facing their society. Within the framed portion of the narrative, incidents like the Golden Day veterans' tempered assault on Norton (Supercargo, in his white uniform and straightjacket, protects the trustee from greater harm by providing a metaphorical equivalent for their anger), the eviction crowd's attack on the white marshals, and the Harlem rioters seething violence

directed toward white shop owners and policemen, epitomize the perilous consequences of denying the complexity of black humanity. Ellison
complements these violent eruptions with cool examinations of particular
facets of American society responsible for promulgating such situations.

One such culprit is the faith Americans place in racially bigoted scientific study. The narrator's opening description of his invisibility launches
his repeated indictment of how scientific research is employed to buttress racial inequality. His insistence that his identity remains unrelated
to the biochemical composition of his epidermis parodies the subject of
H. G. Wells's science fiction classic *The Invisible Man* (1897), which focuses on the protagonist's, Griffin's, quest for power through a scientific
experiment that alters his skin. The unforeseen results of Griffin's successful transformation into an invisible man provide a rich subtext for Ellison's
reformation of the term and hint at the foolhardiness of scientific contributions applied to issues of race. In the Liberty Paints episode Ellison continues his riff. The scientifically precise mixture that produces the company's
most popular paint, "Optic White," includes 10 drops of a black substance
for its whiteness. This foundational product validates the company's logo,
a vow to "keep America pure," and lampoons America's obsessive covering of it's racially mixed heritage, a legacy indicative of violent miscegenation but also the source of immense national vitality. Kimbro's claim
that the paint graces the government buildings and monuments in Washington, D.C., that physically represent American democracy, along with
his authorization of ruined paint for such a project, fuels Ellison's spoof.
Even the naïve narrator discerns the irony of Lucius Brockway's reverence
for the white paint which he proclaims is "so white you can paint a chunka
coal and you'd have to crack it open with a sledge hammer to prove it
wasn't white clear through" (217). His description of Optic White's virtue paradoxically reveals the specious aspect of this scientifically concocted substance: it hides inner complexity. The factory hospital extends
this ambition as the doctors seek to expunge the conflicting aspects of the
narrator's personality. Ellison again considers the insidious underpinning
of scientific experiments that accrue legitimacy through the application
of accepted terms of research, such as the doctor's invocation of gestalt,
rather than the validity of their goals and procedures.

Ellison also examines American ideas that ostensibly justify black humanity even though they are hypocritical and incongruous within themselves. Ellison's name, Ralph Waldo Ellison, drew him to contemplate
Emerson's seminal role in shaping American transcendentalism. Emerson
reacted against the formulism of his Unitarian background to insist upon

man's ability to achieve greatness through intuitive thought. His celebration of the individual soul led him to oppose slavery, but not as vehemently or unequivocally as his philosophy would suggest. This ambivalence in a man whose thinking was so critical to American intellectual history provides rich implications for Ellison's fictional project and shrouds some of the nineteenth-century philosopher's oft-quoted words in irony. Laying out the foundation for transcendentalism, Emerson proclaims, "Standing on the bare ground...all mean egotism vanishes. I become a transparent eye-ball. I am nothing. I see all" (24). Ellison's trope of invisibility clearly has roots in Emerson's sublime statement, but the portrayal of Emersonian ideas throughout the novel acknowledges the dubious aspects of his thought and its incorporation in American culture. Ellison's handling of this issue preoccupies many scholars who analyze *Invisible Man,* and different critics suggest varied methods for understanding the novelist's ultimate outlook on Emerson. Noting the intricacy of Ellison's Emersonian engagement, Kun Jong Lee aptly concludes, "The narrator's underground tinkering with Emerson's ideas, then, suggests both an act of subversion and an attempt at appropriation and redirection. Through these complex efforts, Ellison at once criticizes and claims an Emersonian heritage" (331).

Notwithstanding the density of Ellison's handling of Emerson, his portrayal of white America's general tendency to distort transcendentalist philosophy is clear. Early in the narrator's journey toward self-understanding, he confronts a perversion of Emersonian thought. Norton, in explaining his destiny, inquires about the narrator's familiarity with Emerson. When the young man admits his ignorance, Norton melds his own image with Emerson's: "I am a New Englander, like Emerson. You must learn about him, for he was important to your people. He had a hand in your destiny" (41). The trustee's insinuation that his work with the college, his "first-hand organizing of human life," parallels Emerson's ideas about individual potential contradicts the core of Emersonian thought (42). Emerson eschews any implication that individuals control the destiny of their fellow men, and Norton's words reveal his shallow understanding of transcendental philosophy as well as a sinister comfort with bending ideas to fit his lust for power. Unlike Emerson's idealistic meditations on man's potential, Norton contemplates the black student's advancement strictly in terms of his own accomplishment.

With Emerson Sr. and Jr., the other two characters who directly invoke transcendental ideals through their symbolic names, Ellison offers further comment on popular corruptions of Emersonian thought. The elder Emerson never appears in the text, but his leadership position in an importing firm links him to capitalistic society rather than the pursuit of the fulfilled soul. His son, beleaguered by feelings of filial inadequacy, cautious homosexual urges, and superficial cravings for a bohemian lifestyle, cannot rise above the racial stereotypes surrounding him to see the narrator's possibility for achieving an ideal state. His first instincts lead him to established images of black men: he wonders whether the narrator is an athlete, assigns him to the feminine "nigger Jim" role in their interaction, and offers him the service job of becoming his valet. Both Emersons offer the protagonist no clear vision of Emersonian ideas. Only through his own experiences does he begin to comprehend the importance of Emerson's celebration of intuition, and in the epilogue he ponders how he might achieve personal completion. Yet he ultimately rejects the idealism of transcendentalism in favor of the less morally certain philosophy of existentialism.

Ellison's engagement of existential thought expands his exposé of the American majority's perversion of ideas and also highlights how he revises literary tropes and techniques to achieve his artistic goals. Although he defers his narrator's embrace of existentialism to the end of the novel, the prologue intimates a probable role for this philosophical movement by echoing Fyodor Dostoyevsky's *Notes from the Underground* (1864) in tone and language. The Russian author's novella is a key literary reflection of existential thought and boasts a textual frame and an unnamed narrator that Ellison adapts for his work. Like Dostoyevsky's protagonist, who refers to his home as an "underground hole," engages in mad rants, ruminates on "responsibility," and even describes a climactic bump of an officer, Ellison's invisible narrator, as his prefatory remarks suggest, endures a similar kind of disorientation. Moreover, the tenor of his internal struggles resonates with seminal existential ideas such as an emphasis on individual existence, the necessity of mental freedom and the power to make life choices, and a celebration of subjectivity. The narrator's decision to share the details of his personal experiences in an attempt to arrive at some truth, and thereby accept his social responsibility, colors his quest in key existential terms. As Joseph Frank explains, Ellison casts his narrator in terms reminiscent of Dostoyevsky's protagonist in acknowledgement of the similarity between the Russian novelist's relation to his culture and Ellison "as an American Negro writer in relation to the dominating white culture" (232).

Although the constellation of all the narrator's experiences begets his embrace of a version of existential individualism, the Brotherhood with its commitment to science and antagonism to individuality pushes him most precipitously toward this end. In the climactic scene following

Brother Clifton's funeral, the narrator's assertion of his personal responsibility rejects the organization's ideological foundation. Their celebration of group politics, a clear reference to the tenants of communism, seeks to legitimize the aspect of American culture that Ellison finds most harmful to the advance of blacks, a denial of their individual complexity. His narrator's realization of this, in addition to his intimation that Clifton's contradictions humanize rather than disgrace him, exposes his maturing sense of himself and his community. By contrast, Jack's fake eye and slavish dependence on scientific reasoning displays his ignorance concerning humanity. The narrator's dedication to moving beyond such narrow vision denotes Ellison's insistence upon moving beyond surface understanding. Thus, after the committee meeting, the protagonist perceives Harlem and the Brotherhood through new eyes. Rinehart reifies his suspicions that scientific theory fails to account for much lived experience and history while the Brotherhood theoretician Hambro emerges as "too narrowly logical" to take seriously (500). The narrator needs a new philosophy.

The riot offers him direction. Contemplating the culminating image of the night, Ras on his horse in full warrior attire, the narrator resolves,

> knowing now who I was and where I was and knowing too that I had no longer to run for or from the Jacks and the Emersons and the Bledsoes and Nortons, but only from their confusion, impatience, and refusal to recognize the beautiful absurdity of their American identity and mine. I stood there, knowing that by dying...I would perhaps move them one fraction of a blood step closer to a definition of who they were and of what I was and had been. But the definition would have been too narrow; I was invisible, and hanging would not bring me visibility...(559)

In true existential form, he determines that his anxiety, either over fulfilling definitions imposed by others or achieving images concocted by his ambition, must be acknowledged as an inescapable aspect of his consciousness. Moreover, he sees in this character trait a patently American feature of his character and refuses to continue accepting simplified notions of identity. He realizes that what many deem as absurd rings closer to the inherent complexity defining human existence, and this truth cannot be exemplified by the limited example his sacrificial death would undoubtedly represent. Thus, he decides he must find an alternative route towards visibility, the truthful recognition of his individual character.

As these thoughts race through the narrator's mind, he fights off Ras's men with Tarp's leg chain and his brief case, "running over puddles of milk" and through a "spray of water that seemed to descend from above" in a subconsciously directed quest for Mary's house (560). The milk and water contrast the violent images of the night with icons of birth while the narrator's dependence on the chain gang link and his briefcase symbolizes a dependence on his cultural and personal past. He no longer relies on the dissembling methods of his college or the empty rhetoric of the Brotherhood to save him; instead, he seeks Mary, the embodiment of the folk past and urban present residing in calm harmony. In offering Mary as the narrator's image of salvation, Ellison deftly comments on and revises a well-known aspect of existential thought. Søren Kierkegaard, the nineteenth-century Danish philosopher considered the father of modern existentialism, contends that in order for an individual to lead a life of commitment he must dedicate himself to a personally defined validity that may defy societal norms. In his oft-quoted support for a "leap of faith," Kierkegaard promotes Christianity as the most viable code for staving off despair. Ellison's replacement of Christian faith with Mary cannily adapts Kierkegaard's notion for his black American narrator. Mary's name invokes the mother of Christ but her personality privileges black folk culture over religious doctrine in effecting inner wholeness. Thus, the narrator turns to his heritage, which includes Christian doctrine, for moral salvation.

His failure to reach Mary showcases Ellison's biting wit. By appealing to philosophical traditions extolled by American elites yet distorted by their thirst for racial hegemony, Ellison uncovers the majority's moral and intellectual hypocrisy. His narrator's final decisions, however, celebrate the sophistication of his consciousness that accepts no philosophy completely. Instead, he rises above any single body of thought to form his own conclusions about how to address the issue of American identity. Ellison's naïve black narrator establishes himself as more astute than all those who sought to exploit him. He does not find Mary, but he does locate truth in the glow of the burning documents that set him running towards self-discovery. This dependence on experience combines key elements of transcendentalism and existentialism while his final dream in his hole reduces his antagonists to the violence they embrace instead of reason. The same group he describes as misunderstanding the beauty of American absurdity castrates him to free him from illusion. As he watches his bloody genitals dripping from the bridge, the narrator begins to laugh and explains, "*if you'll look, you'll see... It's not invisible... there hang not only my generations wasting upon the water... but your sun... and your moon... your world*" (570). His final vision pits him against both the black and white forces who sought to determine his identity freeing his achievement of a unified conscious from any racially defined ideology. Consequently, to share his discovery he elects a correspondingly different tack: he rejects the roles of traditional power brokers in preference for the broader, more expansive and morally honest role of the artist. He vows to make his discovery visible through the power of his pen.

FULFILLING ARTISTIC RESPONSIBILITY: ELLISON'S SOLUTION FOR UNDERSTANDING IDENTITY

This final major theme reveals the novel's rationale and pinpoints the narrator's genuine accomplishment. His narrative represents his conscious effort to evaluate the experiences that lead to his underground retreat and acceptance of invisibility, and more importantly, recognition of the responsibility his reflections demand. Throughout the epilogue he admits the compositional process, or "the attempt to write it down," has revealed truths about himself and his countrymen with implications far too great to deny (575). The scope of his final musings casts the major events of his life on the broad stage of American identity formation and reaffirms the role Ellison defines for the American writer. Ellison approaches the art of writing fiction seriously, proclaiming:

> We do become writers out of an act of will, out of an act of choice: and what happens thereafter causes all those experiences which occurred before we began to function as writers to take on a special quality of uniqueness. If this does not happen then as far as writing goes, the experiences have been misused. If we do not make of them a value, if we do not transform them into forms and images of meaning which they did not possess before, then we have failed as artists.
>
> Thus for a writer to insist that his personal suffering is of special interest in itself, or simply because he belongs to a particular racial or religious group, is to advance a claim for special privileges which members of his group who are not writers would be ashamed to demand. (*Collected Essays* 190–191)

As previously noted and reinforced by these quoted words, Ellison's conception of how literature and politics should fruitfully mix stresses his insistence on the generative nature of art. Understanding his position regarding this relationship reveals the rich meaning of several incidents in his novel and shows the profundity of the narrator's decision to accept the obligation of the artist.

Throughout his journey, he embraces various political ideologies in an attempt to realize the success he associates with leadership and power. The multiple lenses through which the narrator peers to assess his position in society press home Ellison's fundamental point: change is most effectively accomplished through art rather than politics. The narrator's battle royal speech and admission that he sees himself as a "potential Booker T. Washington" introduces the subject of black politics in the early twentieth century (18). Washington's notion of black advancement encouraged pragmatic steps towards attaining economic security while brushing aside social inequities. In the shadow of his grandfather's advice, the narrator's commitment to the educator's political philosophy immediately appears problematic. Parroting the speech responsible for gaining traction for Washington's beliefs, the narrator unwittingly exemplifies the naïveté of his words and error of Washington's politics. The road he must travel toward economic success, the four-year path through the Washingtonian black college, is only possible after he endures the brutality promoted and condoned by the segregationist approach to social interaction. His college experiences reiterate the fallacy that black Americans' social and economic fortunes can be divorced from one another and intimate the truth of his grandfather's cryptic admonition: he advocates abandoning submissive practices in favor of penetrating the white majority's mindset through committing oneself to exploiting their hypocrisy.

The Founder's statue, an obvious reference to the Booker T. Washington monument on the Tuskegee University campus, emerges as one of the first images the narrator recollects as he ponders his college years. The bronze statue freezes an image of the Founder holding a veil over a kneeling slave, and the narrator wonders whether he witnesses a "revelation or a more efficient blinding" (36). His revisionist reading of the famous statue hints at the complicated and possibly pernicious nature of Washington's politics, a suggestion that gains weight through Ellison's construction of the college president, A. Herbert Bledsoe. The leader of the school gives Washington's problematic philosophy concrete form and illustrates the dangers of his ideas. To stress this point, Ellison offers a double of Bledsoe in the character of Rev. Homer A. Barbee. As Barbee rises to deliver his address, the narrator admits "I had the notion that part of Dr. Bledsoe had arisen and moved forward, leaving his other part smiling in the chair" (118). The physically blind preacher occupies the third point in the original triangle of power the Founder formed, and Barbee unabashedly invokes his past position to authorize his words. His chapel "sermon" to the captive students exposes the college's willingness to transform any venue into a space for spreading their political philosophy. Instead of preaching the gospel, Barbee exhorts the student's to idolize Bledsoe, the living symbol of the Founder.

The narrator is committed to succeeding in terms the college suggests and his interactions with the college president underscore the hazards of his devotion. When Bledsoe reprimands the narrator for what he deems his treacherous conduct with Norton, the president reveals the doctrine underneath the school. The ability to lie and protect power at all costs secures Bledsoe's position of leadership, and he assumes that the narrator understands and concurs with this policy. In a rare moment of honesty, Bledsoe exclaims, "This is a power set-up, son, and I'm at the controls" so "when you buck against me, you're bucking against power, rich white folk's power, the nation's power—which means government power!" (142). The complicity he suggests between his work, the white majority's ideals, and the government's authority discloses the true aim of not only Washington's philosophy, but the goal of most political machinations: power. The college emerges as an institution promulgating blindness rather than sight, a living equivalent for the ambiguous pose of the Founder's statue.

Ellison does not restrict his consideration of the relationship between black politicians and the role of the artist to an assessment of Washingtonian assimilation. The narrator's arrival to New York introduces him to Ras the Exhorter, a Garveyesque radical advocating the tenets of black nationalism. Ras's dependence on his speaking skills to win adherents for his movement ironically links him to Barbee who also enlists his oratorical dexterity to mesmerize his listeners into surrendering to the college philosophy. Although Ras appears more sincere than the college leaders in his mission of uniting Harlem blacks to fight suppression, his narrow conception of racial triumph and impractical plan of action undermine his well-meaning goals. His dependence on violence to achieve his goals further delegitimizes his politics and highlights the danger of his shortsighted strategy. Like the young participants in the battle royal, Ras and his group willingly fight other blacks to empower themselves. Although he turns his aggression on white law enforcers during the riot, his outrageous costume and foolhardy courage portend his failure. The merger of his two self-proclaimed names, Ras the Exhorter and Ras the Destroyer, makes clear the reason for his fall: he depends on talk and violence instead of crafting a thoughtful, well-reasoned appeal that engages and broadens the minds of Harlem residents.

This aspect of Ras's approach and its similarity to the college strategy subtly points to the problem with the narrator's role in the Brotherhood as well as his general goals for success. He is hired by the communist-styled organization to combat Ras in the streets of Harlem, essentially challenging the Exhorter by appropriating his techniques. In fact, Jack approaches the narrator after hearing his impassioned but specious eviction speech. Although the narrator is prompted to speak by authentic feelings of empathy and anger, when he begins speaking he has yet to translate his emotions into a coherent philosophy. Instead, his oratorical passion emanates from his excitement about his control over the crowd and his desperate desire for their respect and admiration. When the angriest individuals of the group, undoubtedly followers of Ras, take matters into their own hands, the narrator simply tailors his words to their action rather than risk appearing weak. Jack's witness of this turn of events, and his continued interest in the narrator, reveals much about his own philosophy. His rhetoric about science thinly veils his more pressing interest in raw power, and he does not shy away from embracing similar tactics as those he pretends to spurn. The narrator subtly senses this, appealing to the same image in his descriptions of both men. Yet because he, too, is most motivated by a desire to lead, he willingly allows himself to be used for the Brotherhood's purposes in much the same way he played into Bledsoe's schemes.

The narrator's dedication to oratory, another issue often considered by critics, figures prominently in his pursuit of political power and presents an interesting counterpart to his final dedication to writing. Throughout the narrator's search for his identity, his speeches divulge his innocence and inhibit real growth even when he appears on the verge of penetrating the façade covering the workings of American society. His battle royal oration exposes his misguided belief in social submission to achieve economic gains notwithstanding his misgivings over undermining his grandfather's advice; his eviction speech divulges his consuming desire for power and control in the face of his dawning cultural pride; his first Brotherhood address reveals his enslavement to rhetorical flourish even as he strives toward honest revelation and sincere exhortation; and finally, his eulogy at Clifton's funeral succeeds in celebrating Clifton's individuality though his commitment to the Brotherhood leads him to deem his unscientific words a failure. The consistent disconnect between his internal intentions and understanding and his spoken words highlights the artificiality often associated with speech. Like Barbee who skillfully weaves together pictures his physical blindness metaphorically casts doubt on, the protagonist's obsession with speaking exhibits his inability to detect ideas and philosophies underneath surface relations.

In a suggestive scene crafted around Frederick Douglass, Ellison suggests that true political accomplishment is usually linked to writing rather than wholly dependent upon speaking. When the narrator receives a portrait of Douglass from Brother Tarp, he gazes upon the image thinking "there was a magic in spoken words" for had not "Douglass talked his way from slavery to a government ministry"? Contemplating the similarity between his trajectory and the great abolitionist's, he wonders, "hadn't I started out with a speech, and hadn't it been a speech that won my scholarship to college"? He concludes, "Well, I had made a speech, and it had made me a leader" (381). Ellisonian scholars have long pointed out the fundamental misunderstanding the narrator's thoughts display regarding Douglass's success as a leader and politician. Although he was famous for speaking, he never depended solely on his oratorical skill to attain his objectives. The seriousness of his cause called for a form amenable to presenting complicated ideas which his audience could ponder at length. His publication of three autobiographies attests to his dedication to this endeavor and solidified his position as an important figure in American history. In his provoking analysis of the novel as a response to the larger history of black American narratives of ascent and immersion, Robert Stepto surmises the crux of the narrator's misunderstanding of the ex-slave's accomplishment: "Douglass didn't 'talk' his way to freedom; rather, he 'read' his way and... 'wrote' his way" (185–186). The narrator's unfamiliarity with this aspect of Douglass's work emphasizes his misconception of real leadership qualities.

Ellison's allusion to Douglass suggests that his portrayal is spurred less by an inherent antagonism toward political work and more by his desire to underscore the peculiar efficacy of writing. While Ellison does not necessarily consider writing a more honest form of communication, he feels it most successfully facilitates the interrogation of complex ideas while maintaining an admirably tight form. Most importantly, he values the process of writing, especially the composition of fiction, which he believes supremely suited for helping both author and reader arrive at a nuanced understanding of the social condition. The narrator's decision to take up his pen leads to his final extended contemplation of American democracy, which goes beyond the rhetorical flourish he initially favors. As he studies the lessons of his experiences he returns to his grandfather's enigmatic counsel and decides "he must have meant... we were to affirm the principle on which the country was built and not the men, or at least not the men who did the violence." Focusing this logic directly on his race, he speculates, "Was it that we of all, we, most of all, had to affirm the principle, the plan in whose name we had been brutalized and sacrificed...because we were older than they, in the sense of what it took to live in the world with others because they had exhausted in us, some...of the human greed and smallness, yes, and the fear and superstition that had kept them running" (574). As he ponders the weight of this possibility, he admits that he has arrived at this point of through "the very act of trying to put it all down" (579). By struggling to put his chaotic thoughts into writing, he perceives himself, and the undeniable bond linking him to his country's composite self-image, objectively and suggestively. The "pattern" his memoirs provide to the chaos residing in all men leaves him with a new understanding of why he must come out of his hole. The artist's responsibility includes a need for action that his invisibility cannot deny.

At the end of the text, Ellison's artistic creed peeks through the narrator's ponderous conclusions about race and American society. When he accepted the National Book Award for *Invisible Man,* Ellison closed his remarks with words that recall his invisible protagonist:

> [The novelist's] task then is always to challenge the apparent forms of reality—that is, the fixed manners and values of the few—and to struggle with it until it reveals its mad, vari-implicated chaos, its false faces, and on until it surrenders its insight, its truth. We are fortunate as American writers in that with our variety of racial and national traditions, idioms and manners, we are yet one....Through forging forms of the novel worthy of it, we achieve not only the promise of our lives, but we anticipate the resolution of those world problems of humanity...Whenever we as Americans have faced serious crises we have returned to fundamentals; this, in brief, is what I have tried to do. (*Collected Essays* 154)

By building a novel on the multifarious issues challenging a nation committed to celebrating the individual as well as the whole, Ellison succeeds in revealing a cultural reality more truthful and hopeful than those unwilling to look beyond surface tradition.

WORKS CITED

Baker, Houston. "To Move without Moving: An Analysis of Creativity and Commerce in Ralph Ellison's Trueblood Episode." *PMLA* 98 (1983): 828–845.

Burke, Kenneth. *The Philosophy of Literary Form: Studies in Symbolic Action.* 1941. Berkeley: U of California P, 1973.

Ellison, Ralph. *The Collected Essays of Ralph Ellison.* Edited by John Callahan. New York: Modern Library, 1995.

————. *Invisible Man.* 1952. New York: Vintage, 1980.

Ellison, Ralph, and Albert Murray. *Trading Twelves: The Selected Letters of Ralph Ellison and Albert Murray.* Eds. Albert Murray and John F. Callahan. New York: Vintage Books, 2000.

Emerson, Ralph. *Selections from Ralph Waldo Emerson: An Organic Anthology.* Ed. Stephen Whicher. Boston: Houghton Mifflin, 1957.

Frank, Joseph. "Ralph Ellison and a Literary 'Ancestor': Dostoevski." 1983. *Speaking for You: The Vision of Ralph Ellison.* Ed. Kimberly W. Benston. Washington, DC: Howard UP, 1987. 231–244.

Lee, Kun Jong. "Ellison's Invisible Man: Emersonianism Revised." *PMLA* 107 (1992): 331–344.

Nadel, Alan. *Invisible Criticism: Ralph Ellison and the American Canon.* Iowa City: U of Iowa P, 1988.

Spaulding, Timothy. "Embracing the Chaos in Narrative Form: The Bebop Aesthetic and Ralph Ellison's *Invisible Man.*" *Callaloo* 27 (2004): 481–501.

Stepto, Robert. *From Behind the Veil: A Study of Afro-American Narrative.* 1979. 2nd ed. Urbana: U of Illinois P, 1991.

Sylvander, Carolyn. "Ralph Ellison's *Invisible Man* and Female Stereotypes." *Negro American Literature Forum* 9 (1975): 77–79.

Tate, Claudia. "Notes on the Invisible Women in Ralph Ellison's *Invisible Man.*" *Speaking for You: The Vision of Ralph Ellison.* Ed. Kimberly W. Benston. Washington, DC: Howard UP, 1987. 163–172.

Warren, Kenneth. "Ralph Ellison and the Problem of Cultural Authority." *boundary 2* 30 (2003): 157–174.

Wolfe, Jesse. "'Ambivalent Man': Ellison's Rejection of Communism." *African American Review* 34 (2000): 621–637.

Chapter 5

ART

One of Ellison's best known interviews, "The Art of Fiction" (1955), advances his belief that creative writing is a serious artistic process. During this interview the novelist reveals core elements of his training for and conception of crafting great literature. By exploiting the title of a well-known 1884 essay, Ellison announces his intention to amend Henry James's turn of the century meditation on fiction as art. In response to the interviewer's questions, Ellison describes his artistic temperament at the time that he penned *Invisible Man*, discusses the organizational strategies within his text, and considers the book's contribution to the larger body of American literature. Yet the undercurrent of Ellison's answers shows him endeavoring to direct readers' engagement with his novel and to articulate his sense of the contemporary African American literary landscape. Building on the pronouncements of numerous critics, Ellison offers *Invisible Man* as representative of a new tenor in African American fiction and possibly indicative of a fresh direction for future black literary productions.

Ellison's attempts to direct black literary trends suggests that although he titles his interview after James's landmark piece, he wrestles more explicitly with the artistic principles of Richard Wright. The major ideas expressed in "Blueprint for Negro Writing" (1937), Wright's landmark essay about protest literature, continued to dominate African American fiction when Ellison published his blockbuster tome. He would long acknowledge that his friendship with Wright was founded upon their shared "curiosity concerning artistic creation," and he undoubtedly recognized that just as

Native Son (1940) exemplified Wright's artistic philosophy, *Invisible Man* epitomized his own (*Collected Essays* 672). In place of Wright's environmentally determined anti-hero, Ellison creates a protagonist whose experiences in numerous environments both form and inform his identity. Unlike Bigger Thomas, whom Ellison lamented "Wright could imagine" though "Bigger could not possibly imagine Richard Wright," the narrator of *Invisible Man* represents the complexity of African American consciousness (*Collected Essays* 162). To nurture his protagonist's growth, Ellison cultivates a supporting cast of characters who force the boy to evolve his interpretive skills and to accelerate his budding comprehension of his place in American society. Relying upon an episodic structure, Ellison frames the narrator's interactions with these characters using figurative language.

To acknowledge the force of Ellison's rhetorical strategies, this chapter organizes itself around key figures of speech and their role in structuring the protagonist's experiences with important characters and ideas. The chapter begins by considering how irony shapes our interpretation of the narrator's relations with the men who highlight his extreme ingenuousness. The chapter then contemplates Ellison's wielding of satire in creating characters who exemplify the comic profundity of white American psychological angst and the dangerous ignorance of political leaders' well-meaning ideology. Ellison's penchant for parodying canonical texts as well as particular literary genres lends comic, and sometimes tragicomic, texture to his protagonist's exploits. A discussion of metaphor, the most central form of figurative language in the text, demonstrates how the protagonist's more sophisticated sense of black identity and of American society emerges through his mastery of language. The chapter ends with an extended study of symbolism, the modernist marking of the novel and a central component of Ellison's vision of artistic responsibility.

IRONY

Irony, the use of words to convey an idea that departs from its literal meaning, underpins many of the protagonist's earliest experiences. In particular, Ellison's use of structural irony reveals his authorial goals because we, along with the mature writer-narrator whom we meet in the prologue, observe an incredibly naïve central character stumbling towards self-understanding. This pervasiveness of structural irony, or the reader's perpetual sense of knowing more than the narrator, allows Ellison to have fun as he inserts his protagonist into various conundrums. In addition to injecting bursts of humor, the comic aspects of his narrator's experiences facilitate Ellison's artful handling of the weighty issues that he invites readers to explore. The novel's first episode sets this tone. In the battle royal scene, the narrator's earnest recitation of his Washingtonian valedictory speech, one which exhorts his audience of white segregationists to join hands with blacks to attain economic success, reaches the heights of absurdity. His mouth full of blood and his body spent from the violence of the fight and the electrified rug, the narrator's commitment to such a policy emerges as sadly ironic.

The high irony of the smoker scene fittingly brims over into the protagonist's college experiences. Distinguishing his mature sensibility from his youthful acceptance of surface appearances, the narrator commences his recollections of his undergraduate days by reevaluating the statue of the Founder. In his invisible state, he sees the bronze "hands outstretched in the breathtaking gesture of lifting a veil...above the face of a kneeling slave." Yet from his more knowing position, he questions whether he is "witnessing a revelation or a more efficient blinding" thus revealing his ability to analyze the statue, which represents the existent Booker T. Washington Monument (1922) called "Lifting the Veil" located on Tuskegee University's campus, with ironic insightfulness (36). By contrast, the protagonist's experiences as a student underscore his extreme inability to grasp the complicated personalities he meets. His adventure with Norton provides a telling example. He dismisses his observations of the trustee that fail to line up with his preconceived notions of powerful white men. As Norton quixotically declares the protagonist his "fate," the narrator wonders, "But you don't even know my name" (45). Similarly, he detects that the powerful man's violent response to Trueblood's tale of incest is laced with "something like envy and indignation," but he refuses to recognize the irony of Norton's position. Where Trueblood ponders his thorny circumstances and concludes he "ain't nobody but" himself, the millionaire trustee declares he can know himself only through the actions of others and cannot physically handle hearing about socially taboo actions he desired to, but could not, commit (66).

The reader, of course, perceives the irony that the protagonist misses. Thus, when the naive student feels convicted by the blind Reverend Homer A. Barbee's homily, a thinly veiled attempt to inspire undergraduates with renewed reverence for the college's mission and president, readers anticipate his disastrous meeting with Bledsoe. Incensed by the protagonist's conduct with Norton, the college president's candid questions and uncensored revelations throw the narrator into a tailspin, and he only regains his footing when Bledsoe reassumes his duplicitous facade. Looking at the protagonist "like a man about to flip a coin," Bledsoe clearly decides to exploit the boy's inability to read human character (144). His offer to introduce the narrator to powerful men in New York tests the young man's powers of perception: the irony inheres in the protagonist's failure to discern that he faces an exam.

Ellison exploits irony on a larger scale in the novel's overarching structure. The experiences that fill the bulk of the text, along with the narrator's final decision to reproduce his life in written form, denote Ellison's adaptation of the bildungsroman and kunstlerroman. For his purposes, these genres offer a rich template for rendering what he declares the central theme of America, the search for identity. He extols nineteenth-century authors like Mark Twain who craft fiction that probes the country's thorny contemporary dilemmas without compromising artistry. For Ellison, *The Adventures of Huckleberry Finn* (1884), Twain's most celebrated work, symbolizes the essence of what the American novel should accomplish, and he declares its bildungsroman format an integral attribute of its success. After labeling Huck's decision to steal Jim the climax of the novel, Ellison explains that Twain was aware of the "irony" inherent in the romanticized vision of blacks as symbols of man while slavery denied their humanity; accordingly, Huck's "acceptance of the evil implicit in his 'emancipation' of Jim represents Twain's acceptance of his personal responsibility for the condition of society" (*Collected Essays* 89). Huck's development culminates in his demonstration of a cultural maturity matched only by the author who creates him.

Ellison's protagonist, like Twain's, is defined by his unformed, or at least very malleable, view of the world. The structural irony his immaturity establishes contributes more than comic relief. His questioning appraisal of society represents the historical moment that he inhabits. Summing up the aptness of Huck's youth, Ellison asserts "the historical justification for his adolescence lies in the fact that Twain was depicting a transitional period of American life; its artistic justification is that adolescence is the time of the 'great confusion,' during which both individuals and nations flounder between accepting and rejecting the responsibilities of adulthood" (*Collected Essays* 89). *Invisible Man* sets its sights on a similar goal. Ellison considers the mid-century United States an analogous transitional moment and formulates his protagonist's journey accordingly. Unlike the essentially linear trajectory that Huck follows on his developmental journey, physically delineated by the consistently southward flowing Mississippi River, Ellison's protagonist's psychological transformation is marked by his northward movement, which results in a frustrating circularity before the protagonist grasps the irony of his comportment toward society.

SATIRE

Ellison holds our attention amid the meandering experiences of the narrator's slow evolution by satirizing particular personalities. Satire derides in order to correct outside vice or folly and provides what some critics deem the driving purpose for Ellison's text. By depending chiefly on indirect satire, or satire in which the author pokes fun at characters who inadvertently demonstrate their ignorance or absurdity, Ellison hints at how American culture contributes to the confusion surrounding identity formation. Young Emerson supplies a vivid example. In striving to uncover the duplicity of Bledsoe and other figures of power, young Emerson reveals his inability to shed the very condescension that he ostensibly critiques. He stumbles through his quasi-heroic attempt to foil the plans of his father and Bledsoe only to end by asking the narrator to be his "valet," hardly a sign of devotion to egalitarian principles (192). Ellison enhances Emerson's comical image with the young man's tearful plea for the narrator to keep his disclosure secret: "I wouldn't mind, but my father would consider my revelation the most extreme treason.... You're free of him now. I'm still his prisoner. You have been freed" (192). With his Harvard education, expensive clothes, and posh lifestyle, he appears more a craven and spoiled child than a mistreated hostage.

Emerson's melodramatic declaration rings all the more hollow given his initial depiction of his relationship to the narrator. In a bid to prove his knowledge about black life, he insists, "With us it's still Jim and Huck Finn" (188). His words expose an implicit acceptance of the racial dictates ordering their interaction. The white women in the text similarly consent to occupying stereotypical roles in their relations with the protagonist, and Ellison crafts these episodes with heavy satire as well. Following his first speech on the Woman Question, the unnamed woman who invites the protagonist to her apartment confesses that his presentations make her "afraid" because of their "*primitive*" nature; in fact, she declares, he has "tom-toms beating" in his voice (413). Her reliance upon cultural myth rather than on the protagonist's individuality illustrates the pervasiveness of popular images of black male sexuality within purportedly socially advanced organizations. When her husband returns to find her in bed with the protagonist, his dispassionate "Night, and you too," reveals Ellison's satirical presentation of the listless, well-to-do white marriage that is ultimately a victim of the myths white America propagates about black hypersexuality (417). Sybil pushes this satire into the realm of the absurd with her pathetic fantasy of being raped by a black man.

Though the women appear largely comic, Ellison's presentation of political leaders reveals the dangerous nature of wrongheaded notions about race and the necessity for the protagonist to penetrate foolish ideology. Notwithstanding Brother Jack's smooth reliance upon vague political ideas, upon first meeting him, the protagonist remains wary of his intentions. Observing Brother Jack's walk, he admits, "I had a feeling that somehow he was acting a part; that something about him wasn't exactly real" (288). Fresh from the eviction where he has momentarily reconnected with his cultural past, the protagonist sees Jack more clearly than he will once he succumbs to the tantalizing tentacles of Brotherhood power. Yet he eventually realizes that his first notion is correct: Jack and the Brotherhood lack sincerity and true cultural knowledge. Their professed commitment to the people of Harlem stems primarily from a bid for greater power rather than a real understanding of black Americans' struggles. The organization boasts a impressive range of misguided politicos: Brother Tobitt imagines that his commitment to racial equality is legitimated by his marriage to a black woman; Brother Wrestrum cares more about being included in a white organization than the work it accomplishes; and the intellectual Brother Hambro substitutes pedantry for true understanding of black reality. Together, they present a telling commentary on the misguided nature of left-wing politics as well as the absurdity of the protagonist's commitment to their work. Ellison repeatedly denied charges that the Brotherhood corresponded to the Communist Party, or that Ras stood for Marcus Garvey. In fact, a direct correlation seems less important than his broader desire to question the efficacy of particular ideological positions and to contrast his protagonist's response to different, yet equally problematic, political platforms. Ellison's loose satirizing of Marcus Garvey underscores both the flawed nature of the back to Africa movement and the narrator's reflexive dismissal of all-black political agency.

PARODY

In guiding his protagonist toward mature consciousness, Ellison also relies upon parody. A form of burlesque, parody apes the typical style of an author or literary genre for comic effect. Ellison lampoons individual works like Wells's *The Invisible Man* (1897), in which Griffin achieves invisibility through a successful science experiment, and Dostoyevsky's *Notes from the Underground* (1864), a text boasting an existentialist unnamed protagonist who creates many of his own dilemmas. The episode in the El Toro Bar, where Brother Jack gives the protagonist his assignment of being the chief spokesman of the Harlem District of the Brotherhood, gains nuance by Ellison's sly parody of Hemingway's *The Sun Also Rises* (1926). The painted panels of bullfighting scenes recall the importance of this metaphor in Hemingway's text and foreshadow the protagonist's fate within the organization. He simultaneously caricatures particular literary genres. The trajectory the narrator follows parodies the slave narrative genre where South to North geographical movement typically signifies the writer's changing fortunes from slavery to freedom. Ellison's narrator follows a similar route, but his Northern experiences deny the traditional freedom associated with the region. Instead, the narrator's New York life confirms modern black Americans' need for a revised path to emotional freedom.

Ellison proclaims his protagonist's progression along this path by granting him new facility with figurative language. The frames of the text in particular exemplify the mature narrator's fondness for, and mastery of, metaphor, a word or expression in which a comparison is implicit. His opening proclamation, "I am an invisible man," asserts the density of the narrator's perception of his identity (3). Vividly contrasted against his inability to see himself or anyone else in complicated terms throughout the framed portions, his espousal of an invisible status attests to his radical growth. The metaphor also represents Ellison's sense of the appropriate relationship between artistry and politics in fiction. In his rejection of critic Irving Howe's claim that his work lacked legitimacy because it failed to address racial politics directly, Ellison counters that protest might assume different forms: "It might appear in a novel as a technical assault against the styles which have gone before, or as a protest against the human condition. If *Invisible Man* is even 'apparently' free from 'the ideological and emotional penalties suffered by Negroes in this country,' it is because I tried to the best of my ability to transform these elements into art" (*Collected Essays* 183). Accordingly, rather than announce the sociopolitical debate his novel considers, he packages it in metaphor.

METAPHOR

Todd Lieber traces the historical trajectory of the metaphor of invisibility in black American literature where it often refers to the larger American society's refusal to acknowledge black humanity and blacks' purposeful concealment of their identity. He sees Ellison advancing the metaphor by recognizing "that mask-wearing and inherent invisibility are related aspects of the same problem" (87). Ellison not only unites two strands of a metaphorical concept that are usually explored separately, he aims to extend its meaning beyond a description of black existence to render American identity more broadly. With the aid of this rich metaphor, he penetrates the surface discussion of racial invisibility and broaches a discussion of human consciousness. In his preliminary musings, the narrator piles metaphor upon metaphor to portray himself and his society. On the contrary, the narrator dedicates much of the epilogue to translating the central metaphors that confound him throughout his life. His ruminations leave him certain that "the mind that has conceived a plan of living must never lose sight of the chaos against which that pattern was conceived. That goes for societies as well as for individuals" (580). For the narrator, his plan lies squarely in working through the narrative process.

Before he becomes a writer, however, he must confront the one character who is himself a metaphor for identity instability. Just as the protagonist begins harboring serious reservations about Brotherhood dogma related to black consciousness, he discovers Rinehart, the chameleon-like Harlemite who defies simple definition. After being mistaken for Rinehart by vastly different groups, the narrator wonders whether "Rine the runner and Rine the gambler and Rine the briber and Rine the lover and Rinehart the Reverend" could "himself be both rind and heart" (498). His quandary exhibits his willingness to peer beneath the multifaceted surface Rinehart projects as well as his readiness to accept the possibility that Rine comfortably accepts as genuine the incongruity between his outer avatars, the "rind," and his inner self, the "heart." By the novel's end, the protagonist's advance from interpreting Rinehart's metaphorical name to comprehending and rejecting the self-serving, exploitative nature the trickster embodies signifies his readiness to articulate his personal sense of identity.

SYMBOLISM

Symbolism is the final literary trope this chapter considers crucial to the success of Ellison's artistry and central to his manipulation of different forms of narrative representation. In literature, a symbol is defined as "a word or phrase that signifies an object or event which in its turn signifies something, or has a range of reference, beyond itself" (Abrams 311). Analyzing the role of symbol in the novel necessarily initiates a discussion of Ellison's modernist tendencies. Like the other types of figurative language discussed thus far, symbols facilitate Ellison's portrayal of his narrator's inner being, and to a greater extent than other rhetorical moves, systematically chart his growth. T. S. Eliot's theory of an objective correlative offers a formal description of the role symbols occupy in Ellison's text and underscores their modernist roots. Eliot, the poet Ellison credits with steering him away from music toward a serious study of literature, claims "the only way of expressing emotion is by finding an 'objective correlative'; in other words, a set of objects, a situation, a chain of events which shall be the formula of that *particular* emotion" (Abrams 197). Accordingly, he suggests this method should help the reader more easily access and share the emotion the writer strives to express.

Ellison relies on symbols as his primary method for engaging moral quandaries at the center of American identity. In doing so, he aims to correct the oversights of high modernists like Hemingway, whom he greatly admired but felt shirked the moral responsibility of the American author. Ellison takes Hemingway to task for his contention that *Huckleberry Finn* should have ended after Jim is stolen from Huck and concludes that "Hemingway's blindness to the moral values of Huckleberry Finn despite his sensitivity to its technical aspects duplicated the one-sided vision of the twenties" (*Collected Essays* 91). Winking at the knotty dilemma of America's discrimination and violence against blacks, Hemingway latches on to the ritual of the Spanish bullfight, a symbol Ellison describes as representing "amoral violence" in lieu of the morally ridden topic of race (*Collected Essays* 93). Hemingway's propensity towards violent images of animal death links him to human defeat rather than triumph, and consequently, Ellison accuses him of producing literature that celebrates society's failures and absolves readers of their "social irresponsibility" (*Collected Essays* 95).

Ellison writes with no such negligence. He confronts Hemingway directly by incorporating the symbol of the bull into his narrative. The narrator first associates the bull image with Jack as he reminisces over childhood memories before his first Brotherhood speech. Recalling the bulldog, Master, whom he had not trusted as a child, he notes that Jack reminds him of a "toy bull terrier" (338). As previously mentioned, when Jack takes him to the El Toro Bar to inform him of his appointment over the Harlem District, the narrator ponders two panels of bullfight scenes positioned in the normal place for a mirror. The first depicts a matador challenging a bull with elegant artistry, and the narrator marvels at the grace of the image while Jack declares it "sheer barbarism" (358). The second panel pictures the matador being gored. In a seemingly complete change of pace, during his and Clifton's fight with Ras, the narrator describes the Exhorter rocking "like a drunken bull" and looking "bull angry" (369, 370). Changing gears again, as he sleeps with the mystery woman, he dreams of being chased "by a bull" (417). In Ellison's hands, the image that suppressed discussions of moral difficulty for Hemingway becomes a standard bearer for the moral equivocation afflicting myriad aspects of American social interaction. A succinct catalogue of possible interpretations for the recurring bull symbol might respectively connect Ellison's bulls to duplicitous politics, cultural misperception and degradation, white-incited intra-racial violence, and the enactment of racially inflected sexual stereotypes. The interconnected variety of the image displays the pleasure with which Ellison manipulates the symbol while its interspersion corresponds to the narrator's barely perceptible development. Each reference registers his movement from superficially associating Jack and the dog with an impenetrable countenance, to discovering a divergent viewpoint between himself and Jack, to connecting Ras's temperament to Jack's, to sensing the danger of fulfilling derogatory stereotypes. Together, the images indicate the necessity for conscious perception.

Leaving off from ribbing Hemingway, Ellison presents Sambo as a peculiarly American symbol that foregrounds the moral quandary of racism. The term *Sambo* codifies the racist characteristics associated with blacks such as ignorance, unintended comicality, and lasciviousness as well as the exaggerated visual stereotype of blacks with big red lips, black skin, rolling white eyes, and wild hair. Ellison channels the narrator's developing sense of self through the presentation of Sambo. We first witness the narrator encountering the term at the battle royal. As he prepares to scramble for the money on the electrified rug, a blond man encourages, "That's right, Sambo" (26). Instead of feeling insulted or wizened by the term, the narrator simply focuses on the task at hand, signifying an unruffled familiarity with such derogatory language. He has just finished the brutal violence of the fight, but he excitedly vows to seize the most money, thinking "I would use both my hands. I would throw my body against the boys nearest me to block them from the gold" (26). His willingness to physically compromise himself for profit ironically connects him to the other boys whom he scorns for their regular participation in smokers and more pertinently, highlights his inadvertent enactment of the Sambo stereotype.

When the narrator encounters an image of Sambo in Harlem, he exhibits a different sensibility. Awaking in his room at Mary's the morning after his first Chthonian party, he sees the Americana piece that he previously overlooked. Imagining himself newly enlightened, he disgustedly surveys the "cast-iron figure of a very black, red-lipped and wide-mouthed Negro, whose white eyes stared up at [him] from the floor, his face an enormous grin, his single large black hand held palm up before his chest" (319). The memory of the astute Brotherhood members he met the previous night transforms the bank into a sign of Mary's cultural immaturity and his fellow boarders' uncivilized behavior. In a fit of rage, he bangs the iron bank on the metal pipe until its head breaks open in crushed submission. His subsequent inability to dispose of the broken bank wittily identifies the bank with the narrator and symbolizes his continued enactment of the Sambo role. Even his Chthonian invitation to join the Brotherhood is laced with Sambo trappings: Emma inquires whether he is black enough; he foolishly accepts a new name as he holds out his hand for $300; a drunk brother insists that he sing a spiritual since "*all* colored people sing," and he plays the clown to cover everyone's embarrassment with laughter (312). Yet the narrator departs Mary's house thinking that he is privileged to join the scientifically sophisticated Brotherhood.

Ellison's deft analogy between the narrator and the bank displays his complex handling of the Sambo image. It remains a symbol for the disparaging identity white America affixes to blacks, but Ellison refines the many ways it manifests itself in black-white relations. The narrator's physical destruction of the bank artfully signals black Americans' attempts to conquer their abusive past, and his inability to rid himself of the pieces stresses the difficulty of this endeavor. Although the narrator perceives the insulting image the bank represents, a posture that is an improvement over his unquestioning acceptance of the term during the smoker, his obliviousness to the correspondence between his actions and the inanimate object he loathes signals his continued lack of discernment. He remains incapable of inferring from his experience a grasp of the reality of his identity. For Ellison this incapacity offers a rich spin on Melville's construction of a Sambo figure. In *The Confidence Man* (1857), one of the protagonist's avatars is a comic, black-faced, and crippled trickster who swindles passengers out of money through his clever begging. Ellison confided to Murray, "I guess I told you that the bank image in Invisible was suggested by the figure of Black Guinea. That son of a bitch with his mouth full of pennies!" (Ellison and Murray 79). His exuberant appreciation of Melville's multifaceted formulation of the American charlatan, that admirable rogue embodying the ingenuity and charm basic to American success, accentuates the problem he creates for his narrator. Melville's manipulative confidence man plays (or at least uses) Sambo to exploit the stereotype for monetary gain and the scene reflects Melville's study of the moral consequences involved in both enacting and accepting such roles. Ellison's narrator cannot detect this tension.

When he confronts Clifton's outrageous Sambo doll, the narrator is dumbfounded by the former brother's injudiciousness. After an onlooker in Clifton's audience laughs at the narrator's angry response to the mocking doll and connects his childish anger to the doll's merry performance, the narrator wonders how Clifton could forget that the Brotherhood protects them from "being empty Sambo dolls," an "obscene flouncing of everything human!" (434–435). He senses that something more is at stake in Clifton's act but cannot detect the rationale provoking the youth leader's behavior until he witnesses the Brotherhood's duplicity. Ellison's sly assembly of Clifton's insinuating spiel, the narrator's discovery of the controlling black string, and Jack's revelation of the Brotherhood's view of the narrator together invest the Sambo doll with a critical task. It triggers the narrator's ultimate realization of his role in society. When he apprehends the Brotherhood's part in inciting the riot that tears Harlem apart, his own Sambo status dawns on him. The complexity with which Ellison creates this sequence emphasizes the brilliance of his artistry.

The narrator's eventual sense of clarity regarding Clifton's tortured embrace of Sambo begs a reconsideration of his earlier assumption regarding Mary's bank. He originally concludes the decorative piece attests to Mary's cultural ignorance, an emblem of her unsophisticated sense of race. His final desire to return to Mary's suggests otherwise. Contrary to proving her lack of judgment, the Sambo bank conveys her racial wholeness. Unlike the narrator, she comfortably exists within the contradictions that define her life. In fact, the relationship Ellison creates between Mary and Sambo dramatizes another way in which his use of symbols relates to modernist literary technique. The density of the Sambo symbol exposes his tendency to invest with great meaning words and images tied to the folk heritage of black Americans. This predilection fuels his more expansive argument that black writers must not restrict their refutation of society's denial of their humanity to realistic, documentary-styled literature; rather, they must discover and present black consciousness artistically. Ellison points to Picasso as a master of this truth. He expounds:

> [Picasso is] the greatest wrestler with forms and techniques of them all. Just the same, he's never abandoned the old symbolic forms of Spanish art: the guitar, the bull, daggers, women, shawls, veils, mirrors. Such symbols serve a dual function: they allow the artist to speak of complex experiences and to annihilate time with simple lines and curves, and they allow the viewer an orientation, both emotional and associative, which goes so deep that a total culture may resound in a simple rhythm, an image. (*Collected Essays* 213–214)

For Ellison, the most meaningful symbolic forms of black life were found in folklore, and he believes these forms also represent an essential part of American culture. The varied expressions and images comprising black folklore embody both the black and white history of the nation, and Ellison insists that minority artists must integrate these forms into art helping define American identity.

His contention stems from his expansive study of modernist literature. In an explanation of the roots of his artistry he contends, "I use folklore in my work not because I am Negro, but because writers like Eliot and Joyce made me conscious of the literary value of my folk inheritance" (*Collected Essays* 111–112). What is more, he credits his familiarity with works such as *The Waste Land* (1922) and *Ulysses* (1922) for exemplifying how "ancient myth and ritual were used to give form and significance to material," leaving the responsibility to recognize and transform them to the work of the artist (*Collected Essays* 216). Thus, Sambo becomes more than an image of a very dark person with exaggerated features. It is a marker of the racist attempt to deny black American humanity; it embodies the confusion haunting American identity formation; it characterizes the extent to which black and white experience is intertwined. Ellison's artistic transformation of an intended symbol of racial bigotry into a method for exploring consciousness goes to the heart of what he values in the integration of folk materials into art. He notes a range of episodes, sayings, and images in *Invisible Man* indebted to the wealth of black folklore. More than any particular saying or image, he suggests that their import for readers lies in the willingness to find the interconnections that grant the narrative meaning.

The narrator's experience at the eviction provides a case in point. Directly following his cathartic experience of eating a yam in the streets, the narrator stumbles upon an array of objects he initially mistakes for junk. When he realizes he is witnessing an eviction, he imbues the articles with new meaning, contemplating them individually and collectively. Items ranging from a portrait of the old couple to knocking bones to a breast pump to freedom papers mingle in the dirty snow and elicit new emotions from the narrator. Moved beyond understanding at the sight he wonders, *"why were they causing me discomfort so far beyond their intrinsic meaning as objects? And why did I see them now, as behind a veil that threatened to lift"* (273). The old couple's household goods attest to the varied history of black Americans, visually tying them to the folk past the narrator rediscovered in the yam, and they give his cultural awakening definition. The pedestrian aspect of the individual objects recedes as the force of their symbolism hits him. The veil he imagines, an echo of the veil held by the

Founder's statue at the college, clearly denotes the emotional and ideological baggage blocking his move toward a clearer perception of society. Like
the vibrant and layered lore that captures the lives of folk like the Provos,
the random artifacts combine to tell an intricate story of their life.

The destruction of symbolic objects and images during the riot and
its aftermath offers a final example for contemplating the importance of
symbolism in Ellison's art. This episode also ushers the narrator into his
ultimate procurement of personal and cultural insight and manifests what
some critics identify as the postmodernist strain in *Invisible Man*. Although neither the term modernism nor postmodernism is easily defined,
the signature characteristics of both literary modes illuminate Ellison's
narrative shifts. In "The Art of Fiction," he ends his discussion of the
dominant styles in the novel by noting that "during [the narrator's] fall
from grace in the Brotherhood, it becomes somewhat surrealistic. The
styles try to express both his state of consciousness and the state of
society" (*Collected Essays* 220). His description of the latter portions
of the narrative as surrealist gives meaning to the bizarre, dream-like
atmosphere he creates and indicates his move beyond a modernist approach. If modernism identifies the literary movement committed to
making things new while lamenting the fracturing of culture as we know
it, postmodernism accepts this fracturing with less distress and locates
a generative quality in the breaks. Postmodernists accept the reality
of chaos, celebrate the intertextuality of contradictory parts, find value
in the illogical thought of subconscious states, and revel in the endless interpretations that produce personal vision. As the narrator lugs
his briefcase toward the destruction of the Harlem riot, he is primed for
adopting such a perspective.

The physical destruction of Harlem signifies the mental and emotional
devastation its residents endure daily. In the unreality of the dark, the
narrator witnesses the explosion of their inner turmoil with a changing
sense of perception. He progresses from applauding their self-sufficiency
to recognizing the futility of their outburst to accepting his culpability in
bringing the events to pass. Amidst violent injuries, deaths, and sense-
less waste, the narrator grasps the meaning of his identity. Confronting Ras on his horse, he concludes "I . . . recognized the absurdity of the
whole night and of the simple yet confoundingly complex arrangement
of hope and desire, fear and hate, that had brought me here still running, and knowing now who I was and where I was" (559). He com-
prehends the necessity for Harlem's expression of its discontent, but he
also apprehends the need for them to move forward through a positive

understanding of their complicated consciousness. When he falls into the hole and dreams of being castrated, he metaphorically associates physical fragmentation with the path to wholeness and celebrates this accomplishment notwithstanding the pain involved. His dream serves as a prelude to his decision to burn the contents of his briefcase, a physical symbol of his past, and displays his newfound ability to assess other characters perceptively.

The narrator's ironic assertion to the white men who accost him before he falls into the manhole that he has them in his briefcase, notwithstanding their ignorance of his identity and their blindness to their position, highlights his expanding vision of society. In the blackness of the hole, he discovers the light of self-knowledge as he destroys the documents and paper artifacts signifying his past experiences. After burning his high school diploma, a symbol of the extremity of his naïveté, he burns Clifton's Sambo doll. By the light of the "stubbornly" burning doll, he lights the anonymous letter (568). Taking out the paper on which Jack scrawled his Brotherhood, he realizes the papers have the same handwriting. The shock of this discovery propels him into the darkness of the hole and the light of self-discovery. Ellison suggests that only through such a violent fracturing of all his protagonist thinks is stable can he begin to perceive the reality of his life and position in society. The destruction, then, is not lamentable but celebratory; it paves the way toward a discovery of the truth of his human condition. In this way, Ellison suggests the universal implications of his narrator's journey.

Ellison's sophisticated handling of figurative language underpins his creation of the protagonist who embodies his artistic agenda. In many ways, he travels a parallel journey with his fictional rabble-rouser turned writer. Just as the narrator's growing facility with language indicates his evolving mental state, Ellison announces his own artistic maturity through the publication of his first novel. Emerging out of the shadow of his friend and mentor, Richard Wright, Ellison demonstrates rhetorical skills that vouch for his artistic excellence and announce his creative potential. His deployment of figurative twists and turns lends both density and lightness to his narrative, congealing a text remarkable for its serious exploration of race and simultaneous dedication to art. Ellison erects his house of fiction upon the variegated literary foundation of past, contemporary, and developing movements, but to peer through his novel's windows reveals his vivid sense of the architectural future of fiction. For all who are game, he eloquently beckons.

WORKS CITED

Abrams, M. H. *A Glossary of Literary Terms.* Fort Worth, TX: Harcourt Brace, 1999.

Ellison, Ralph. *The Collected Essays of Ralph Ellison.* Edited by John Callahan. New York: Modern Library, 1995.

Lieber, Todd. "Ralph Ellison and the Metaphor of Invisibility in Black Literary Tradition." *American Quarterly* 24 (1972): 86–100.

Murray, Albert, and John F. Callahan, eds. *Trading Twelves: The Selected Letters of Ralph Ellison and Albert Murray.* New York: Vintage Books, 2000.

Chapter 6

RECEPTION

Almost from the moment of its publication, *Invisible Man* has inspired thoughtful and impassioned debate. In June 1952, Saul Bellow toasted the book's willingness to confront the "enormously complex and difficult American experience" (28). That same month, John Oliver Killens, lamenting among other things its lack of activist frenzy, called the novel "a vicious distortion of Negro life" (qtd. in Butler xxii). From one vantage, these disparate views merely reveal the complicated agendas that circulated in post–World War II America; still, when one considers the unresolved tensions that to this day surround *Invisible Man,* a more complex reality must be acknowledged. What impressions lead Houston Baker to label Ellison's first book "a colorblind, literarily-allusive prison house of language" that ultimately embraces "the 'presentist simplicity' of ... industrial, imperialist, xenophobic American myth making," while Ross Posnock fetes the novel and its author as quasi-prophetic witnesses for "the renewed promise of cosmopolitan democracy" ("Failed Prophet" par. 18, par. 11; 1)? However difficult it may be to answer that question, one quickly senses that time-bound exigencies cannot adequately explain the fierce and enduring divergence that *Invisible Man* prompts. For more perspective on the stakes of Ellisonian position-taking, a peculiar fact of laboring with the word must be remembered.

Because statutes once declared that black slaves could not read or write, literacy has often carried a talismanic status in African American experience (Gates 127–132). By the mid-1940s when Ellison began composing

Invisible Man, legal restrictions on black literacy were long gone, but shades of their legacy persisted in the unique contest over the cultural complexion of blackness. Richard P. Barksdale, discussing African American literature in light of the transformations in post–World War II literary inquiry, presciently observed that the pursuit of beauty must always be juxtaposed with a realization that the struggle against dehumanizing assignations rarely recedes (33–34). Thus, art, the archetypal chase after beauty, for blacks simultaneously strives to express a transcendent truth even as it aims to encourage practical redress. Between the Harlem Renaissance and World War II, many African American writers insistently felt that they played too small a role in the fight for improvements in black existence. Apprehensive about the purpose of the literary experiments during the Roaring Twenties, they sought an approach to writing and a set of stories that unambiguously announced their allegiance to a progressive future. The result was a style and content termed "Protest Literature." Richard Wright's essay "Blueprint for Negro Writing" (1937) expressed the ideological assumptions of protest, and his book *Native Son* (1940), hailed by Noel Shraufnagel as a marker of "the birth of the modern Negro novel," is the manifest text of the protest movement because it earlier and more forcefully than any other extended fiction declared the fact and the consequences of America's inhumanity to blacks (ix). The critical reaction to *Invisible Man* forever emerges against the backdrop of Wright's aesthetic. Recognizing this fact, the present chapter offers a large cross section of opinions about Ellison's novel and attempts to document trends in the reactions to it. Beginning with a sample of the initial reviews of the novel, it will then consider how literary/cultural historians and literary critics have discussed the book. In the section on reviews, responses from representative national publications will be perused; after that, selected perspectives from radical and African American periodicals are examined. The second segment on literary/cultural history will examine how commentators have fit *Invisible Man* into discussions of black and Anglo-American artistic development. The final part of this chapter, literary criticism, will present the different approaches that analysts of this novel have employed. The intent here is to document the rich variety of secondary material that exists and to organize this material under useful headings.

REVIEWS

The national press heralded the publication of *Invisible Man* with a flurry of reviews, the quantity of which suited the latest offering from a

seasoned veteran rather than the initial sustained product of a rank ama-
teur. While Ellison had published fairly extensively before his first novel
appeared, his works usually graced the pages of leftist journals like *New
Masses* and *Daily Worker,* not spaces where the tastemakers of the mainstream literary establishment usually turned for the newest talent. Despite
this, shrewd promotion, rampant curiosity, and formidable accomplishment prompted wordsmiths of all stripes to weigh in on the novel. Wright
Morris, writing in the *New York Times,* stated that "*Invisible Man* belongs
on the shelf with the classical efforts man has made to chart the river Lethe
from its mouth to its source" (par. 9). Embellishing his claims with an
extended allusion to Dante's *Divine Comedy,* Morris also conjured Dos-
toevsky and Virgil in his praise of Ellison's serious and sensitive portrayal
of the underworlds of the human consciousness. For this reviewer, "the
traumatic phase of the black man's rage in America" too often stands in
the way of creative mastery; however, he believes that Ellison "handles"
the "surrealist" facets of black experience "with so much authority," "ma-
cabre humor," and "detachment, that the reader is justified in feeling that
in the process of mastering his rage, [Ellison] has also mastered his art"
(pars. 7, 5) The significance of *Invisible Man* emerges quite conspicuously when one considers that Orville Prescott wrote another review of the
book for the *New York Times* only three days after Morris's. Where Morris
stresses the novel's conversations with global literary classics, Prescott sets
the tone and the terrain of his consideration with this opening statement:
"Ralph Ellison's first novel, *Invisible Man* is the most impressive work of
fiction by an American Negro which I have ever read." He continues in
this vein differentiating Ellison from Richard Wright and Willard Motley,
who achieve their effects "by overpowering their readers with documentary detail." For Prescott, *Invisible Man* profitably exploits melodrama
powering it with "poetic intensity and immense narrative drive" (19). In
doing this, he completes a "tough, brutal and sensational" novel that "no
one interested in books by or about American Negroes should miss" (20).
    Jacqueline Covo, one of the more thorough cataloguers of critical ap-
praisals of *Invisible Man,* cautions against a glib painting of all the early
reactions as laudatory. In fact, she stresses the measured comments of
most observers: "Perhaps [the] sheer bulk [of reviews of *Invisible Man*]
accounts for the impression that the book elicited unanimous [positive]
reviews; curiously, the impression persists even after one notes the fairly
general technical criticism directed at the novel" (11). Covo senses an eva-
sive tendency even in those critics who applaud Ellison's book. Instead
of grappling with the complexity and the challenges of his portrayals, she

believes that commentators latch onto "esthetic" and philosophical features by way of ignoring the prominent racial conflicts that permeate the novel. This phenomenon allows them to clap without completely entering the consciousness at "the core of the novel" (Covo 12).

Robert Butler, author of the landmark compendium, *The Critical Response to Ralph Ellison* (2000), sees the reviews and the reviewers differently. While he acknowledges that "the early reviews of *Invisible Man* were not without criticism," he argues that "these criticisms...must be put into context as relatively minor objections within otherwise glowingly positive assessments" (xxi). Far from viewing mainstream critics like Orville Prescott as myopic readers who selectively mine the text and marginalize its major preoccupations, Butler quotes them as evidence of the considerable chorus of "highly influential critics who hailed Ellison as a writer of genuine importance" (xx). Neither does Butler express Covo's ironical view of this coronation. Where Covo reads the mainstream literary establishment's attitude towards Ellison as enthusiastic, yet uncomprehending endorsement, Butler asserts that not only do "the early reviews of [*Invisible Man*] clearly demonstrate that the publication of the novel was an event of great cultural and literary importance," but also that "the spirited and fruitful debate over the precise nature of the [novel's] extraordinary impact" signals a far-reaching understanding of the exact merits and demerits of this landmark work (xxiii).

Covo's survey, *The Blinking Eye: Ralph Waldo Ellison and his American, French, German and Italian Critics, 1952–1971,* was published in 1974, while Butler's collection appeared in 2000. Although it is tempting to account for their different perspectives via the quarter-century span between their publication dates, the simple fact is that the initial reviews of *Invisible Man* have not changed at all even unto this day. So, if both critics are responding to the same reviews, what explains their alternate conclusions? Covo believes that Ellison produced a great book that was championed for if not disingenuous, then certainly self-serving reasons. To put it more directly, Covo seems to sense in many mainstream reviewers of *Invisible Man* a ready desire to hallow an apparently palatable depiction of black life as an echo of the interminable angst that at least since the turn of the century had affected the mainstream American psyche. In doing this, the black and white advocates of the novel, according to Covo, too often dismissed its fundamental implication of institutional racism, embracing instead its equally prominent, yet less inflammatory message of the abiding need for self-determination. While Covo detects in this tendency a troubling incompletion, Butler, embellishing the perspective of commentators like Alan Nadel, Ross Posnock, and even Ellison himself, identifies in these critical assessments the seed of the master narratives of *Invisible Man*'s most profound interrogation. It is not then that early critics missed crucial subtexts of Ellison's exploration of segregation's absurdity; rather, Butler avers that their crafting of "the fundamental questions" surrounding Ellison's novel penetrates the merely superficial narrative of black repression by racial inequality (xxiii).

If one kind of ambivalence typifies immediate national reactions and subsequent interpretations of those views, then complexity of another sort emerges when one considers the responses of radical and black commentators. Lloyd L. Brown, the African American author of the novel *Iron City* (1950), not only resents the anti-Communist energy that he detects in Ellison's portrayal of the Brotherhood, but also, anticipating an accusation that Chester Himes later levels, he indicts *Invisible Man* as a fiction that curries to the literary fashions of the day. He begins his review "The Deep Pit" (1952) with this observation:

> "Whence all this passion toward conformity?" asks Ralph Ellison at the end of his novel, *Invisible Man.* He should know, because his whole book conforms exactly to the formula for literary success in today's market. Despite the murkiness of his avant-garde symbolism, the pattern is clear and may be charted as precisely as a publisher's quarterly sales report. (31)

Where some Communist Party stalwarts signal Ellison's betrayal purely in terms of his less than flattering allegories that impugn the organization, Brown's suggestion of a hunger for social ascendancy behind Ellison's artistry betrays both an ideological dogmatism and perhaps an unintended glimpse into the younger novelist's psyche. The suspicion of Ellison's version of social scaling stokes many black reviewers' allegations of creative irresponsibility.

Abner Berry, an acquaintance of Ellison's from his early days in leftist circles, plainly entitles his *Daily Worker* review, "Ralph Ellison Shows Snobbery, Contempt for Negro People" (1952). Emphasizing this same charge, Roi Ottley, while giving his *Chicago Sun Tribune* piece the more equivocal moniker, "Blazing Novel Relates A Negro's Frustrations" (1952) complains about Ellison's defeatist portraits of black life. Perhaps the most strident critic of this facet of *Invisible Man* was Marguerite D. Cartwright who in two pieces for the *Amsterdam News* lamented what she saw as Ellison's defamatory accounts of black masculinity (Butler xxii). On one level, contemporary critics correctly identify Cartwright, Ottley, and Berry as less than ideal readers; nevertheless, notwithstanding that the substance of their objections reflects anxieties tied to racial identity in the context of the struggle for racial equality, these kinds of indictments also reveal the charged subtexts of how one should achieve middle-class security in a world slowly ambling towards integration. Many spectators detected in Ellison's art a willingness to cannibalize black existence. Their authorized versions of African American life not only required the kind of ennobling that W.E.B. Du Bois discussed in his famous essay "The Criteria of Negro Art" (1926), but also a sort of entrenchment in black liberation pre-occupations that *Invisible Man*'s plot and protagonist seems to mock. The tensions that instantly sprang up around Ellison's novel have not receded, and as Robert Butler points out, the "early reviews" of the book "set up the basic framework for" an ongoing "lively critical debate" (xxiii). The way that the novel is deployed in literary history ratifies this contention.

LITERARY/CULTURAL HISTORY

Robert Bone, just over a decade after the publication of *Invisible Man,* imbued the novel with one of its earliest defenses as an epoch-making text. Writing in his seminal work *The Negro Novel in America* (1965), Bone suggests that the "first and basic impulse" of the post-Depression African American novel was "social protest" (156). Describing in celebra-tory terms how Ellison distanced himself from earlier black writers, he contends that the post–World War II novelist was "forced to revise [his] literary goals... Superimposed on his old impulse to protest was a new im-pulse... to transcend the parochial character of Negro experience" (156). Bone argues that Ellison strikes "out in the direction of a more universal art," and in the novelist's example, he sees the resolution of a more abiding dilemma: "From the beginning, the Negro novelist has been torn between the conflicting loyalties of race and art. On the one hand, he has sought to be a spokesman for his people; on the other, to be accepted on his merits as an artist" (243). Bone's thesis is thought-provoking if incredibly presump-tive, and the fact of its existence so soon after the publication of Ellison's novel suggests just how emphatically *Invisible Man* influenced the consti-tution of the American and the African American literary landscape. For if Bone's book includes Ellison because of its author's professed interest in the "Negro Novel," then Marcus Klein's extended discussion of El-lison in *After Alienation* (1964) suggests that very early *Invisible Man,* in accordance with its author's wishes, occupied an identifiable place in the mainstream American canon.

After Alienation examines how post–World War II American novels turn away from the radical estrangement that defined key fictions of the post–World War I era. Using *Invisible Man* as an example of this more pervasive tendency, Klein, in a substantial chunk of his study, discusses how Ellison's protagonist shunts, confronts, and ultimately embraces the challenges of joining the American community. In many ways Klein's analysis reflects not only the idylls of the protagonist, but also those of the novel itself. Consider that R.W.B. Lewis in his 1955 classic *The American Adam* placed *Invisible Man* beside the work of J. D. Salinger and Saul Bellow by way of suggesting its exemplary portrayal of a national character (Butler xxiii). Likewise, Leslie Fiedler, in *Love and Death in the American Novel* (1966), implicitly ties Ellison to the novels of a nineteenth-century master like Edgar Allan Poe. Fiedler implies that Ellison's handling of the gothic in black experience places him in a richer vein than that mined by previous African American novelists (493–494). Robert Butler, alluding specifically to Ihab Hassan's *Radical Innocence* (1961) and Jonathan Baumbach's *The Landscape of Nightmare* (1965), aptly summarizes the exalted status of *Invisible Man* when he observes that "clear evidence of the extremely positive critical response to Ellison's work... is the fact that several influential books on [post–World War II] American fiction devoted whole chapters to detailed analyses" of Ellison's text (xxiv). If the two decades following *Invisible Man*'s publication included unequivocal assertions of its centrality to American and African American literary history, then it must be acknowledged that, especially during the 1960s, dissenting views on the value of Ellison and his novel also surfaced.

Black Fire (1968), co-edited by LeRoi Jones and Larry Neal, continues a tradition of literary history via anthology that extends all the way back to Benjamin Brawley, Sterling Brown, and Arthur P. Davis. Attempting to exemplify the aims and the priorities of the Black Arts Movement, Jones and Neal's volume not only presented key new voices, but also it examined how the way forward for black creative expression depended on understanding key precursors in African American writing. Neal's perspective on *Invisible Man,* offered fittingly in an "Afterword: And Shine Swam On," suggests that "the things that concerned Ellison are interesting to read, but contemporary black youth feels another force in the world today." Continuing, he asserts that since the younger generation is not "invisible at least not to each other," they are frustrated by the Ellison's fixation on "a white light of confusion and absurdity" (652). The contours of this frustration emerge more clearly when one considers Addison Gayle's book-length study of the African American novel, *The Way of the New*

World (1975). Gayle senses in *Invisible Man* a profound portrait of the suspension between what Arthur P. Davis called "two worlds": a world of segregation "not yet dead" and a world of integration "not fully born" (Davis 606). He sympathizes with Ellison's dilemma at such a crossroads and even states that as *Invisible Man*'s protagonist narrates "the movement of black people from slavery to the modern era," a reader can vividly "glimpse the fluidity and variety of the black experience," an achievement that Gayle honors by saying that the novel "has...soul" (204). Despite these merits, Gayle feels that the conclusion of *Invisible Man* shows Ralph Ellison and his protagonist embracing "individualism instead of racial unity" (212). This choice in Gayle's mind occurs because the author "has accepted...the modern idea of a raceless world" without acknowledging that "those who have proposed such an existentialist solution...have never stepped outside of their own race, religion, and nationality" (212). Gayle's deep ambivalence about *Invisible Man* is summed up in a telling simultaneity; at the same moment he deplores the novel's "assimilationist denouement" and "Ellison's tendency to act the role of Rinehart to his white critics," he considers it "among the twenty best...published in the last thirty years" and a beacon of "the creative direction of the coming years" (213, 210, 213). A development late in the 1960s dramatizes the stakes of Gayle's schizophrenia.

In 1965, the *New York Herald Tribune*'s "Book Week" poll, conducted by what William Walling called "an essentially white group of authors, editors, and critics" (124–125), identified *Invisible Man* as the most accomplished novel printed between 1945 and 1965. Discussing Ellison's achievement, F. W. Dupee commented that while Ellison was young and relatively inexperienced, his book "could scarcely have been more ambitious if he had been writing novels for half a lifetime" (4). As Dupee was lauding *Invisible Man,* other sentiments were percolating among younger black writers. These stirrings emerged in a 1968 *Negro Digest* survey where Richard Wright was named "the most important black American writer of all time" (Fuller 13). Reinforcing that perception, Eldridge Cleaver, in his 1968 pièce de résistance *Soul on Ice,* declared that "Richard Wright reigns supreme for his profound political, economic, and social reference" while Ellison is merely "noisy" (105, 96). The tension in these estimates of *Invisible Man* and its author betray the tumultuous environment of 1960s America, a moment replete with vigorous war protests, escalated agitations for civil rights, and a wistful hunger for reassurance about the nation's traditional virtues. In this context, the uses that literary and cultural scholars made of *Invisible Man* are indexes of position-taking in broader debates about the appropriate form of American and African American identity. The preponderance of essay collections that the novel inspires in the 1970s indicates one conclusion that intellectuals and publishers were reaching.

In the early 1970s, *Invisible Man* and its author prompt no fewer than four essay collections. All of these, *Twentieth Century Interpretations of "Invisible Man"* (1971), *The Merrill Studies in "Invisible Man"* (1971), *A Casebook on Ralph Ellison's "Invisible Man"* (1972), and *Ralph Ellison: A Collection of Critical Essays* (1974), appear within a scant three-year span. In part, the publication of Ellison's first essay collection *Shadow and Act* (1964) explains this outpouring; nonetheless, the larger message of these compendiums is the firm canonization of *Invisible Man*. Prentice Hall began publishing the Twentieth Century Interpretations series so that representative essays that covered "the major areas of critical concern" within a single literary text could be compiled in a convenient volume (O'Hara 207). This series in 1968 produced guides on works like *Tom Jones* (1749), *The Portrait of a Lady* (1881), and *The Sound and the Fury* (1929). For *Invisible Man* to join this company in 1971, the same year that an *Absalom, Absalom!* (1936) entry was published, indicates how quickly and how thoroughly Ellison's novel saturated the curricula of colleges and universities. Consider for example that Richard Wright's *Native Son,* notwithstanding its publication in 1940, did not receive a Twentieth Century Interpretations treatment until over 20 years later in 1972. *Invisible Man,* throughout the 1970s, provided academic defenders of fledgling African American literature specializations a much-needed exemplum of black modernist genius. As the place of these specializations grew more secure, the chorus of commentators who dipped into the book's riches would expand.

Extended studies of African American literature that were published during the 1970s evolved away from the biographical and thematic dynamic evident in books like Edward Margolies's *Native Sons: A Critical Study of Twentieth-Century Negro American Authors* (1968). In place of the older approach, critics were envisioning black literary history through more selective templates. Glimmers of this can be detected in Roger Rosenblatt's *Black Fiction* (1974), where his premise is expressed as follows: "What distinguishes the black character's situation is not that he is oppressed, but that a great part of the nature of his oppression is prescribed by a physical characteristic" (7). Grappling with Ellison's energetic confounding of skin-based prejudice's absurd assumptions, Rosenblatt concludes that *Invisible Man*'s protagonist ultimately realizes that "it was his efforts to make himself seen" that "got him into difficulties." Recognizing this, the narrator will now try to "thrive on invisibility," an attempt that Rosenblatt feels "there is no evidence" to believe will be successful (197). *Black Fiction* connects *Invisible Man* to other texts by African Americans, but it does so not through mere chronology; rather, it tries to situate the book via its affinity to other narrative tendencies and plot devices. This impulse reaches landmark heights in analyses from the late 1970s to the mid-1980s.

If Noel Shraufnagel, in his 1973 study *From Apology to Protest,* charts a movement of black novels from accommodation to militancy, with Ellison's book indicating "that protest can be an integral part of a supreme artistic creation," then later analysts change the terms of the discussion concentrating more emphatically on how *Invisible Man* relates to the broader development of African American narrative (ix-xiv, 87). One of the earliest scholars to position the novel in this more subtle trajectory is Robert Stepto in his classic *From Behind the Veil* (1979). Describing the relationship between prior narratives and how their generic qualities inform later works thereby creating a formal tradition, Stepto argues that "what is narratively new in *Invisible Man*" is "its brave assertion that there is a self and form to be discovered beyond the lockstep linear movement within imposed definitions of reality" (168). This perspective, focusing prominently on the formal logic of Ellison's novel, unlocks some of the most ground-breaking interpretations that will emerge in the twentieth and twenty-first centuries. This chapter will consider those positions at greater length in the "Literary Criticism" section; however, Stepto's unique take on Ellison not only signaled an underexplored dimension of a pivotal text, it also pointed to an ideological contest in African American letters that would reach a fever pitch in the 1980s.

In a review of *Chants of Saints* (1979), a book that Robert Stepto co-edited with Michael Harper, and *From Behind the Veil,* John Edgar Tidwell writes that "both of these books have liberated the study of Afro-American literature from its entanglement in the web of socio-political approaches to the study of literature" (236). Implicitly alluding to the "street scholars and gypsy artists" of 1960s Black Arts Movement literary analysis, Tidwell suggests that "linguistic" interpretations of black literature would better serve not just professional academic advocates, but also the overall under-standing of the works themselves (Wright "Chimed Saints" 218; 236). Tidwell's remarks indicate not only the reemergence of the art versus pro-paganda theme that has intermittently spiced African American literary debate, but also it reveals the specific analytical climate of the early 1980s.

The conflict regarding the appropriate form of black literary criticism is charged with profound questions about the nature of culture and the advisability of accepting interpretive modes that privilege values foreign to those who create the works. *Invisible Man*'s recurrent centrality in these discussions, almost 30 years removed from its publication, is a testament to the revolutionary nature of the novel's narration and its irrefutable status as an urtext of black and American letters.

While Stepto initially exemplified the advisability of probing *Invisible Man*'s form for a commentary on African American identity, one of his colleagues Michael G. Cooke picked up the thread of his thinking in a novel, if alternative way. Cooke, using intimacy or "a sound and clear orientation toward the self and the world" as his index of narrative complexity, argues in *Afro-American Literature in the Twentieth Century* (1984) that *Invisible Man,* while stimulating, ultimately fails because its protagonist overlooks the benefits of community, a sincere engagement with which would lead to a more successful character (x). Thus, the hopefulness that Stepto observes in Ellison's abandonment of linear movement becomes for Cooke a lamentable submission to the broader post–World War II fascination with an abdicating alienation. Two studies in the late 1980s raise serious questions about Cooke's pessimism. Keith Byerman's *Fingering the Jagged Grain* (1985) senses a phenomenological vitality in The narrator's indeterminacy. In fact he believes that the protagonist's resistance of a fixed identity mirrors *Invisible Man*'s rejection of linear narration. These denials, according to Byerman, do not signal betrayal of communal belonging; rather, they point the way towards both a "radically protean" selfhood and a usefully antagonistic mode of expression (Butler xxxiii). For Byerman, this posture is a hallmark of the modernization of black fiction. *In the African-American Grain* (1988), by John Callahan, likewise attends to the ways that *Invisible Man* offers a narrative that is formally ground-breaking; in doing so Callahan persuasively contends that call and response rituals underlie any effective comprehension of what Ellison achieves. His contention is important because it addresses Cooke's anxieties about alienation not with a plot resolution, but with a formal detail. Callahan argues that *Invisible Man* is a testament to Ellison's belief that "the struggle with form is bound up with America" (184). Thus, the protagonist's transformation from an oratorical performer into a writer is not essentially dissociative; rather, it is the necessary prerequisite to his refined "awareness of diversity and complexity, possibility and limitation," the binaries that initiate one into active democratic citizenship (183). Callahan believes that Jack the Bear isolates himself not to "lead his audience but to make contact on an equal individual basis" (182). In many ways, as Callahan's comments on the jazz-inspired posture of the protagonist make clear, this type of connection is more intimate than an unproblematic embrace of solidarity.[1] If Byerman and Callahan deftly express *Invisible Man*'s formal achievements, then Valerie Smith and Henry Louis Gates, Jr., complement their efforts, offering systematic treatments of the novel's narration and bold claims for its literary historical significance.

Valerie Smith's *Self-Discovery and Authority in Afro-American Narrative* (1987) probes the relationship between earlier narrative techniques and the ways that later black artists question and refine these conventions. In her analysis of *Invisible Man,* she is interested in its status as a fictional autobiography and in how Ellison uses that form to explore "the artist's power and responsibility" (90). Acknowledging the controversy over "Ellison's rhetoric of rebellion," Smith nevertheless feels that the protagonist's discovery of how "the act of naming is linked inextricably to issues of power and control" reflects the writer's belief in an artist's transformative potential (90). Where Smith qualifies The narrator's control over this potential, Henry Louis Gates ascribes Ellison an unabated mastery. In *The Signifying Monkey* (1989), Gates argues that a special kind of "formal revision," what he calls "critical signification," is a "metaphor for [African American] literary history" (107). He believes that Ralph Ellison, critiquing disparate earlier writers especially Richard Wright, pioneers "a new manner of representation." Explaining this innovation, he says of Ellison's approach: "I cannot emphasize enough the major import of this narrative gesture to the subsequent development of black narrative forms" (107). Where Michael Cooke's focus on plot and characterization connect the novel's form to existentialist texts, Gates, like Byerman and Callahan, places the book within a dense network of prior African American works and senses a peculiar profundity in Ellison's manipulation of both narrative organization and tropes. That Gates uses such formal concerns as a basis for literary history shifts the ground of analysis considerably. A look at other 1980s estimates of Ralph Ellison and *Invisible Man* illuminate why.

Houston Baker in *The Journey Back* (1980) discusses the ambivalent relationship between "the black writer" and "Western history" (58). For him, Ralph Ellison, along with James Baldwin and Richard Wright, exemplify this tension in mid-twentieth-century America. Describing what he called an "artistic revolution" in the 1950s, Charles T. Davis, in "The Mixed Heritage of the Modern Black Novel" (1979), wrote: "We know now that it is not simply Ellison that we must thank or damn, but Wright and Baldwin too, whose more modest participation must be counted" (324). Bernard Bell reinforced this position in his book *The Afro-American Novel and Its Tradition* (1987):

> In retrospect, then, the most significant development in the tradition of the Afro-American novel between 1952 and 1962 was the rediscovery of myth, legend, and ritual by Ralph Ellison and James Baldwin...Ellison and Baldwin were both influenced by the achievement of Richard Wright in naturalism, but each chose a different approach to the novel. (233)

These statements of Ralph Ellison's importance depend on his accomplishment in *Invisible Man,* and each establishes the novel's significance via a chronological survey. These survey treatments do not ignore the novel's formal attributes; however, they do, in making longitudinal assessments, emphasize the moment of *Invisible Man*'s publication. Gate's approach, while not strictly ahistorical, ignores particularities of 1950s era experiences in favor of constructing a sort of compositional continuum. This trend answers the call for linguistic-centered analyses that Tidwell's review sounded, and it reflects one reaction against the Black Arts Movement's demand for politically activist literary analysis. Although such impulses gained momentum in the late 1980s, the traditional focus on historically informed analyses not only influenced African American literary histories, but also it guided some late 1980s revisions of Anglo-American literary/cultural history.

Concerned that perspectives on 1950s American culture were dominated by images of an idyllic utopia, many commentators in the 1980s cast a critical eye on that decade and presented a counternarrative of what Josh Lukin calls "a monolithic age of oppression" (1; Lukin 1–7). Thus poised between contradictory accounts of an epoch, one defined by "*Happy Days* nostalgia" and the other by a pervasive "dark age with perhaps a single bright spot," revisionist scholars struggled to construct a viable portrait of America's mid-twentieth-century status (Lukin 1, 2). Perhaps quite aptly, *Invisible Man* invariably wiggled into these conversations. In 1988, Lary May edited the collection *Recasting America.* Within that volume, he included the essay "To the Battle Royal: Ralph Ellison and the Quest for Black Leadership in Postwar America" by John S. Wright. Wright's essay engaged Ellison's extended meditation on leadership in *Invisible Man,* and he suggested that this meditation, far from an abstraction, actually dwelled on particulars of the black dilemma in a post–World War II world. For Wright, the mature protagonist's apprehensions about middle-class uplift narratives like those proffered by Bledsoe, Barbee, and even Brother Jack underscores a broader, if still delimited tendency by segments of Anglo-American society to question sanctioned routes to success. That Ellison synchs with this sort of national soul-searching should not be surprising given his bold advocacy for it in his essays; despite this, it takes a work like W. T. Lhamon's *Deliberate Speed* (1990) to suggest the connections of Ellison's efforts to a wider consensus-cracking streak in 1950s America.

Deliberate Speed, echoing the ambitions of Lary May and his compeers, sets out to refute "the usual theory about the 1950s," namely that the decade "lacked serious culture" (1). For W. T. Lhamon, *Invisible Man* joins a set of "apparently disparate," yet "subsequently important" mid-twentieth-century texts that converged around the fact that "they were born fighting the forces ignoring and suppressing them" (6). Thus, Lhamon feels that *Invisible Man*'s motley depictions of half-naked young black pugilists, horse-riding nationalists, and an interracial one-night stand are less abstract tableaus and more so precise engagements of "diverted cultural reflectors" (1). The upshot of this diversion is a deferment of the realization that, as many commentators have argued, the black experience to a marked degree epitomizes American-ness. Capturing Ellison's contribution to American post–World War II existence, Lhamon writes, "*Invisible Man* is the novel that enacted the process of rebirth after the war": it "showed people how to admit their differences from the shibboleths of high modernism," and by championing "the process of rediscovering vernacular shape," the book "showed its characters and its readers how to resume responsible action" (51). If Lhamon looks at *Invisible Man* as a recuperative literary experiment, then Thomas Hill Schaub, situating the novel more rigorously within the socio-intellectual context of post–World War II liberalism, judges it less generously. Charting Ellison's early engagement with leftist organizations and publishing venues, Schaub sees the writer's first novel as mediation on the appropriate role for art in vexing political circumstances. To him Ellison's choice of a "mythic form" for *Invisible Man* not only signals his rejection of "conventionally realistic modes of fiction" but also his embrace of a specific way of critiquing daily sociopolitical realities (Schaub 92; Butler xxxiii). In Schaub's view, Ellison's "radically surrealistic novelistic form" mutes the power of his political commentary, giving it at times an impression of aesthetic indulgence (Butler xxxiii). If Schaub qualifiedly echoes earlier charges of Ellison's ivory-tower political reserve, then Jerry Gafio Watts expansively expresses the belief that *Invisible Man* is compromised by aesthetic conformity and its author's covetousness of social status.

Like the cultural and intellectual historians of the 1980s who debate the contours of the 1950s American spirit, Jerry G. Watts, in *Heroism and the Black Intellectual* (1994), is simultaneously looking at Ralph Ellison the novelist and using Ellison the black thinker as a case study to ponder "antagonistic tendencies," which he terms "the hyperpoliticized" and "the depoliticized," in the execution of early 1990s intellectual criticism (11). While Watts announces in his introduction that he will not "engage in a literary analysis of *Invisible Man,*" his conclusions bear not only on the understanding of that novel, but also on the way that the literary critics who analyze it should be viewed (12). Watts acknowledges the hybrid-ist convictions at the center of Ellison's notion of America; nonetheless, while others view such cultural inter-penetration triumphantly, he argues that Ellison's tenacious assertion of "interracial cultural cross-fertilization within a society in which socially, politically, and economically based ra-cial differences were so distinct may have appeared disingenuous" (13). Thus, Watts's study returns to Tidwell's ruminations on sociopolitical ver-sus linguistic criticism and tries to redeem the efficacy of the former. On one level, the interdisciplinary approach of his work and his American studies affinities explain some of his distrust of purely aesthetic estimates. Still, the deeper challenge in Watts's work is his questioning of the ex-tent to which avant-garde literary critical techniques conceal portions of phenomenon that might otherwise enhance comprehension. To see Ralph Ellison as a writer, Watts believes, one must look upon more than just his texts. The evolution of literary critical studies of *Invisible Man* suggests that such scrutiny is at the very least felicitous.

LITERARY CRITICISM

If one commonplace of literary theory is that lovably diffuse idea, the interpretive community, then *Invisible Man,* over its 55-year history, has prompted diverse neighborhoods to coalesce into a veritable metropolis of interlocking literary analyses. Robert Butler's *The Critical Response to Ralph Ellison* usefully divides the territory into four quadrants: "1) the early reviews, 2) scholarly articles and chapters in books written from the mid-fifties to the mid-sixties, 3) commentary produced from the late sixties to the late seventies, and 4) critical and scholarly work from the early eighties to the present" (xix). The beginning of this chapter mean-dered over all of Butler's divisions, paying particular attention to news-paper and journal reviews of *Invisible Man* and to books or parts of books that in some way illuminated the novel. In this section with a few exceptions, Butler's final category will be engaged, giving equal attention to journal articles, chapters of books, and book-length studies. While the chronological impulse that guides Butler's taxonomy will be honored, this segment unfolds via the recurrent themes that define criticism of *Invisible Man*. To ease access to and digestion of a dizzyingly varied output, the information here is arranged under four headings that reflect these themes: 1) "Folk Redemption"; 2) "Integration Poetics"; 3) "Modernism"; and 4) "Gendered Meditations." Designed to tame an unruly set of approaches and conclusions, these headings, as Butler remarks about his own, should be taken suggestively rather than summarily. They try to reveal signature moments in a nearly 60-year history, and by creating broad categories, they risk oversimplification in an attempt to efficiently direct the reader to the material most relevant to her interest.

FOLK REDEMPTION

Opinions regarding Ellison's use of folk materials in *Invisible Man* begin appearing along with the earliest reviews of the novel. Thus, it is fitting that among the first more capacious readings of the book are several addressing its handling of folklore. Floyd R. Horowitz's "Ralph Ellison's Modern Version of Brer Bear and Brer Rabbit in *Invisible Man*" (1963) presents the protagonist as the easily duped Brer Bear, who through a series of encounters with Brer Rabbits, figured here as Trueblood, the blueprint carrying cartman, Lucius Brockway, and Brother Jack, completes his journey from "rural copse to cosmopolitan forest" (38). This journey pushes the narrator away from "the tradition of Booker T. Washington" and towards "the hypocrisy which alone means survival for the natively talented Negro," a movement that is so disorienting that he "has no choice but to hide" (32, 36, 38). George Kent in "Ralph Ellison and the Afro-American Folk and Cultural Tradition" (1970) argues that more than any one reference, *Invisible Man* presents a "complex" network of "folk and cultural tradition[s]," one replete with "motifs...situations, symbols, and strategic appearances of...blues, spirituals, and...rhymes" (155). The effect of this inclusion is both the novel's capacity to move instantly "into the privacy, tensioned coherence, toughness, terror and beauty of Black experience" and its recognition that the folk's "basic *attitudes* and *forms* of response to existence" are indispensable for "confronting" the fluidity of "darkness" (160, 162). As early as 1966, Larry Neal pointed to Ralph Ellison as a writer who had explored the "possibilities and ramifications" of "Afro-American folk culture" ("The Black Writer's Role" 7–9). By the time he published "Ralph Ellison's Zoot Suit" (1973), Neal had completed a 360 degree turn in his assessment of his elder, and his claims about Ellison's vernacular vestments were even stronger: "Ellison's spiritual roots are...deep in the black American folk tradition" (103). Neal's essay thoroughly unpacks Ellison's depictions of black urban style, figured in *Invisible Man* as zoot-suited youngsters, and shows how such style might be a source of revelatory humanity. The genius of his reading stems from its recognition of Ellison's sensitivity to the black folk's dynamism. Zoot-suited youngsters tie rural impulses to urban exigencies, and Neal, gleaning the purpose of Ellison's defense of individuation, reminds even the originator of this insight that the full-throated, carefree ranging that he exults in should not be stinted in his prescriptions for the next generation of black artists. Ironically, Susan Blake, escalating Neal's gentle chiding to the pitch of his *Black Fire* days, sees several problems with Ellison's folk applications.

In "Ritual and Rationalization: Black Folklore in the Works of Ralph Ellison" (1979), Blake argues that instead of allowing black cultural traditions to retain their own meaning, Ellison alters them by equating them with "similar elements of American or Western mythology" (122). This equation, for Blake, results not in fecund integrationist synthesis but in the pernicious conclusion that "a change in mental context can change social reality" (135). Such thinking is especially damaging because in Blake's mind it suggests that the inequities in black-white relations can be dismissed merely as creations "in the minds of the victims" (135). Blake's apprehension marks one pole of critical anxiety regarding the modernist techniques of Ellison's novel; however, most scholars have seen the cultural blending in *Invisible Man* as commendably cosmopolitan. In particular, their remarks on the novel's folk-tinged musical and oratorical facets reveal profound admiration for Ellison's "almost godlike knowledge of blackness" (Kent 162). A consideration of the criticism treating *Invisible Man*'s deployment of music makes this abundantly clear.

Albert Murray, in *Omni-Americans: Some Alternatives to the Folklore of White Supremacy* (1970), has written that Ellison's *Antioch Review* essay, "Richard Wright's Blues" (1945) opened up what was "represented, symbolized" and "ritualized" in Wright's 1945 autobiography *Black Boy* (161). The tool that Ellison used to pick the lock was the blues, and in his own turn, Murray repeated the favor for his dear friend. He says that "*Invisible Man* was *par excellence* the literary extension of the blues" combining as it did "the naturalistic, the ridiculous, and the downright hallucinatory" (167). Houston A. Baker, in "To Move Without Moving: An Analysis of

Creativity and Commerce in Ralph Ellison's Trueblood Episode" (1983), pushes Murray's assertion to its logical conclusion and beyond. Returning to the uneasy interplay between folklore and "an extant, identifiable tradition of Western literary art," the very combo that gave Susan Blake so much pause, Baker states while "it seems mere evasion to shy from the assertion that Ellison's criticism ranks folklore below literary art," such a "distinction...collapses in his creative practice" (829). For Baker, Ellison's casting of Trueblood as a blues-implicated embracer of his unreformed black masculinity signals an artist who knows "the value of Afro-American folk forms." If Ellison's critical remarks "modify" the significance of black folklore, then in Baker's mind this is mere "merchandise[ing]," an attempt via "skillful" strategizing and speaking "to turn a profit from...monumental creative energies." Such maneuvering places Ellison alongside classic African American performers who tricked out their wares "to make" them "commensurate with a capitalistic marketplace" (843). Baker is not the last critic who sees music and its exigencies as a key to Ellison's art.

Thomas Marvin's "Children of Legba: Musicians at the Crossroads in Ralph Ellison's *Invisible Man*" (1996) presents an Afro-centric analysis of music's function in the novel. Positing the African figure of musical mastery "Papa Legba" as a crucial emblem of Ellison's portrayal of cultural fusion, Marvin argues that "to understand the full importance of musicians as characters" in *Invisible Man,* one should consider how they bridge "liminal sites" in the protagonist's budding consciousness (588). He considers folks like Trueblood, the blueprint-carrying cartman, and Louis Armstrong suggesting that each tutors The protagonist, providing him a model of transcending the "whole sordid history of American race relations" (603). Such transcendence depends on a delicate balancing between swirling cultural energies, a topic that resurfaces in Berndt Ostendorf's article, "Ralph Waldo Ellison: Anthropology, Modernism, and Jazz" (1988). Arguing that "jazz is an example and chief exhibit for Ellison's conception of a pluralist culture," Ostendorf sees this music as the force that resolves Ellison's conflicted allegiance to anthropology and modernism (96). He admits that some commentators think Ellison's subordination of folklore "to the high seriousness of Modernism" robs "it of its antinomian power," yet to Ostendorf, this thinking misses the fact that jazz as an emblem of "black-inspired American culture" effectively mediates the nation's seemingly insurmountable "cultural contradiction" (117). Thanks in part to the ground-clearing positions explored above, the latest analyses of Ellison and music admit the efficacy of the pairing and spend considerably more time placing the exact action of the artist in a clearer light.[2]

Andrew Radford's "The Invisible Music of Ralph Ellison" (2003) concentrates on *Invisible Man*'s allusions to Louis Armstrong. Juxtaposing the figure of Charlie Parker as he emerges in Ellison's jazz criticism and engaging the perils of excess that Rinehart represents, Radford argues that Armstrong embodies for Ellison the ability "to improvise an imaginative response that denies nothing of the force and power of disorder but will affirm" humanity "without supine acquiescence to a numbing stasis" (59). Where Radford captures the jazz that Ellison loves, Kevin Bell's "The Embrace of Entropy: Ralph Ellison and the Freedom Principle of Jazz Invisible" (2003) probes the relationship between Ellison as "a pivotal theorist... of improvisational music" and his aversion to free jazz, a genre that he and his buddy Albert Murray "imagine to be musical nonsense" (23, 24). Bell argues that notwithstanding the novelist's "apparent disdain" for how free jazz stalwarts like Andrew Hill and Sun Ra practice improvisation, his "novelistic work [Bell references only *Invisible Man*] can be argued to set into literary and philosophical motion some of the vital creative impulses that propel the music of free jazz" (25). Veering away from the projective impulse that fuels Bell's argument, two 2004 essays strive to reconstruct the facts and the logic of Ellison's musical debts.

Timothy Spaulding's "Embracing Chaos in Narrative Form: The Bebop Aesthetic in Ralph Ellison's *Invisible Man*" counters the tendency to ascribe only formal and thematic valences to Ellison's use of jazz. For Spaulding, the most specific understanding of music's place in the text emerges when one notes that "the novel is...a product of a particular moment in history and the jazz tradition: the evolution of bebop" (498). Recounting the particulars of Ellison's immersion in bebop, "the form of jazz that achieved the height of its popularity between...1945–1950, the time during which Ellison wrote" *Invisible Man,* Spaulding meticulously connects the conundrum of identity and artistic dignity experienced by bebop musicians to that endured by Ellison's protagonist and by Ellison himself (481). A similar documentary quality defines Steven C. Tracy's "A Delicate Ear, a Retentive Memory, and the Power to Weld Fragments" (2004). Contending that "we should understand Ralph Ellison as a literary artist in the context of musical traditions" namely those associated with "the nationalist nineteenth century Romantic" and the "twentieth-century modernist aesthetics," Tracy, alluding to figures as varied as Antonín Dvořák, Duke Ellington, Louis Armstrong, Ida Cox, and Big Bill Broonzy, chronicles the pantheon from which Ellison's musical sensibilities were hewn and concludes that the writer among other things completed a specific kind of cultural recovery in his novel (90). For Tracy, Ellison's writing reflects a wish "to illuminate the unfathomed world of African American music," a world that had been unduly neglected (111).

While music dominates one node of recent interest in *Invisible Man*'s folkloric content, another important vein is the novel's oratorical depictions. Lloyd W. Brown in "Ralph Ellison's Exhorters: The Role of Rhetoric in *Invisible Man*" (1970) engages the novel's speaking scenes and dividing them into robotic utterances and genuine moments of "self-expression," he lauds the latter as models of the folk's anchoring potential (290). Robert Bataille's "Ellison's *Invisible Man:* The Old Rhetoric and the New" (1978) documents the density of *Invisible Man*'s concern with "rhetorical situation[s]" (43). Cataloging the protagonist's movement from the smoker to the Brotherhood and culminating with remarks on the Provo's eviction, Bataille uses the binary of "old rhetoric (manipulative and deliberate)" and "new rhetoric (spontaneous and candid)" to suggest that the overlapping possibilities of these modes allow the narrator to convince the reader to take the "leap of faith and imagination" that transforms consciousness (43, 45). Dolan Hubbard's chapter, "The Sermon Without Limits and the Limits of the Sermon," (1994) analyzes Ellison's use of the folk preacher and offers perhaps the most comprehensive conclusions about *Invisible Man*'s depictions of oration. Arguing that "the variety of preachers that the nameless narrator encounters attest to the vitality and dynamic character of the sermon in the black community," Hubbard concludes that it is the protagonist's shift from a desire to conceal these cultural purveyors to a commitment to evoke their "culturally rich linguistic tradition," which marks the conjoining of "his vision with the vision of the community" (93, 92). Such a conciliatory view challenges the visions of folklore as a burden, and Darryl Dickson-Carr, in *African American Satire* (2001), shares Hubbard's optimism. While conceding that Ellison's aesthetics are risky, Dickson-Carr, looking in particular at the novelist's engagement of "the bear and the lion in some trickster story cycles," concludes that "*Invisible Man* proved that black folklore and its concomitant ironies and satirical commentaries could and should form the bases for black arts" (101, 110). Dickson-Carr's perspective creates an intriguing portal through which to enter critical contemplations of Ellison's hybrid aesthetics.

INTEGRATION POETICS

The claims about Ralph Ellison's culturally integrated achievements in *Invisible Man* crop up quickly, and as the years pass, their sophistication and their scope increase. Early articles like Earl H. Rovit's "Ralph Ellison and the American Comic Tradition" (1960), Barbara Fass's "Rejection of Paternalism: Hawthorne's 'My Kinsman, Major Molineux' and Ellison's *Invisible Man*" (1971), and Stewart Rodnon's "*The Adventures of Huckleberry Finn* and *Invisible Man:* Thematic and Structural Comparisons" (1972) tie *Invisible Man* to canonical American texts and writers suggesting that not only do they share formal and aesthetic tendencies but also they are bound by a remarkably consistent national ethos. These kinds of treatments are not limited to Anglo-American writers; Ellison's work is rapidly analyzed alongside the leading lights of a broader Western literary continuum. Marcia Lieberman in "Moral Innocents: Ellison's *Invisible Man* and *Candide*" (1971) examines the artistic affinities between Ellison and Voltaire. In "Ralph Ellison's Use of *The Aeneid* in *Invisible Man*" (1974), Charles Scruggs shows that the character of Sybil and the notion of home in Ellison's novel arise from his consideration of Virgil's work. Dostoyevsky's *Notes from Underground* (1864) and *House of the Dead* (1860) show their writer mining and collecting the "richness and depth" of "Russian peasant culture" (Frank 235). For Joseph Frank, who records his thoughts in the article "Ralph Ellison and a Literary 'Ancestor': Dostoevski" (1983), this example provides Ellison both a prestigious and professionally efficacious literary forebear. John S. Wright, Robert O'Meally, and Alan Nadel pioneer even more profound deployments of Ellison's artistic hybridism.

"Dedicated Dreamer, Consecrated Acts: Shadowing Ellison" (1980) is John S. Wright's contribution to a *Carleton Miscellany* issue that followed Brown University's "A Ralph Ellison Festival." Demonstrating systematically the shape of "Ellison's syncretic drive to combine, reconcile, and reintegrate competing cultural realities," Wright explains how T. S. Eliot, André Malraux, Kenneth Burke, Constance Rourke, Alain Locke, and W.E.B. Du Bois, among others, nourish the "pluralist social thought" at the center of Ellison's artistry (155, 165). Wright's remarks signal a rigorous, yet variegated historicizing of Ellison's multicultural intellectual development that continues unabated for the next 25 years. Robert O'Meally's efforts in "The Rules of Magic: Hemingway as Ellison's 'Ancestor'" (1985) show the direct effects of these energies on the analysis of *Invisible Man*. Complete with a thorough synopsis of Ellison's vacillating estimate of Hemingway in his essays, "The Rules of Magic" ultimately turns to Ellison's first novel. In examining that text, O'Meally stresses the relationship between *Invisible Man's* ritualized violence and Hemingway's recurrent presentation of a "heroic attitude toward life's troubles and changes." To O'Meally, the protagonist's endurance of life's bumps and bruises owe a lot to Ellison's admiration of Hemingway's imperturbable sufferers, characters whose "resiliency and steadfastness" Ellison ultimately "would connect with the blues" (247). This identification of a definitive moment of profound cultural collusion consistently crops up in Reagan-Era (1980–1992) analyses of *Invisible Man.* Alan Nadel's book *Invisible Criticism* (1988) is among the most deliberate and sustained attempts to document the intensity of this interplay.

Arguing via "a radical approach to the use of allusion," Nadel suggests that Ellison "consistently and effectively" raises "the issue of canonicity" (xii). Far from an ancillary concern, Ellison's canonical preoccupations are analogues to the separatist absurdity that his protagonist confronts. For Ellison, the slant of vision that occludes the moral significance of blackness in the national discourse surrounding literature is symptomatic of the broader misperception of where African Americans fit into daily life. To address this quandary, he presents, as Nadel terms it, "a novel which achieves" the "literary critical ends" of forcing readers at once to confront both their myopia and the maelstrom of black presence (xiii). As earlier examples in this chapter show, these themes had been sounded before; however, the range of Nadel's execution was unprecedented. Dealing extensively with models and foils as varied as Herman Melville, Mark Twain, Ralph Emerson, and Lewis Mumford, Nadel contends that Ellison's sparring with these participants in and commentators on nineteenth-century American culture not only reflect an "entering . . . into a dialogue with tradition" but also a "revivifying" of "the past by changing it" (150). This contention becomes the foundation of a perspective on Ellison and *Invisible Man* that guides a critical strain of late twentieth-century responses. Just looking at the pieces that focus on *Invisible Man* and Ralph W. Emerson gives a glimpse of what Nadel and his approach portend.

Kun Jong Lee "Ellison's *Invisible Man:* Emersonianism Revised" (1992) explores how "Ellison brings Emerson into his genealogy while subverting and expanding Emersonianism in the process" (342). Emphasizing how "Emerson's transcendentalism" and Ellison's fiction bristle upon contact because both are "steeped in the question of race," Lee believes that too often scholars herald a sort of "Emersonian universalism" in *Invisible Man*'s protagonist without fully appreciating the importance of his "racial identity" (332). This claim echoes earlier fears about Ellison's technique, namely that his penchant for overlaid allusions somehow obscures racial peculiarities in *Invisible Man.* Despite these anxieties, Lee's interpretation is but one example of how deftly scholars have cleared misperceptions and advanced their belief that correctly reading Emerson can help unlock Ellison's artistic methods. James M. Albrecht pursues similar work in "Saying Yes and Saying No: Individualist Ethics in Ellison, Burke, and Emerson" (1999). Refuting the widespread view that Ellison simply engages in a "scathing rejection of Emersonian individualism" (47), Albrecht opines that a fuller assessment would note Ellison's attraction to the "Emerson whose obsession with self-reliance" acknowledges "the political task of exploring the individual's connections to and conflicts with others" (60). Thus, the difference between Emerson as he is chronicled by Lewis Mumford and the evocation that Ellison offers in the Norton and the young Emerson episodes must be attenuated with a careful regard for the protagonist's hole-bound epiphanies about individual responsibility. Albrecht concludes that submission to the satirical momentum of the set pieces distracts from the harder work of precisely parsing the place of Emersonian philosophy in the protagonist's identity.

If juxtaposing Emerson and *Invisible Man* defines one tack in analyzing Ellison's integration poetics, then twenty-first century scholars have also chosen more variegated strategies. Considering the novel's relationship to central political developments in American democracy, a concept that for many captures the most aggressively interracial impulses in Ellison's thinking and his art, several critics have produced nuanced perspectives on *Invisible Man*. Kenneth Warren in *So Black and Blue* (2003) thoughtfully ponders whether *Invisible Man* is a document "of civilization written precisely to expose and denounce history's barbarisms" (5). While such a function would generate no stint of admiration, Warren wonders whether "*Invisible Man*'s eloquent evocations of the particularities of race in midtwentieth-century America" lost their "resonance" as civil rights era gains quickened (4). *So Black and Blue* concludes that the philosophical capaciousness of Ellison's novel preserves its profundity; nevertheless, Warren believes that the enduring significance of the work also owes much to the fact that Ellison was around to manage its reception for over 40 years after its publication. *Ralph Ellison and the Raft of Hope: A Political Companion to Invisible Man* (2004), a collection of 12 essays edited by Lucas E. Morel, exemplifies several major tendencies in sociopolitical analysis of *Invisible Man*. Touching on topics as varied as the novel's relationship to *Brown v. Board of Education* (1954), its meditations on democratic citizenship, and its depictions of political power, these commentaries synthesize trends that began swirling in the 1990s, and they poignantly capture the contemporary tendency to redeem Ellison's assertion that at base his novel seeks to recall interracial democracy to its loftiest possibilities. If a domestic emphasis prevails in certain estimates of Ellison's integrationist efforts, then the critical interest in *Invisible Man*'s modernist pedigree lends a distinctly global dimension.

MODERNISM

With its prominent use of dream scenes and stream of consciousness narration, *Invisible Man* instantly inspired critical comparisons that evoked modernism, usually via a reference to psychological interiority. Lynn M. Grow's "The Dream Scenes of Invisible Man" (1974) and Robert E. Abrams's "The Ambiguities of Dreaming in Ralph Ellison's *Invisible Man*" (1978) are two early examples of this trend. Other observers interested in the novel's modernist lineage examined its dense allusions. Remarking a stylistic affinity between Ellison and other American modernists like Stephen Crane, William Faulkner, and Ernest Hemingway, critics mostly in passing suggested the rich effects of his experiments with pastiche and bricolage. By the 1980s, these casual references were giving way to full blown considerations of how *Invisible Man* continued and re-imagined the formal experiments and moral meanderings of writers as disparate as T. S. Eliot, Franz Kafka, Gertrude Stein, and James Joyce. Recurrent foci in these examinations were psychoanalysis and the representation of consciousness. In the 1990s, a focus on visuality joined psychoanalytic concerns, giving rise to a view of *Invisible Man* as a technically accomplished novel that ratifies the insights of towering European intellectuals like Mikhail Bakhtin and Michel Foucault. On one level, these readings could be viewed as extensions of the integration poetics that were mentioned in the prior section. They nonetheless deserve discrete chronicling both because of how voluminous they have become and also because of the crucial transnational energy that they bring to the critical engagement of *Invisible Man.* This section will consider modernist views of Ellison via psychoanalytical and visual studies readings.

Philip Brian Harper's "'To Become One and Yet Many': Psychic Fragmentation and Aesthetic Synthesis in Ralph Ellison's *Invisible Man*" (1989) is an attempt "to situate *Invisible Man* squarely within the problematic of literary modernism" (682). Alluding to Georg Lukacs and Frederic Jameson, pivotal theorists of modern subjectivity, Harper contends that Ellison's depiction of "the essential dividedness...and, hence, *specificity* of black experience" rejects the notion that such fragmentation "poses the primary threat to black identity"; rather, the greater risk is an evasion of complexity that mistakenly posits "black culture's simpleness" (699). Harper's optimistic view of psychic fragmentation not only acknowledges Ellison's belief in diversity's edifying principle but also in aesthetic terms it shows that *Invisible Man*'s representational strategies, while resembling those of certain white Western artists, serve a decidedly black purpose. William Lynne in "The Signifying Modernist: Ralph Ellison and the Limits of the Double Consciousness" (1992) returns to this consideration of the ultimate significance of Ellison's modernist tendencies. Lynne notes that Ellison's "trafficking in the motifs and artistic techniques of the Euro-American literary tradition" afford him tremendous power, yet he also admits that these aesthetics have "attracted continual and vociferous criticism" (320). Concluding that critical observations about Ellison's relationship to modernist impulses have erroneously been viewed as strictly laudatory, Lynne argues that Ellison "uses the strategy of African American vernacular signifying and the blues to turn modernism back on itself and show its blindness to the social and economic circumstances of oppression" (329). This position synchs with Harper's belief in Ellison's redemptive appropriation of the Western master's tools, but for Lynne modernism also marks Ellison and *Invisible Man* as testaments to entrapment. Although signifying and the blues can point to ailment, in Lynne's opinion, they are ineffective remedies for such sickness.

In contrast to those who see Ralph Ellison and *Invisible Man* as irrefutably ensconced "in the modernist tradition," Robert Genter's "Toward a Theory of Rhetoric: Ralph Ellison, Kenneth Burke, and the Problem of Modernism" (2002) suggests that Ellison and his novel were less modernist and "much closer to the tradition of American pragmatism" (193, 195). Appealing to Kenneth Burke and his rhetorical theories, Genter claims that *Invisible Man* strives to "overcome the depoliticized character of postwar modernism without falling into the trap of social realism" (195). Implicit in Genter's argument is a belief that Ellison must be delivered from modernism. Unlike Harper and Lynne who proffer Ellison's formal experiments as a resourceful harnessing of modernism's apparatus, Genter consistently rebuffs attempts to tie Ellison's use of folklore, especially the blues and by extension dense allusion or even allegory, to anything other than a practical rhetoric that affirms "a common humanity and a common political faith amidst cultural, racial, and ethnic differences" (211). If his interpretation forecloses some expressions of modernism's hold on *Invisible Man,* then the visual studies readings of the novel return quite vigorously to identifying and examining the aesthetic jousts at its center.

A host of early responses to *Invisible Man* remark upon the ingenuity of its central metaphor, invisibility. Charles Glicksberg's "The Symbolism of Vision" (1954), Alice Bloch's "Sight Imagery in *Invisible Man*" (1966), and

A. Robert Lee's "Sight and Mask: Ralph Ellison's *Invisible Man*" (1970) are strong indications of this propensity. Notwithstanding these examples, it is not until the twenty-first century that critics emphatically take up the fertile cues regarding visuality offered by Robert Stepto (175–178). Karen Jacobs in the chapter "One-Eyed Jacks and Three-Eyed Monsters: Visualizing Embodiment in Ralph Ellison's *Invisible Man*" (2001) examines how Ellison uses "the trope of invisibility" to link "subjective transcendence" and "the representational world of social conditions" (148). According to Jacobs, Ellison's use of invisibility "takes its bearings…from a range of discourses largely contemporary with the novel"; nevertheless, like "a characteristic modernist," Ellison has a "manifest stake in the myth of the isolated man of genius" (148, 149). Thus, he cloaks his technique behind a narrative of "individual invention," offering readers only glimpses of "his eclectic assimilation of intellectual resources, many European in origin" (148, 149). Jacobs carefully examines how Ellison's invisibility engages key elements of folklore, the philosophy of Ralph Waldo Emerson, and the existentialism of Jean Paul Sartre. Revealing how these tools enabled Ellison to reject the limitations of sociology, she argues that while he escapes documentary circumscription, Ellison and his protagonist still evade "the real challenges to African-American political and cultural agency," namely the successful situation of "the self within the collectivities of race and nation" (198). Where Jacobs sees Ellison's manipulation of invisibility in *Invisible Man* as only partially effective, Hsuan Hsu sees greater efficacy in the novel's visual politics.

In "Regarding Mimicry: Race and Visual Ethics in *Invisible Man*" (2003), Hsu explores how Ellison questions the logic of "the racial gaze," a term which Herman Beavers designates as a "mode of voyeurism" that perpetuates racist assumptions by fixing blacks in an inescapable frame (qtd. in Hsu 107). Contending that Ellison sees the gaze as a ruse meant to reify racial division, Hsu suggests that instead of accepting the "fixed terms of identity politics," *Invisible Man* posits "an ethics of visuality" motivated by "heterogeneous alliances" (108). Hsu's argument alludes liberally to Jacques Lacan, Frantz Fanon, and Homi Bhahba, and he puts these theorists' conception of the gaze in conversation with Ralph Ellison's own evocation of the privileged looker, the little man at Chehaw Station. Insisting that the little man is one model of the productive or "enabling" gaze, Hsu suggests that this sort of seeing allows the individual to "discover and participate in potentially transformative collectivities" (131). Kimberly Lamm's "Visuality and Black Masculinity in Ralph Ellison's *Invisible Man* and Romare Bearden's Photomontages" (2003) while stating Ellison's awareness of the "impediments to remaking visual representations of the black male" also affirms *Invisible Man*'s success in "reconfiguring" the effects of racism on black manhood (813). Describing how the novel "map[s] and sketch[es] screens of vision that the eyes of black men look within and across in order to forge perceptions and images of themselves," the essay focuses on Tod Clifton's relationship with the Sambo doll arguing that this characterization includes a "play with the external 'scaffolding' of black masculinity" (815, 832). Lamm believes that Ellison's portrayal of Clifton "attests to the role visual art can play" in "developing a malleable perceptual apparatus" that fruitfully registers black manhood in America (832). Another account of visual art's role in *Invisible Man* is on display in Sara Blair's "Ellison, Photography, and the Origins of Invisibility" (2005).

Declaring that photography just as much as jazz or the blues influences the narrative strategies of *Invisible Man,* Blair establishes the scope of Ellison's interest in picture-taking and the elaborate ways in which his text "riff[s] on photographic history and effect" (67). Connecting the documentary facets of photography to its more self-conscious reflection on how images are created, she concludes that the "double understanding of documentary images, as both a source for devastating misrepresentations of black Americans and a resource for combating it, helps explain how the visual genre that Ellison at times so powerfully critiques remains central to his self-imagination as a writer" (65). Blair reinforces these claims with readings of the Provos' eviction and the figure of the mannequin that emerges in the riot that closes *Invisible Man.* By charting an arc from "the fact of documentary eye-witnessing to a more complex form of self-expression," these scenes to Blair reveal both Ellison's "subtle appropriations" of "post-war photography['s] . . . imagery" and the more sympathetic contours of his "controversial commitment to an Afro-Euro-American aesthetic" (71, 78). If, as Blair's allusion to controversy suggests, judgments of Ellison's modernist experiments vacillate between indictment and approval, lately tipping decidedly towards the latter, then the critical evaluation of *Invisible Man*'s depictions of women may be if anything more tempestuous.

GENDERED MEDITATIONS

Carolyn Sylvander's "Ralph Ellison's *Invisible Man* and Female Stereotypes" (1975) levels the charge that "both Black and white female characters in *Invisible Man* reflect the distorted stereotypes established by the white American male" (77). Alluding to Ellison's analysis of stereotyping in *Shadow and Act,* Sylvander scrutinizes his portrayals of the blonde at the smoker, Mary Rambo, Emma, and Sybil and determines that these women, in contradiction of Ellison's own admonitions about successful characters, "operate as nothing more than symbol" (79). For Sylvander, these females exemplify the very dehumanization that *Invisible Man* ostensibly exposes and resists. Counseling that such a reading may miss "what lies hidden beneath the mask," Claudia Tate in "Notes on the Invisible Women in Ralph Ellison's *Invisible Man*" (1987) contends that even if the novel's women appear stereotypical, then it does not follow that they do not promote an awareness of the "broader aspects of the humanity of all of us" (163). She embellishes this position by claiming that "like the underground station masters of the American slave era...female characters assist the Invisible Man along his course to freedom" (164). Looking at the same cast as Sylvander with the addition of "the old slave woman in the Prologue" and "the anonymous, rich white woman" who seduces the narrator, Tate argues that the protagonist's interactions with these victimized women "force him to recognize" that he shares their "plight" (165, 169, 164). This recognition does not mean that he will leave "the inanimate womb of the underground"; however, Tate believes that his richer purpose may be to deliver a message about the infectiousness of "utter and devastating disillusionment" (171). Although Tate's sentiments momentarily shift the debate about Ellison's gender dynamics, two late 1980s articles forcefully express a feminist censure and an allegorical potential that holds for the next decade.

Mary Rohrberger's "'Ball the Jack': Surreality, Sexuality, and the Role of Women in *Invisible Man*" (1989) reasserts the legitimacy of Sylvander's critique and suggests that *Invisible Man*'s preoccupation with fathers and sons overwhelms its scant interest in women. Frankly diagnosing this situation, she states, "Nowhere in [the novel] is there a woman not characterized as automaton-prostitute or mother" (130). Hortense Spillers in "'The Permanent Obliquity of an In(pha)llibly Straight': In the Time of the Daughters and the Fathers" (1989) implicitly assesses Rohrberger's premise via an analysis of incest in the Trueblood episode. Although Spillers notes that Kate and Matty Lou "are deprived of speech," her suggestion that their silence may be a convention of "incest fiction" complicates any attempt to read her argument as merely an indictment of Ellison's portrayal (235). In fact she seems to conclude that this scene, with its complicated figurations of Matty Lou as a prophylactic, a protean signifier of her father's interracial fantasies, and as ultimately "a different and informing femininity," teaches the protagonist the limits of phallic signification (241, 242). Spiller's wary recourse to Freudian interrogation and her daring verve in reading Ellison's deployment of female bodies anticipates the most recent directions in gender-centered interpretations of *Invisible Man;* still, it is her emphasis on silencing that is taken up anew by Ann Folwell Stanford.

Stanford in "He Speaks for Whom?: Inscription and Reinscription of Women in *Invisible Man* and *The Salt Eaters*" (1993) states that "both black and white female characters throughout the novel are constructed along a spectrum that replicates the classic duality embodied in representations of women—madonna or whore, mother or seductress" (20). Considering the motley array of females that *Invisible Man* distributes under this binary, Stanford concludes that "it is...Mary Rambo, who stands out as the only positively memorable woman character" (21). That Mary's fuller presence in the novel was cut from the final draft indicates for Stanford "the terrain of absence, silence, or invisibility that inheres" in *Invisible Man's* "gender bias" (24). Laura Doyle's chapter "Burning down the House: Interruptive Narrative in *Invisible Man*" (1994) strives to make the significance of black women's silencing more obvious. Focusing on his interactions with race mothers, figures who represent "a bodily and collective past," Doyle argues that the protagonist wants "to leave behind all racial mythologies and in doing so" gain the ability to "speak as an 'individual,' not as a race brother or race son" (6, 175). While this intention is preeminent, the protagonist and Ralph Ellison in Doyle's view manifest "a complex self-consciousness" regarding their projects (187). If the protagonist's encounter with the old slave woman in the Prologue inscribes his determination to submerge "the story of the black mother figure's rape," then Ellison's portrayal of recurrent engulfing "mother narratives" like those evident in the Trueblood and Mary interludes reveal not only an awareness of the tenacity of those narratives' demands, but also an "ambivalence" regarding what identification with a white male world at the cost of "a genuine intimacy with black women" might mean (188). Thus, in a complication of Tate's view, Doyle believes that the protagonist's interplay with a series of women is crucial and that Ellison's depictions while tinged with the outlines of types reveals the complicated place of women in the narrator's attempt to negotiate individual identity while managing the complicated obligations of race and gender. This reading establishes a posture towards women's interlocutory role in the protagonist's development that resurfaces in two twenty-first-century analyses.

James Smethhurst's "'Something Warmly, Infuriatingly Feminine': Gender, Sexuality, and the Works of Ralph Ellison" (2004) revisits *Invisible*

Man's portrayals of females and concludes that while "there are really no fully positive representations of women... in it," the "ideological and artistic project of the book" makes women "absolutely central" (117, 138). This oxymoronic statement is plausible for Smethhurst because the protagonist's "heroism relies on strangely dependent relationships with... women that are both mothering and murderous" (137). Although the narrator ultimately "rejects [these] relationships," they are pivotal aids in his preparation to "liberate" himself (138). "Female Iconography in *Invisible Man*" (2005) by Shelly Eversley demonstrates exactly how the book's women provide that preparation. Convinced that critics should read "the debased iconography of women in the novel" as "vivid renderings of the logic of invisibility," Eversley argues that "Ellison purposefully crafts female presences in the novel so that, on first glance, readers only see a form without substance, highly visible objects without meaningful significance" (173, 180). Prodding the reader and the protagonists towards "closer scrutiny," the novelist makes these women vehicles for "a cogent lesson in illumination," an illumination that depends on "discomfort" to deliver its "revelation of truth" (180). Eversley addresses the blond at the smoker, Matty Lou and Kate from the Trueblood episode, Mary, "the woman framed by the Renoir," and Sybil, yet it is the protagonist's reaction to the "gingham pinafore-d" woman atop the "milk wagon" that signals his recognition of "the poignancy of ambivalence and contradiction" (185). His ability to read beyond her status as a "symbolic mammy" indicates his mature awareness not just of her own complexity but also his own. This according to Eversley is the ultimate purpose of Ellison's female iconography.

The tentacles of *Invisible Man*'s reception persistently outstrip containment; thus, a word about two previously unmentioned strands in reactions to the novel is in order here. The first regards discussions of the book's Communist themes. Although Donald B. Gibson's chapter "Ralph Ellison's *Invisible Man:* The Politics of Retreat" (1981) presents a decidedly Marxist perspective, it is not until the late 1990s that the specifics of Ellison's depictions of Communism are fully engaged (59–60, 93–94). Barbara Foley's "The Rhetoric of Anticommunism in *Invisible Man*" (1997), "Roads Taken and Not Taken: Post-Marxism, Antiracism, and Anticommunism" (1998), and "From Communism to Brotherhood: The Drafts of *Invisible Man*" (2003) all burnish the author's position that *Invisible Man*'s depiction of the Brotherhood may reflect Ellison "deliberately ascending—and helping to steer—the anti-communist bandwagon" ("Rhetoric" 532). For Foley, as her research in "Reading Redness: Politics and Audience in Ralph Ellison's Early Short Fiction" (1999) and

"Ralph Ellison as a Proletarian Journalist" (1998–1999) makes clear, this development acquires even greater poignancy when one considers that the young Ralph Ellison manifested considerable sympathy for the Communist Party. Jesse Wolfe, ignoring Foley's offerings, enters this discussion with "'Ambivalent Man': Ellison's rejection of Communism" (2000), a meditation on Hegel, Reinhold Niebhur, and Ellison and Wright's ironic portrayal of the Communist Party's reenactment of "old forms of oppression" and "new forms of discord" (622). Brian Roberts's "Reading Ralph Ellison: Synthesizing the CP and the NAACP" (2004) announces itself on one level as a "counterpoint" to Foley in its stressing of the continuity "between Ellison's Cold War era novel *Invisible Man* and his early proletarian story 'A Party Down at the Square,' which Ellison wrote in the late 1930s" (89). While Roberts enters the additional claim that he admires Foley's "acutely argued and meticulously researched scholarship," his salvo nonetheless inspired a rejoinder from Foley, "Ralph Ellison, Intertextuality, and Biographical Criticism: An Answer to Brian Roberts" (2004), that emphatically defends the legitimacy of her position. William J. Maxwell's "'Creative and Cultural Lag': The Radical Education of Ralph Ellison" (2004) ponders how Ellison's sojourn in "Harlem Communism" reasserts itself in key aspects of "*Invisible Man*'s pointed deliberations on time and history" (82, 79). Acknowledging certain "strengths" in Foley's contentions, Maxwell nevertheless argues that far from perceiving "a presumptive isolation of Ellison's radical and liberal careers" as Foley does, he senses in the prologue's comments on time and the image of a trio of zoot-suited boys a fusion of "the radical and liberal Ellisons" (79, 80).

A second recent development involves *Invisible Man*'s appearance in queer studies theory. *Blacks in Eden* (1996) by J. Lee Greene is not predominantly concerned with sexuality, still it stands as one of the earliest sustained attempts to read the Emerson Jr. episode in explicitly homosexual terms. Green concludes that Ellison's portrayal of Emerson Jr. "the feminized white male" intersects with a broader "counteroffensive" in mid- twentieth-century black novels (219, 222). To oppose the "Negrophobic discourse that projected the black male as a sex-crazed brute mono-maniacally driven to rape white women," Ellison drawing on Freud, Whitman, and Twain, sketched a homoerotic scene that dramatized the proliferate circulation of horror in the American psyche (222). Probing this horror more meticulously, Daniel Y. Kim's "Invisible Desires: Homoerotic Racism and its Homophobic Critique in Ralph Ellison's *Invisible Man*" (1997) applauds the book's exposition of the "specifically erotic gratification" that white men elicit "from their racist practices" (309). Despite this

Kim see in the novel's "disturbingly homophobic symbolism" a problematic figure of "racial subordination" (309). Specifically, Kim argues that the battle royal and the unincluded excerpt "Out of the Hospital and Under the Bar" exemplify Ellison's homophobic explanation of white male racism, namely that "white men seek to subordinate black men" so that they can "use the black male body to" fulfill an "essentially homosexual" eroticism (324). Pointing to strengths in Kim's interpretation, Douglass Steward in "The Illusions of Phallic Agency: *Invisible* Man, *Totem and Taboo,* and the Santa Claus Surprise" (2003) nevertheless concludes that "Ellison's novel demonstrates something more complex and salutary than 'homophobic logic'" (525). The protagonist's colloquy with young Emerson, in particular its use of Freud's *Totem and Taboo* (1913) along with the Sybil scene, cause Steward to assert that while "the abjection of women and homosexuals" initially seems a route to a more "endurable" existence for the protagonist, Jack the Bear eventually discards this route, recognizing it as "a myth on the order of Santa Claus" (533). Roderick A. Ferguson in *Aberrations in Black: Toward a Queer of Color Critique* (2004) looks at a discarded Woodridge scene from *Invisible Man* and argues that it "critiques sociology and literature as sites of knowledge production about African Americans" (54). This critique extends then to "formations of sexuality, racialization, and citizenship" because just as national unity "pressures subjects to conform" politically, it also encourages them to submit to "the sexual ideals of the nation" (55, 56). Complicating an idea that he introduced in 1997, Kim produced a full-length study *Writing Manhood in Black and Yellow: Ralph Ellison, Frank Chin, and the Literary Politics of Identity* (2005) that fuses queer studies interest and the sort of comparative energy that inspired *Invisible Man*'s relevance to postcolonial studies.[3]

Taken together, this chapter's rendering of the many wending avenues in *Invisible Man*'s reception bespeak both the chaos and the creativity that the book unleashes. Such madcap adventure would no doubt delight the novel's progenitor given his penchant for recurrent depictions of riotous behavior. Still, the joy of indeterminacy remains a transcendent staple of both Ellison's and *Invisible Man*'s personalities. Given this fact, the vexations of the novel will multiply, and one can be sure that there will ever be game pursuers of its evanescent truths.

NOTES

1. Callahan, describing the musical interplay between one and many, writes that "A jazz group achieves its full effect only if the musicians test each other's

skill and, through improvisation explore the full range of each member's un-
tapped potentialities" (154). For him, this situation explains Ellison's notion of
democratic citizenship. Only by allowing each citizen to possess and perform his
individual potential can the nation achieve its most audacious incarnation.

　　2. One other example of jazz in *Invisible Man* emerging as a terrain of ideological wrangling is James M. Harding's chapter "Adorno, Ellison, and the Critique of Jazz" (1997). There, Harding posits "a surprising correlation between the
attitudes of the narrator in Ellison's novel and of Adorno in his criticism of jazz"
(98). This is significant in part because Adorno's controversial views on jazz had
often fueled accusations that he was a racist. By linking Adorno to the *Invisible
Man*'s narrator and Ellison, Harding strives to redeem the philosopher from indictment as a "cultural elitist," an activity not too far removed from the crucial
activities of Ellison apologists (116).

　　3. For a sampling of critics who do comparative work on postcolonial literature and *Invisible Man,* see Tang Soo Ping's "Ralph Ellison and K. S. Maniam:
Ethnicity in America and Malaysia, Two Kinds of Invisibility" (1993) and Judith
Tabron's *Postcolonial Literature from Three Continents: Tutuola, H. D., Ellison,
and White* (2003).

WORKS CITED

Abrams, Robert E. "The Ambiguities of Dreaming in Ralph Ellison's *Invisible
　　Man.*" *American Literature* 49 (1978): 592–603.
Albrecht, James M. "Saying Yes and Saying No: Individualist Ethics in Ellison,
　　Burke, and Emerson." *PMLA* 114 (1999): 46–63.
Baker, Houston A., Jr. "Failed Prophet and Falling Stock: Why Ralph Ellison was
　　Never Avant-Garde." *Stanford Humanities Review* 7.1 (1999): 25 pars. July 25,
　　2007 <http://www.stanford.edu/group/SHR/7–1/html/baker.html>.
———. *The Journey Back: Issues in Black Literature and Criticism.* Chicago:
　　U of Chicago P, 1980.
———. "To Move Without Moving: An Analysis of Creativity and Commerce in
　　Ralph Ellison's Trueblood Episode." *PMLA* 98 (1983): 828–845.
Barksdale, Richard. "Critical Theory and Problems of Canonicity in African
　　American Literature." *Praisesong of Survival: Lectures and Essays, 1957–
　　1989.* Urbana: U of Illinois P, 1992. 32–40.
Bataille, Robert. "Ellison's *Invisible Man:* The Old Rhetoric and the New." *Black
　　American Literature Forum* 12 (1978): 43–45.
Bell, Bernard. *The Afro-American Novel and Its Tradition.* Amherst: U of Mas-
　　sachusetts P, 1987.
Bell, Kevin. "The Embrace of Entropy: Ralph Ellison and the Freedom Principle
　　of Jazz Invisible." *boundary 2* 30 (Summer 2003): 21–45.
Bellow, Saul. "Man Underground." 1952. *Ralph Ellison: A Collection of Critical
　　Essays.* Ed. John Hersey. Englewood Cliffs, NJ: Prentice-Hall, 1974. 27–30.

Benston, Kimberly, ed. *Speaking for You: The Vision of Ralph Ellison.* Washington, DC: Howard UP, 1987.

Berry, Abner W. "Ralph Ellison's Novel *Invisible Man* Shows Snobbery, Contempt for Negro People." Rev. of *Invisible Man* by Ralph Ellison. *Daily Worker* June 1, 1952: 7.

Blair, Sara. "Ellison, Photography, and the Origins of Invisibility." Posnock 56–81.

Blake, Susan. "Ritual and Rationalization: Black Folklore in the Works of Ralph Ellison." *PMLA* 94 (1979): 121–136.

Bloch, Alice. "Sight Imagery in *Invisible Man.*" *English Journal* 55 (November 1966): 1019–1021.

Bone, Robert. *The Negro Novel in America.* 1958. Rev. edition. New Haven: Yale UP, 1965.

Brown, Lloyd. "The Deep Pit." Rev. of *Invisible Man* by Ralph Ellison. June 1952. Butler 31-33.

Brown, Lloyd W. "Ralph Ellison's Exhorters: The Role of Rhetoric in *Invisible Man.*" *CLA Journal* 13 (March 1970): 289–303

Butler, Robert, ed. *The Critical Response to Ralph Ellison.* Westport: Greenwood, 2000.

Callahan, John F. *In the African American Grain: The Pursuit of Voice in Twentieth Century Black Fiction.* Urbana: U of Illinois P, 1988.

Cartwright, Marguerite D. "S.P.D.N.M." *Amsterdam News* March 7, 1953: 14.

———. "The Neurotic Negro." *Amsterdam News* March 14, 1953: 16.

Cleaver, Eldridge. *Soul on Ice.* 1968. New York: Laurel, 1992.

Cooke, Michael G. *Afro-American Literature in the Twentieth Century: The Achievement of Intimacy.* New Haven: Yale UP, 1984.

Covo, Jacqueline. *The Blinking Eye: Ralph Waldo Ellison and His American, French, German, and Italian Critics, 1952–1971.* Metuchen, NJ: Scarecrow, 1974.

Davis, Arthur P. "Integration and Race Literature." 1956. *Black Voices: An Anthology of Afro-American Literature.* Ed. Abraham Chapman. New York: Mentor, 1968.

Davis, Charles T. "The Mixed Heritage of the Modern Black Novel." *Black is the Color of the Cosmos: Essays on Afro-American Literature and Culture, 1942–1981.* Ed. Henry Louis Gates, Jr. New York: Garland, 1982. 313–328.

Dickson-Carr, Darryl. *African American Satire: The Sacredly Profane Novel.* Columbia: U of Missouri P, 2001.

Doyle, Laura. "Burning down the House: Interruptive Narrative in *Invisible Man.*" *Bordering on the Body: The Racial Matrix of Modern Fiction and Culture.* New York: Oxford UP, 1994. 174–205.

Dupee, F. W. "On 'Invisible Man.'" *Chicago Sunday Sun-Times Book Week* September 26, 1965: 4, 26–27.

Eversley, Shelly. "Female Iconography in *Invisible Man*." Posnock 172–187.

Fass, Barbara. "Rejection of Paternalism: Hawthorne's 'My Kinsman, Major Molineux' and Ellison's *Invisible Man*." *CLA Journal* 14 (Spring 1971): 317–323.

Ferguson, Roderick A. *Aberrations in Black: Toward a Queer of Color Critique.* Minneapolis: U of Minnesota P, 2004.

Fiedler, Leslie. *Love and Death in the American Novel.* 1960. 2nd ed. New York: Anchor-Doubleday, 1992.

Foley, Barbara. "From Communism to Brotherhood: The Drafts of Invisible Man." *Left of the Color Line: Race, Radicalism, and Twentieth-Century Literature of the United States.* Eds. Bill V. Mullen and James Smethhurst. Chapel Hill: U of North Carolina P, 2003. 163–82.

———. "Ralph Ellison as Proletarian Journalist." *Science and Society* 62 (1997): 24 pars. Aug. 1, 2007 <http://victorian.fortunecity.com/holbein/439/bf/foleyreleft2.html>.

———. "Ralph Ellison, Intertextuality, and Biographical Criticism: An Answer to Brian Roberts." *JNT: Journal of Narrative Theory* 34 (2004): 229–257.

———. "Reading Redness: Politics and Audience in Ralph Ellison's Early Short Stories." *JNT: Journal of Narrative Theory* 29 (1999): 323–339.

———. "The Rhetoric of Anticommunism in *Invisible Man*." *College English* 59 (1997): 530–547.

———. "Roads Not Taken and Not Taken: Post-Marxism, Antiracism, and Anticommunism." *Cultural Logic* 1.2 (Spring1998): 11 pars. July 26, 2007 <http://clogic.eserver.org/1–2/foley.html>.

Frank, Joseph. "Ralph Ellison and a Literary 'Ancestor': Dostoevski." 1983. Benston 231–244.

Fuller, Hoyt. "A Survey: Black Writers' Views on Literary Lions and Values." *Negro Digest* Jan. 1968: 11–27.

Gates, Henry Louis, Jr. *The Signifying Monkey: A Theory of African-American Literary Criticism.* New York: Oxford UP, 1988.

Gayle, Addison. *The Way of the New World: The Black Novel in America.* Garden City, NJ: Anchor, 1975.

Genter, Robert. "Toward a Theory of Rhetoric: Ralph Ellison, Kenneth Burke, and the Problem of Modernism." *Twentieth Century Literature* 48 (Summer 2002): 191–214.

Gibson, Donald B. "Ralph Ellison's *Invisible Man:* The Politics of Retreat." *The Politics of Literary Expression: A Study of Major Black Writers.* Westport: Greenwood, 1981. 59–98.

Glicksberg, Charles. "The Symbolism of Vision." 1954. Reilly 48–55.

Greene, J. Lee. *Blacks in Eden: The African American Novel's First Century.* Charlottesville: UP of Virginia, 1996.

Grow, Lynn M. "The Dream Scenes of Invisible Man." *Wichita State University Bulletin* 50.3 (1974): 3–13.

Harding, James M. "Adorno, Ellison, and the Critique of Jazz." *Adorno and "A Writing of Ruins": Essays on Modern Aesthetics and Anglo-American Literature and Culture.* Albany: SUNY P, 1997. 97–116.

Harper, Philip Brian. "'To Become One and Yet Many': Psychic Fragmentation and Aesthetic Synthesis in Ralph Ellison's *Invisible Man.*" *Black American Literature Forum* 23 (Winter 1989): 681–700.

Horowitz, Floyd. "Ralph Ellison's Modern Version of Brer Bear and Brer Rabbit in *Invisible Man.*" 1963. Reilly 32–38.

Hsu, Hsuan. "Regarding Mimicry: Race and Visual Ethics in *Invisible Man.*" *Arizona Quarterly* 59.2 (Summer 2003): 107–140.

Hubbard, Dolan. "The Sermon Without Limits and the Limits of the Sermon: *Invisible Man.*" *The Sermon and the African American Literary Imagination.* Columbia: U of Missouri P, 1994. 64–93.

Jacobs, Karen. "One-Eyed Jacks and Three-Eyed Monsters: Visualizing Embodiment in Ralph Ellison's *Invisible Man.*" *The Eye's Mind: Literary Modernism and Visual Culture.* Ithaca: Cornell UP, 2001. 145–199.

Kent, George. "Ralph Ellison and the Afro-American Folk and Cultural Tradition." 1970. *Blackness and the Adventure of Western Culture.* Chicago: Third World, 1972. 152–163.

Kim, Daniel Y. "Invisible Desires: Homoerotic Racism and its Homophobic Critique in Ralph Ellison's *Invisible Man.*" *Novel* 30 (Spring 1997): 309–328.

———. *Writing Manhood in Black and Yellow: Ralph Ellison, Frank Chin, and the Literary Politics of Identity.* Stanford: Stanford UP, 2005.

Lamm, Kimberly. "Visuality and Black Masculinity in Ralph Ellison's *Invisible Man* and Romare Bearden's Photomontages." *Callaloo* 26 (2003): 813–835.

Lee, A. Robert. "Sight and Mask: Ralph Ellison's *Invisible Man.*" *Negro American Literature Forum* 4 (March 1970): 22–33.

Lee, Kun Jong. "Ellison's *Invisible Man:* Emersonianism Revised." *PMLA* 107 (March 1992): 331–344.

Lhamon, W. T., Jr. *Deliberate Speed: The Origins of a Cultural Style in the American 1950s.* Washington, DC: Smithsonian, 1990.

Lieberman, Marcia. "Moral Innocents: Ellison's *Invisible Man* and *Candide.*" *CLA Journal* 14 (September 1971): 64–79.

Lukin, Josh. "Under Gray Flannel: Introduction to *Fifties Fiction.*" *Paradoxa* 18 (2003): 1–7.

Lynne, William. "The Signifying Modernist: Ralph Ellison and the Limits of the Double Consciousness." *PMLA* 107 (1992): 318–330.

Marvin, Thomas. "Children of Legba: Musicians at the Crossroads in Ralph Ellison's *Invisible Man.*" American Literature 68 (1996): 587–608.

Maxwell, William J. "'Creative and Cultural Lag': The Radical Education of Ralph Ellison." Tracy 59–83.

Morel, Lucas E., ed. *Ralph Ellison and The Raft of Hope: A Political Companion to "Invisible Man."* Lexington: UP of Kentucky, 2004.

Morris, Wright. "A Tale From Underground." Rev. of *Invisible Man,* by Ralph
    Ellison. *The New York Times* April 13, 1952. 9 pars. Aug. 1, 2007 <http://
    www.nytimes.com/library/books/072098ellison-invisible.html>.
Murray, Albert. *Omni-Americans: Some Alternatives to the Folklore of White
    Supremacy.* New York: Da Capo, 1970.
Nadel, Alan. *Ralph Ellison and the American Canon.* Iowa City: U of Iowa P,
    1988.
Neal, Larry. "Afterword: And Shine Swam On." *Black Fire.* 1968. Eds. Leroi
    Jones and Larry Neal. New York: Morrow, 1971. 637–656.
———. "The Black Writer's Role." *Liberator* 6 (June 1966): 7–9.
———. "Ralph Ellison's Zoot Suit." 1973. *Ralph Ellison's "Invisible Man": A
    Casebook.* Ed. John Callahan. New York: Oxford UP, 2004. 81–108.
O'Hara, J. D. "Reviews of *Twentieth Century Interpretations of 'Tom Jones'*
    and *Twentieth Century Interpretations of 'The Portrait of a Lady,'"* by
    M. C. Battestin and Peter Buitenhuis. *The Modern Language Journal* 53
    (March 1969): 207–208.
O'Meally, Robert. "The Rules of Magic: Hemingway as Ellison's 'Ancestor.'"
    1985. Benston 245–271.
Ostendorf, Berndt. "Ralph Waldo Ellison: Anthropology, Modernism, and Jazz."
    New Essays on Invisible Man. Ed. Robert O'Meally. Cambridge: Cam-
    bridge UP, 1988. 95–121.
Ottley, Roi. "Blazing Novel Relates a Negro's Frustrations." Rev. of *Invisible
    Man,* by Ralph Ellison. *Chicago Sun Tribune* May 11, 1952: 4.
Ping, Tang Soo. "Ralph Ellison and K. S. Maniam: Ethnicity in America and Ma-
    laysia, Two Kinds of Invisibility." *MELUS* 18.4 (Winter 1993): 81–97.
Posnock, Ross, ed. *The Cambridge Companion to Ralph Ellison.* Cambridge:
    Cambridge UP, 2005.
Prescott, Orville. "Books of the Times." April 16, 1952. Butler 19–20.
Radford, Andrew. "The Invisible Music of Ralph Ellison." *Raritan* 23 (Sum-
    mer 2003): 39–62.
Reilly, John M., ed. *Twentieth Century Interpretations of "Invisible Man."* Engle-
    wood Cliffs, NJ: Prentice-Hall, 1970.
Roberts, Brian. "Reading Ralph Ellison: Synthesizing the CP and the NAACP:
    Sympathetic Narrative Strategy, Sympathetic Bodies." *JNT: Journal of
    Narrative Theory* 34 (2004): 88–110.
Rodnon, Stewart. "*The Adventures of Huckleberry Finn* and *Invisible Man:* The-
    matic and Structural Comparisons." *Negro American Literature Forum* 4
    (1972): 45–51.
Rohrberger, Mary. "'Ball the Jack': Surreality, Sexuality, and the Role of Women
    in *Invisible Man.*" *Approaches to Teaching Ellison's Invisible Man.* Eds.
    Susan Resneck Parr and Pancho Savery. New York: MLA, 1989. 124–
    132.
Rosenblatt, Roger. *Black Fiction.* Cambridge: Harvard UP, 1974.

Rovit, Earl H. "Ralph Ellison and the American Comic Tradition." 1960. Reilly 56–63.

Schaub, Thomas Hill. *American Fiction in the Cold War.* Madison: U of Wisconsin P, 1991.

Scruggs, Charles. "Ralph Ellison's Use of *The Aeneid* in *Invisible Man.*" *CLA Journal* 17 (March 1974): 368–378.

Shraufnagel, Noel. *From Apology to Protest: The Black American Novel.* Deland, FL: Everett Edwards, 1973.

Smith, Valerie. *Self-Discovery and Authority.* Cambridge: Harvard UP, 1987.

Smethhurst, James. "'Something Warmly, Infuriatingly Feminine': Gender, Sexuality, and the Works of Ralph Ellison." Tracy 115–142.

Spaulding, Timothy. "Embracing Chaos in Narrative Form: The Bebop Aesthetic in Ralph Ellison's *Invisible Man.*" *Callaloo* 27 (2004): 481–501.

Spillers, Hortense. "'The Permanent Obliquity of an In(pha)llibly Straight': In the Time of the Daughters and the Fathers." 1989. *Black, White, and in Color: Essays on American Literature and Culture.* Chicago: U of Chicago P, 2003. 230–250.

Stanford, Ann Folwell. "He Speaks for Whom?: Inscription and Reinscription of Women in *Invisible Man* and *The Salt Eaters.*" *MELUS* 18.2 (Summer 1993): 17–31.

Stepto, Robert. *From Behind the Veil: A Study of Afro-American Narrative.* 1979. 2nd ed. Urbana: U of Illinois P, 1991.

Steward, Douglass. "The Illusions of Phallic Agency: *Invisible* Man, *Totem and Taboo,* and the Santa Claus Surprise." *Callaloo* 26 (2003): 522–535.

Sylvander, Carolyn. "Ralph Ellison's *Invisible Man* and Female Stereotypes." *Black American Literature Forum* 9 (Fall 1975): 77–79.

Tabron, Judith L. *Postcolonial Literature from Three Continents: Tutuola, H. D., Ellison, and White.* New York: Peter Lang, 2003.

Tate, Claudia. "Notes on the Invisible Women in Ralph Ellison's *Invisible Man.*" Benston 163–172.

Tidwell, John Edgar. "Afro-American Literature Reinterpreted." *Callaloo* 8/10 (1980): 233–236.

Tracy, Steven C., ed. *A Historical Guide to Ralph Ellison.* New York: Oxford UP, 2004.

———. "A Delicate Ear, a Retentive Memory, and the Power to Weld Fragments." Tracy 85–114.

Walling, William. "'Art' and 'Protest': Ralph Ellison's *Invisible Man* Twenty Years After." *Phylon* 34 (1973): 120–134.

Warren, Kenneth. *So Black and Blue: Ralph Ellison and the Occasion of Criticism.* Chicago: U of Chicago P, 2003.

Watts, Jerry Gafio. *Heroism and the Black Intellectual: Ralph Ellison, Politics, and Afro-American Intellectual Life.* Chapel Hill: U of North Carolina P, 1994.

Wolfe, Jesse. "'Ambivalent Man': Ellison's Rejection of Communism." *African American Review* 34 (Winter 2000): 621–637.

Wright, John S. "Chimed Chants from Dark and Dutiful Dyelis: A Review Essay." *A Ralph Ellison Festival.* Spec. issue of *Carleton Miscellanny* 18.3 (1980): 215–230.

———. "Dedicated Dreamer, Consecrated Acts: Shadowing Ellison." *A Ralph Ellison Festival.* Eds. Michael Harper and John S. Wright. Spec. issue of *Carleton Miscellany* 18.3 (1980): 142–199.

BIBLIOGRAPHICAL ESSAY

As the bulk of the previous chapter suggests, the chorus voicing opinions about *Invisible Man* rarely finds itself wanting for members. Notwithstanding the consistency and the voluminous nature of critical interest in this text, a few developments that could be considered belated still surround it. For example, the publication in 2002 of Lawrence Jackson's *Ralph Ellison: Emergence of Genius* marks the first sustained biographical treatment of *Invisible Man*'s author. Although a veritable bevy of interviews, sketches, and tributes exist, the appearance of this work facilitates the kind of scrutiny and inspired debate that scholars of Melville enjoyed in 1996 when the first volume of Herschel Parker's indefatigable tome was published. With Arnold Rampersad's completion of *Ralph Ellison: A Biography* (2007), the initial volume that treats the writer from the cradle to the grave, what had been speculative regarding the whole span of Ellison experiences can now at least peremptorily be tested. These two biographies are significant in themselves; however, their generative impact on the broader production of criticism can already be glimpsed. Between 2002 and 2007, no fewer than nine full-length books were printed that treated Ralph Ellison exclusively. To gain perspective on this output's importance, consider that in the entire decade from 1990 to 2000, only six such studies were produced. This acceleration bodes well for those who welcome proliferating points of entry to *Invisible Man;* nonetheless, a precise sense of what the past holds benefits not only Ellison's protagonist, but also his meaning-seeking readers. To that end this chapter presents and summarizes some of the most fruitful sources for secondary research on *Invisible Man.*

Divided into two parts "Classic Criticism" and "The Impact of Biography," this chapter predominantly focuses on extended studies. Occasional references to a single article or chapter will occur, but the aim is to point the reader towards volumes whose overall handling of Ralph Ellison or *Invisible Man* makes them valuable. "Classic Criticism" engages single-author works or edited anthologies that provide indispensable takes on Ralph Ellison or his first novel. Considering many of the texts published during the 55 years since *Invisible Man* appeared, this segment identifies and summarizes those that either because of their aggregation of viewpoints or their unparalleled grasp of the novel's subtleties are definitive. In "The Impact of Biography," the texts of Jackson and Rampersad receive sustained attention. All of this information should allow a reader quick transit to the materials most relevant to his curiosity. In doing so satiety both for the novice and the specialist will be the most welcome byproduct.

CLASSIC CRITICISM

John M. Reilly's *Twentieth Century Interpretations of "Invisible Man"* (1970) deserves mention as the first anthology that solely treats Ralph Ellison's initial novel. In addition its inclusion of oft-reprinted articles by Robert Bone and Floyd R. Horowitz and full reviews by Lloyd Brown and Anthony West make it a useful starting point for those seeking early impressions of *Invisible Man*. Joseph Trimmer in *A Casebook on Ralph Ellison's "Invisible Man"* (1972) pioneers an approach that considerably enriches the reader's understanding of the novel's milieu. Providing excerpts from people like Booker T. Washington, W.E.B. Du Bois, and Marcus Garvey, Trimmer uses them to supplement the eight literary critical analyses that he includes. The effect is not only profound intellectual orientation but also a capacity for deeper, more ambitious interpretations. Such a capacity follows in the wake of John Hersey's *Ralph Ellison: A Collection of Critical Essays* (1974), yet it achieves its power not by introducing the reader to voices from the past rather by confronting its audience with some of the sharpest tongues in its present. Front-loaded with insightful pieces from Robert Penn Warren, Saul Bellow, Stanley Edgar Hyman, and James Alan McPherson, all in varying degrees close acquaintances of Ellison, this collection also benefits from its editor's unencumbered access to its subject. The result is an opening interview that many consider one of Ellison's most candid discussions of craft. When the appearance of reprints of Larry Neal's "Ellison's Zoot Suit" (1970) and George Kent's "Ralph Ellison and the Afro-American Folk and Cultural Tradition" (1970) is considered, one could profitably argue that Hersey's book stands as the finest compendium of the first 25 years of Ellison scholarship.

Published in 1980, Robert O'Meally's *The Craft of Ralph Ellison* is the first book-length, single author study of the writer and his corpus that is produced in America. This work, complete with a biography, a sustained reading of *Invisible Man,* a productive look into Ellison's shorter fiction, and ample attention to the essays, sets a firm foundation for later scholarship. In particular, O'Meally's willingness to read developmentally is quite useful. Instead of considering *Invisible Man* as a masterwork that emerged out of a void, his interpretations stress the book's interrelatedness not only with other writers and thinkers but also with Ellison's own evolving awareness and abilities. Mark Busby's *Ralph Ellison* (1991) possesses a similar strength. Its biography and its selected bibliography are especially useful since they update the Ellison record accounting for developments from 1980 to 1990. In addition Busby's discussions of Ellison's post–*Invisible Man* fiction clarifies both the chronology and the content.

Boasting no fewer than 25 separate pieces, *Speaking for You: The Vision of Ralph Ellison* (1987) edited by Kimberly Benston remains the first place to turn when one is looking for a take on Ellison or *Invisible Man.* In part this reality stems from the convenience that the volume's extensive reprints offers. For example, nowhere else can a reader find Claudia Tate's "Notes on the Invisible Women in Ralph Ellison's *Invisible Man*" (1987) keeping company with Hortense Spillers's "Ellison's 'Usable Past': Toward a Theory of Myth" (1977). Aside from mere handiness though, this collection's range of perspectives, diverse kinds of material, and ease of availability make it a watershed work. Add to its other merits the presence of a thorough bibliography and a comprehensive index, and the reasons for this book's reputation as an indispensable resource becomes obvious.

Divided into three parts that offer windows into rural, artistic, and urban facets of African American existence, Eric Sundquist's *Cultural Contexts for Ralph Ellison's "Invisible Man"* (1995) makes the excerpting motif that typified a section of Trimmer's book the central basis for its organization. It includes over 30 entries, and in an attempt to show how *Invisible Man* posits a kind of "blueprint of African American culture," Sundquist rigorously documents the range of works, among them legal briefs, sociological studies, speeches, and songs, with which the novel converses (23). The values of Sundquist's volume rest on its combination of a fine introduction and a well-selected set of excerpts. The former lucidly captures the editor's reasons for choosing and arranging as he did, and the latter truly unlocks the complex intellectual universe that Ellison saw himself engaging. *Cultural Contexts for Ralph Ellison's "Invisible Man"* not only illuminates in its own right but also stimulates new analytical directions in the critical examination of Ralph Ellison's writings.

Jacqueline Covo's *The Blinking Eye: Ralph Waldo Ellison and His American, French, German and Italian Critics, 1952–1971* (1974) still stands as one of the most ambitious bibliographies within the canon of Ralph Ellison criticism. Apart from its distinctive catalogue of international output, its annotations effectively sketch major developments in the analysis of *Invisible Man.* At this point, its chief limit is its vintage, and Robert Butler's *The Critical Response to Ralph Ellison* (2000) considerably augments that deficiency. While Butler's book confines itself to criticism that is published in the United States, two features make it requisite. First, his introduction to *The Critical Response to Ralph Ellison* includes the most thorough annotation to date of articles, book chapters, and books about *Invisible Man.* Additionally, its section on "Early Reviews of *Invisible Man*" conveniently collects eight such responses, an invaluable service.

Since 2000, a spate of books examining some facet of Ellison's artistry has appeared. Many of them include articles or chapters that are treated in this book's "Reception" section; still, a word or two about their status as essay collections or monographs is in order. Horace A. Porter's *Jazz Country: Ralph Ellison in America* (2001), Herbert William Rice's *Ralph Ellison and the Politics of the Novel* (2003), and John S. Wright's *Shadowing Ralph Ellison* (2006) consider the full span of Ellison's productions, and they use music, politics, and intellectual history respectively to analyze the writer's corpus. Arguing that *"unity, ambiguity, possibility, discipline,* and *transcendence"* are "major chords" in Ellison's expression of "his principal themes," *Jazz Country* takes the music that so deeply informs the content and the aesthetics of Ellison's work and uses it to read these chords as crucial touch-points in explicating the novelist's oft-misunderstood and always controversial views of democratic pluralism (8). Focusing on the abiding "incompleteness" of his characters' and by extension Ellison's own "political gestures," *Ralph Ellison and the Politics of the Novel* analyzes Ellison's statements about the novel's civic obligations and the implications of these remarks for *Invisible Man* and the writer's sparse fictional output (3). *Shadowing Ellison* evokes the notion of "a metaphysical manhunt," and in implicitly linking itself to this trope, it relentlessly reinserts Ellison's writings into the socio-intellectual contexts from which they issued hoping to show how the novelist turned "a blue fog" into "a near-tragic, near-comic *transbluency*" (3, 11). The capaciousness of each of these studies lends their pronouncements a redeeming fullness, and each presents a reading of *Invisible Man* and a systematic portrait of Ellison's overall mission that through its synthesis of selected prior treatments becomes a critical primer in brief. For a grasp of longstanding tensions in the analysis of Ellison and *Invisible Man,* these books are quite good.

Kenneth Warren's *So Black and Blue: Ralph Ellison and the Occasion of Criticism* (2003), Beth Eddy's *The Rites of Identity: The Religious Naturalism and Cultural Criticism of Kenneth Burke and Ralph Ellison* (2003), and Patrice D. Rankin's *Ulysses in Black: Ralph Ellison, Classicism, and African American Literature* (2006) reveal another tendency in recent studies of Ralph Ellison. Instead of looking at the writer's fictional output in isolation, these works place it within the context of his actions as a public intellectual. This entails careful scrutiny of his essays, editorials, and addresses, and a meticulous contemplation of both his intellectual indebtedness and his ideological independence. *So Black and Blue* raises questions about the ultimate importance of *Invisible Man* and Ralph Ellison by juxtaposing the aesthetics of the writer and his novel with the historical realities of segregation, embattled racial leadership, and controversial academic methodology. By showing how specific scenes and particular facets of Ellison's thinking intersect with these larger phenomena, it weighs the broader question of how one establishes literary worth. *The Rites of Identity* systematically examines what has long been deemed a pivotal and generative relationship, that between Ralph Ellison and Kenneth Burke. After identifying signature concepts in Burke's philosophies, it suggests how Ellison in his writing incorporates, extends, and objects to Burkean notions. *Ulysses in Black* shifts the ground that situates Ellison's classical allusions as markers of his Eurocentric affinities, and describing among other things the figure of the "Black Ulysses," it contends that the long tradition of black literature that appropriates classical references should be viewed as a translation mechanism, a vehicle whereby writers seek to establish the universality of black characters' experiences. Warren, Eddy, and Rankin all demonstrate the part to whole strategies that will continue to illuminate *Invisible Man*'s nuances. If your interests among other things involve socio-cultural history, Kenneth Burke, or Afro-Classicism, then their works will edify.

Remarks about three recent collections will round out this survey. *Ralph Ellison and the Raft of Hope: A Political Companion to Ralph Ellison* (2004) indicates the current allure of analyzing *Invisible Man* as a quasi-irascible parable of American democracy. Edited by Lucas E. Morel, the collection contains 10 chapters in addition to a framing prologue and epilogue. Of these 12 parts, 8 betray an explicit interest in *Invisible Man* while the 4 that do not make liberal use of the text. *Ralph Ellison and the Raft of Hope* profitably underscores the merits of attending to Ellison's politically inflected views of the novelist's task, yet given the intellectually responsible choices available, the relative lack of dissenting voices regarding Ellison's political odyssey produces gaps. Distinguished by a succinct, yet informative biography, a thorough bibliographical essay, and an innovative chronology, Steven C. Tracy's *A Historical Guide to Ralph Ellison* (2004) admirably supplements the collections that strive to give readers an introduction to Ralph Ellison. Its critical essays, touching in part on Ellison's leftist dispensation, his encyclopedic manipulation of music, and his posture towards culture and race, fit into fissures in the larger, well-defined categories of criticism about Ellison. As such they provide a less triumphal, yet never stinting view of the man and his work. Ross Posnock's *The Cambridge Companion to Ralph Ellison* (2005) gathers 12 essays that point to the promising, variegated future of criticism on Ellison and *Invisible Man*. Engaging topics like biography, religion, photography, music, politics, science, and black-Jewish relations, these pieces extend the insights afforded by well-established topics in Ellison scholarship and suggest new directions that might yield greater comprehension. Readers will benefit from its panoramic perspectives.

THE IMPACT OF BIOGRAPHY

There have been innumerable advancements in the criticism of *Invisible Man,* but the appearances of Lawrence Jackson's *Ralph Ellison: Emergence of Genius* and Arnold Rampersad's *Ralph Ellison: A Biography* should fundamentally alter subsequent approaches both to the novel and the novelist. This section will not allow even a cursory unpacking of the many insights afforded by these texts; however, in sketching a brief overview of each biography's content and prevailing portrait of Ellison, it will give readers a glimpse of the distinct treasures that each holds.

Pointing to Ellison's manipulation of his birth date, his abiding disinclination for returning to Oklahoma, and the writer's inability to complete the novel that takes the Midwestern frontier as its canvas, *Ralph Ellison: Emergence of Genius* casts *Invisible Man* both in story and acclaim as its author's attempt via discipline and literary success to craft "a justification and a pattern for the decisions that [he] had made in his own life" (viii). With this connection in mind, the book concludes that Ellison and his masterpiece are best understood through the exultant attractions and the emotional demons that each strives to balance. It spends considerable energy charting the wondrously resonant fiction and the abundance of casualties occasioned by such a search for equilibrium. Because he is most interested in *Invisible Man* and its relationship to Ellison's early life, Jackson concludes his treatment with the year 1953. This leaves him open to charges of arbitrary incompletion; nonetheless, the logic of his plan and the thoroughness of its execution formidably answer those charges. By unearthing the details and the contexts of Ellison's formative years in Oklahoma, Alabama, and New York, Jackson provides a view of the poverty, the tragedy, and the intellectual crucible out of which Ellison's indomitable appetite for artistic excellence emerged. Observing this mélange grants readers the opportunity to analyze the novelist and his craft via the orienting refractions of his multivalent experiences. For a meticulous look into how Ellison went from artistic anonymity to the "red-cock crowing on a hill," *Ralph Ellison: Emergence of Genius* is necessary (qtd. in Jackson, vii).

The long-awaited *Ralph Ellison: A Biography* renders its subject within a magisterial full-life sweep. As the authorized account of the novelist's existence, it profits from access to all of the materials in the Ellison archives at the Library of Congress. This access edifies not only because it enables expanded appreciation of a Tuskegee figure like Walter B. Williams, along with richer texture in the characterization of Ralph and Fanny Ellison's marriage, but also because it affords Arnold Rampersad a greater confidence as he reaches conclusions about the overarching trajectory of Ellison's personal and professional movements. Exploiting this confidence, *Ralph Ellison: A Biography* depicts Ellison as a man who went from a life suffused by black culture and its institutions to one defined by upper echelon white acquaintances and membership in their most exclusive social and cultural organizations. The book sees within this development one possible reason for Ellison's inability to finish a second novel. Never merely a lament though, Rampersad's text chronicles the durable convictions and the personal stubbornness that simultaneously enamored and infuriated the writer's observers. To Rampersad, this binary in Ellison's character becomes a paradoxical prod. It explains his professional triumphs and his oxymoronic status as probably the most influential, yet least munificent black artistic elder of his day. *Ralph Ellison: A Biography* will chafe Ellison's boosters and detractors with equal intensity. Despite this vexation, its smoothly presented information will endure assisting readers admirably.

WORKS CITED

Benston, Kimberly, ed. *Speaking for You: The Vision of Ralph Ellison.* Washington, DC: Howard UP, 1987.

Busby, Mark. *Ralph Ellison.* Boston: Twayne, 1991.

Butler, Robert, ed. *The Critical Response to Ralph Ellison.* Westport: Greenwood, 2000.

Covo, Jacqueline. *The Blinking Eye: Ralph Waldo Ellison and His American, French, German, and Italian Critics, 1952–1971.* Metuchen, NJ: Scarecrow, 1974.

Eddy, Beth. *The Rites of Identity: The Religious Naturalism and Cultural Criticism of Kenneth Burke and Ralph Ellison.* Princeton: Princeton UP, 2003.

Hersey, John, ed. *Ralph Ellison: A Collection of Critical Essays.* Englewood Cliffs, NJ: Prentice-Hall, 1974.

Jackson, Lawrence. *Ralph Ellison: Emergence of Genius.* New York: Wiley, 2002.

Morel, Lucas E., ed. *Ralph Ellison and The Raft of Hope: A Political Companion to "Invisible Man."* Lexington: UP of Kentucky, 2004.

O'Meally, Robert G. *The Craft of Ralph Ellison.* Cambridge: Harvard UP, 1980.

Porter, Horace A. *Jazz Country: Ralph Ellison in America.* Iowa City: U of Iowa P, 2001.

Posnock, Ross, ed. *The Cambridge Companion to Ralph Ellison.* Cambridge: Cambridge UP, 2005.

Rampersad, Arnold. *Ralph Ellison: A Biography.* New York: Knopf, 2007.

Rankin, Patrice D. *Ulysses in Black: Ralph Ellison, Classicism, and African American Literature.* Madison: U of Wisconsin P, 2006.

Reilly, John M., ed. *Twentieth Century Interpretations of "Invisible Man."* Englewood Cliffs: Prentice-Hall, 1970.

Rice, Herbert William. *Ralph Ellison and the Politics of the Novel.* Lanham: Lexington Books, 2003.

Sundquist, Eric J., ed. *Cultural Contexts for Ralph Ellison's "Invisible Man."* Boston: St. Martin's Press, 1995.

Tracy, Steven C., ed. *A Historical Guide to Ralph Ellison.* New York: Oxford UP, 2004.

Trimmer, Joseph F., ed. *A Casebook on Ralph Ellison's "Invisible Man."* New York: T. Y. Crowell, 1972.

Warren, Kenneth. *So Black and Blue: Ralph Ellison and the Occasion of Criticism.* Chicago: U of Chicago P, 2003.

Wright, John S. *Shadowing Ralph Ellison.* Jackson: U of Mississippi P, 2006.

INDEX

About the Authors

MICHAEL D. HILL is assistant professor of English and African American Studies at the University of Iowa. His research interests are African American novels of the 1950s and black culture during the Reagan era.

LENA M. HILL is assistant professor of English and African American Studies at the University of Iowa. She was previously a Mellon postdoctoral fellow in the university writing program at Duke University.